The Entrepreneur in Local Government

Edited by
Barbara H. Moore
ICMA Staff

**International
City
Management
Association**

PRACTICAL MANAGEMENT SERIES
Barbara H. Moore, Editor

The Entrepreneur in Local Government
Capital Financing Strategies for Local Governments
Human Services on a Limited Budget
Telecommunications for Local Government

Library of Congress Cataloging in Publication Data
Main entry under title:
The entrepreneur in local government.
   (Practical management series)
     1. Local government—United States—Addresses,
essays, lectures. 2. Municipal services—United
States—Addresses, essays, lectures. 3. Entrepreneur
—Addresses, essays, lectures. I. Moore, Barbara H. II. Title.
III. Series.
JS341.E58   1983   352.073   83-10806
ISBN 0-87326-039-2

Printed in the United States of America.
12345 • 89888786858483

Foreword

Responding to fiscal and other pressures, local government managers are becoming increasingly entrepreneurial—making public services pay for themselves, seeking new sources of revenue, applying marketing and other profit-oriented techniques to public services, and generally looking beyond the traditional boundaries of their jobs to create and take advantage of new opportunities.

The Entrepreneur in Local Government presents selections that examine this new way of thinking—showing how a new breed of managers are encouraging a fresh look at the role of government in providing services and generating dollars. It also contains numerous case studies from localities that have implemented entrepreneurial programs.

This is the fourth book in ICMA's Practical Management Series, devoted to serving local officials' needs for timely information on current issues and problems. The editor has drawn on current literature and on reports from innovative managers to bring a wealth of material to the busy reader's hands.

We are grateful to the managers and others who prepared original articles for this book and to the organizations that granted ICMA permission to reprint their material. Thanks also go to Barbara H. Moore, editor of the volume, and to David S. Arnold, Editor, Municipal Management Series, who was of great help in planning the entire Practical Management Series.

Mark E. Keane
Executive Director
International City
Management Association

The Entrepreneur
in Local Government

The International City Management Association is the professional
and educational organization for chief appointed management executives in local government. The purposes of ICMA are to strengthen
the quality of local government through professional management
and to develop and disseminate new approaches to management
through training programs, information services, and publications.

Managers, carrying a wide range of titles, serve cities, towns,
counties, and councils of governments in all parts of the United
States and Canada. These managers serve at the direction of elected
councils and governing boards. ICMA serves these managers and local governments through many programs that aim at improving the
manager's professional competence and strengthening the quality of
all local governments.

The International City Management Association was founded
in 1914; adopted its City Management Code of Ethics in 1924; and
established its Institute for Training in Municipal Administration in
1934. The Institute, in turn, provided the basis for the Municipal
Management Series, generally termed the "ICMA Green Books."

ICMA's interests and activities include public management education; standards of ethics for members; the *Municipal Year Book*
and other data services; urban research; and newsletters, a monthly
magazine, *Public Management*, and other publications. ICMA's efforts for the improvement of local government management—as represented by this book—are offered for all local governments and educational institutions.

About the Authors

Following are the affiliations of the contributors to *The Entrepreneur in Local Government* at the time of writing.

Donald D. Brown, Assistant City Manager, Fairfield, California

Calvin A. Canney, City Manager, Portsmouth, New Hampshire

William V. Donaldson, President, Philadelphia Zoological Society

Fred Fisher, Director of Program Development, College of Human Development, Pennsylvania State University

Ted A. Gaebler, City Manager, Visalia, California

Steve Garman, City Manager, Pensacola, Florida

James A. Goodrich, Associate Professor, School of Business and Public Administration, University of the Pacific, Stockton, California

Douglas Harman, City Manager, Alexandria, Virginia

Harry P. Hatry, Director, State and Local Government Research Program, The Urban Institute, Washington, D.C.

James L. Hetland, Jr., Senior Vice President, First National Bank of Minneapolis, and President of the Citizens Forum on Self-Government, National Municipal League

Rosabeth Moss Kanter, Professor of Organization and Management and of Sociology at Yale University, and Chairman of the Board, Goodmeasure, Inc., a management consulting firm in Cambridge, Massachusetts

Norman R. King, City Manager, Palm Springs, California

Anne M. Kirlin, specialist in land development, Dickenson, Peatman, and Fogarty, Napa, California

John J. Kirlin, Professor of Public Administration, University of Southern California, Sacramento Public Affairs Center

Ted Kolderie, Senior Fellow, Hubert H. Humphrey Institute of Public Affairs, University of Minnesota

Eberhard Laux, Director, WIBERA, private consulting firm spun off from German local government associations

J. Scott McBride, President, Marketing General, Inc., Washington, D.C.

Gary R. McDonnell, Director of Parks and Recreation, Lakewood, Colorado

James L. Mercer, President, James Mercer & Associates, Atlanta, Georgia

David Morris, President, Institute for Local Self-Reliance and author of *Self-Reliant Cities: Energy and the Transformation of Urban America*

Arthur E. Pizzano, Director, Department of Economic Development, East Orange, New Jersey

J. Edward Tewes, Budget Management Officer, Long Beach, California

Charles W. Thompson, City Administrator, Huntington Beach, California.

Paula R. Valente, Director, Transportation Project, ICMA, Washington, D.C.

Gordon E. Von Stroh, Professor of Management and Public Administration, College of Business Administration, Graduate School of Business and Public Administration, University of Denver

Kenneth M. Wheeler, Director, Department of Communications and Marketing, Norfolk, Virginia

B. Gale Wilson, City Manager, Fairfield, California

Susan W. Woolston, Intergovernmental Specialist, U.S. Environmental Protection Agency

Contents

PART 4
Conclusion

PART 1

A
New
Outlook

The Entrepreneurial Manager

Ted A. Gaebler

The impetus for entrepreneurism in local government

Shortly after the passage of California's Proposition 13 in 1978, Dr. Robert Biller, Dean of the School of Public Administration of the University of Southern California, addressed the League of California Cities. In that speech he made the seemingly contradictory assertion that Proposition 13 passed *not* because local government is *so bad*, but precisely because it is *so good*. His point was that the well-established mechanisms which exist at the local level for responding to citizen needs and providing services made this level of government uniquely vulnerable to attack in the face of rampant discontent over government policies at all levels. Local government, because of its accessibility and its historic role as the provider of service, became a lightning rod for citizen anger and doubt about who, in reality, government serves. The message Proposition 13 resoundingly delivered was: Government is not serving me; it is providing services to "others," so why should I pay for it?

Proposition 13 launched government into a new era. It dramatized changes in public perception about the value of government as we've come to know it since the Roosevelt years, and it dramatized the reality of our limits—fiscal and psychological. Not only have we reached the saturation point in terms of (local) government's fiscal ability to provide *all* services to meet *all* community needs; we also have reached the limits of our psychological desire to do so. People now resent paying taxes that go toward something they don't personally use. We have become a society of particularistic interests; and to the extent that government policies and services are geared to meet *mass* needs, an increasing number of *individual* voters will continue to be dissatisfied.

What these altered perceptions about the value of government reflect are the massive changes taking place in society as a whole, changes which are radically reshaping this society and the role of local government in it. You need only to read Alvin Toffler's books and look around you to understand the magnitude of these changes and their impact on people and institutions. When you see what is happening in formerly stable industries such as banking, housing, and automobiles, you realize that the very fabric of American society is being reworked.

Local government is not immune from these forces. We need only look at the financial crisis facing one state—California—to grasp how acutely our industry has been affected. The state itself faces billion-dollar deficits in the current and upcoming fiscal years, and 34 cities in California face dissolution or bankruptcy. We simply are not going to have the same sources of revenue that we had years ago. We are being forced to find new revenue sources and to leverage our dollars with dollars in the private sector. Our survival will depend on our ability to adapt.

Entrepreneurs: who they are and how they function

As managers, collectively and individually, we are being challenged to *change*—to change our attitude and our approach to management, to unlock different and hopefully more exciting solutions to new and pressing problems. I think we are being challenged to become entrepreneurs.

What does it mean to be an entrepreneur? Webster says an entrepreneur is one who assumes risk for the sake of profits. *Risk* and *profits*: two words not generally heard in the ranks of public management—until recently when traditional revenue sources began to dry up. Now we have all kinds of new ventures springing up with local governments as active partners. Change forces us to adapt, and entrepreneurism is one of the strategies that can help us adapt. It literally and psychologically pays off.

Seven traits characterize entrepreneurial managers:

1. They are *goal oriented*, not task oriented. Entrepreneurs organize their agencies and personal schedules to work on what they choose, and not what others dictate.
2. Entrepreneurs are *flexible*. They look for and seize opportunities; they are aware of external forces.
3. They constantly *challenge* what is and *question* what could be. They do not see existing laws, rules and regulations, practices, or tradition as insurmountable barriers to change.
4. Entrepreneurs are *future oriented*. They have a long-term outlook and don't care much about what happens today. They have somebody else who cares about today.
5. Entrepreneurs are *risk-takers*, not with crazy projects, but with calculated risks. If you don't take risks, you are doomed

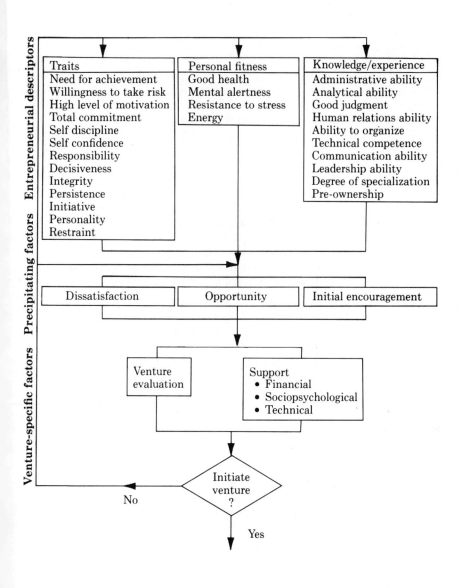

A model of factors leading to the initiation of new ventures.

Source: Adapted from: "A Model of Entrepreneurship: Moving Toward Precision and
Complexity," by James Donald Powell and Charles F. Bimmerle, *Journal of
Small Business Management*, January 1980, p. 35.

to the lowest common denominator. You won't have any failures, or not too many, but you also won't have any successes.

6. Entrepreneurs are *profit-* or *bottom-line oriented*. They care at least as much about increasing revenues as they do about controlling costs. They regularly review their organizations to see which subsidiaries, which product line, or which services should be divested, or stopped, or acquired. The creative juices flow much more freely when you ask yourself how you might profit from a problem rather than how you might avoid the problem.

7. Entrepreneurs have a *sense of ownership*; they are owners, not bureaucrats. How many managers regularly test their recommendations to the city council by asking themselves: "If this were *my* money, would I make this recommendation?" Local government will improve if we can get ourselves, our top managers, and maybe our middle managers, to feel, think, and act like they're owners, not employees.

Entrepreneurism is a more proactive approach to management, and more fun. You set the agenda rather than letting other people and their problems set it. You initiate change rather than just reacting to it. You, in effect, make the future happen. Although such active management of the environment is common in the private sector, it is largely foreign in the public sector. For example:

1. Most cities do not perform *economic base analyses* to determine why the community exists economically and what the economic trends and forecasts are.

2. Cities commonly do not develop *economic models* to test assumptions about proposed programs and service levels *prior to* establishing them—in effect projecting future affordability based on today's costs.

3. Cities do little *market research* to measure systematically and regularly the impact of services and programs; nor do they market the few programs they do have that break even or make money.

4. Public sector managers expend little time or effort educating the public about government—that is, shaping a positive image in the public's eye about who they are, what they offer, and how they perform.

These are just a few of the techniques the public sector needs to borrow from the private sector corporate model.

Stimulating entrepreneurism in the organization

Being entrepreneurial also means *creating a climate for change* in the organization, a climate in which innovation is encouraged, creativity rewarded, and errors tolerated. In creating this climate for change, top management support is critical. You need to provide incentives for all employees, not just management employees, to act as *owners*. One way to do this is through a top-down budgetary system. Such a system takes the previous year's appropriations (dating back to the Proposition 13 era) and adds a formula increase of one-half of the cost-of-living index (CPI), plus an increase equal to the actual percentage increase in population. That number gives the previous year's base, and that is what department heads get each year. They have to operate with that amount of money, regardless of what salary increases the city council may give subsequently. Any savings stay within the department until it chooses to spend it.

This kind of a budgeting system creates a departmental *incentive to save* money instead of spending it. It changes the entire look of budgeting for all employees, not just managerial employees. The pay system also can be an effective tool for encouraging innovation and creativity. You need to have an open pay system with no cap on earnings. You need to give cash bonuses for jobs well done and pay some employees on a commission, rather than a salary, basis.

Redefining the government's role

The key, however, to becoming entrepreneurial lies with *redefining the role of local government*. The mission of local government usually is said to be providing services. This definition is too narrow and constraining. We need one that will give us more options. I propose that the mission of local government is not to provide services, but rather to provide a forum for determining community consensus, for identifying the needs and the desires of citizens, and for actively *matching those needs with* all *available community resources*, not just governmental resources and tax dollars. Local government is a forum where citizens can state their needs and where the manager helps to broker the community's resources to satisfy those needs.

This new definition puts city government at the very heart of what happens to the community in all areas—from economic development to education, from cultural affairs to health issues—without the assumed responsibility for actually providing these services. Although you don't need to assume ownership for providing services, you are involved in making sure that the needs are satisfied.

Local governments have an important role to play in the evolution of community life, but that role is not necessarily always that of an exclusive service provider. We have been shackling our creative energy in the face of revenue constraints by continuing to view our role as provider of a historically preset mix of services. Be a catalyst, be a broker, but don't be a doer.

You probably think these ideas sound good in theory, but don't work in reality. But they do. The following questions and examples of what we are doing in Visalia may illustrate both this point and, more important, the attitude of the entrepreneurial approach.

How many cities can you think of that have more money than they can spend? We do, in Visalia, not because we are rich (we are a rural agricultural community), but rather because we are a totally entrepreneurial organization. Our council adopted a mission statement and a set of corporate goals. Our operating slogan is "Get off the fix by '86"—meaning no more federal or state money.

Does your agency regularly divest itself of programs and services? We gave the library to the county, the ambulances to private hospitals, day care to churches and the junior college, historic preservation to a private not-for-profit group, recycling to a private not-for-profit group, public relations activities to the chamber of commerce (we pay them a fee), and animal control to the humane society. We sold the baseball franchise to the private sector, and gave a theater to the private sector.

Have you ever considered buying industrial land, selling it for a profit in another city, and installing a regional vice president to manage it off the commissions she would make? How recently have you examined your city's policy on inventions and on the split on royalties that the employee and the city would share? Is it possible that just discussing this kind of thing could turn loose the creative juices in your organization and improve morale, loyalty, and profits?

How many of you charge for solid waste pickup? How many charge on the solid waste bill for street sweeping? How many sell street signs to high school kids (to cut vandalism and make money)? How many have run for and been elected to the chamber of commerce's board of directors?

The *value* of entrepreneurism in the public sector is the flexibility it gives us to continue providing the community with the services citizens want and need without taxing them to do it. It frees us from the Catch-22 choice of either stopping services because of decreasing revenues, or finding another hidden tax mechanism to support them. Most important, entrepreneurial methods help target both services and the dollars to pay for them to particular publics in the community, those with interest in that investment, and therefore a willingness to support it. Taking a more entrepreneurial approach to managing public resources could well be the key to restoring the public's faith in government and in our capacity to manage their resources effectively.

The New Entrepreneurs

Fred Fisher

The term *entrepreneur* is, in large measure, a wholly owned subsidiary of the private business world. And even within the private sector, the term is largely reserved for those rugged individuals who have invested their time, talent, and resources in a risky venture and, incidentally, have been successful. Did you ever hear of an unsuccessful entrepreneur? Those who fail at such ventures are usually thought to be poor managers.

Entrepreneur is an old word, as far as economics and management goes. J. B. Say, a French economist and disciple of Adam Smith, coined it back in the early 1800s to identify the person who directs resources from less productive into more productive investments, thus creating wealth. Say believed it was the genius of development and not production that was the generator of wealth.

The genius of development or the entrepreneurial venture is not doing the same thing in more abundance but rather doing things differently. Peter Drucker says, "The manager has to create tomorrow, to slough off yesterday and to render obsolete what already exists and is already known."[1] This, it seems to me, is the role of the entrepreneur and I believe it is one which is not the sole domain of the private manager but has been and continues to be a valuable role for those who labor in the public vineyards, as well.

Noted researcher Henry Mintzberg once analyzed other people's research about the manager's job. Among other things, he said that we perpetuate a lot of myths about managers and how they carry out their roles (like the myth that entrepreneuralism is only private sector business). Mintzberg's greatest contribution to management theory and thought, however, was his identification of ten primary roles that he believes are central to the management process and the effec-

Reprinted with permission from *Public Management*, June 1981.

tive manager. One of these ten is the role of entrepreneur, that of helping the organization adapt to the changing conditions in the environment.[2] It is a role which public managers, particularly those at the grass roots level of our society, can identify with and one in which many find their greatest challenge.

Hustling the unneeded, performing the unnecessary

While Mintzberg has identified the role of entrepreneur as integral to the management process, I would like to argue that it is also an unnecessary role in organizations or society as it exists at any particular point in time. The entrepreneur is really someone who exploits opportunities to solve non-pressing problems. In other words, the entrepreneur is someone who hustles the unneeded, who opens doors, and explores opportunities that are not necessary for personal or organizational survival at that particular point in time. Granted, the discoveries and changes brought about by the entrepreneur make for a more interesting, rich, and diverse future, but from the standpoint of an organization's here and now survival, they don't much matter. If this line of thinking bothers you, ponder for a moment any new invention and the environment in which it was created. Henry Ford and his noisy contraption, for example, took a lot of flak when they descended into the lives of the horse and hay generation. Or, consider the public concern that currently surrounds the work of the genetic engineers and the potential change (or havoc) they could perpetrate upon an unwitting society. Who needs it? That's the question often asked in the face of change.

I belabor the point because it is important in considering the role of the entrepreneur and how it gets nurtured, and protected, particularly within the public domain. The entrepreneurial role has never been one associated openly and directly with the public manager (ever see it in a city manager's job description or contract?). From the standpoint of managing an organization (maintaining what is), it's probably unnecessary. This, of course, is very different from saying the role is desirable and perhaps even necessary from a future perspective. For example, I heard on the radio that the city of Minot, North Dakota, is going into the banking business.

Since they don't own and operate a bank at the present time, one could argue convincingly that they don't need it. After all, other cities get along perfectly well without performing this role and Minot, somehow, has managed to exist over the years in unvaulted fashion. And my guess is that whoever initially thought of this unconventional role for their city can bank on receiving their fair share of grief before the decision is finally made, not to mention what will happen if it is unsuccessful. On the other hand, city-owned and operated banks might become as fashionable on Main Street as the ubiquitous golden arches (whoever said 34 trillion belches ago that we needed Big Macs to survive?).

First things first

The first thing the manager needs to come to grips with, as he or she thinks in entrepreneurial terms, is the unconventionality of this role in the public sector and the largely unnecessary character of its function from the immediate point of view. If the manager is not only responsible for maintaining today but also partially responsible for creating tomorrow, then the role of entrepreneur is, if not necessary, highly desirable and needs to be thought about in public terms. It becomes even more important as we face greater uncertainty about the role of the public sector as the glue that holds communities and societies intact.

The foregoing dialectic about the necessity of the entrepreneur, particularly within the public sector, is crucial for any manager who wittingly incorporates this role in his or her bag of tricks these days. Two reasons stand out. First, the resources for being venturesome (and perhaps adventuresome) are much scarcer today than they were in recent years. There is widespread recognition these days that resources are not unlimited. C. W. Mills, in his many writings over several decades, referred to the entrepreneur and contrasted the old entrepreneur with the new. In the past, the entrepreneur operated "in a world opening up like a row of oysters under steam," whereas "the new entrepreneur must operate in a world in which all the pearls have been grabbed up and are carefully guarded."[3] With the pearls "grabbed up and guarded," it's more difficult than ever to be an entrepreneur.

It's also risky business. Albert Low reminds us that "new ideas are not enough, one must be willing to expose himself to a potentially hostile environment."[4] The entrepreneur must be prepared to risk his/her reputation and to invest time and energy into the realization of ideas that are only defendable on future outcomes, not on current gains. Not only are the gains future in orientation, entrepreneurial work causes conflict. As Low so aptly puts it, the entrepreneur risks becoming a stranger in his/her own organization. "To the extent that a man is doing entrepreneurial work, he is without a manager, he is a stranger and exposed to the risks of a stranger."[5]

Maxims to maximize the entrepreneurial spirit

Our discussion thus far might lead you to believe that I would counsel the manager to turn his or her back on this business of being the entrepreneur. Not at all, but I must say it's not a role for the unimaginative or the faint-hearted. On the other hand, there are some things we can do to ensure that first, the role is a bit less risky and second, the outcomes are more predictable. Let's explore a few propositions by which one might more productively, and with less anxiety, pursue the entrepreneurial process.

I. The effective entrepreneur works the fringes and not the mainstream of societal ventures   The entrepreneurial ventures that pay the greatest dividends are those that begin at the periphery of our thinking and move toward the center of activity. Donald Schon uses the term "ideas in good currency" to identify concepts and strategies that ultimately become conventional. The trick is to buy a McDonald's franchise when it is inexpensive, not when they cost a fortune and all the good spots are taken. Better yet, invent the idea and sell it to others.

II. Never go pearl diving alone in shark-infested waters   Some people call it co-venturing these days, or collaboration, or simply a willingness to share the risks and the gains. Whatever you call it, teaming up with others (individuals, organizations, coalitions) makes eminent sense in a time of scarce resources. The Kettering Foundation, it seems to me, has worked this strategy successfully. As an operating foundation, they seek relationships that are mutually rewarding. Unfortunately, some of their collaborators have been bothered by the need to share power and responsibility—perhaps because it violates norms established by other, more traditional foundations.

III. Sharing power and ideas is not the same as giving them away   The entrepreneur who becomes secure enough to share his or her ideas and the power that these ideas might ultimately command in the marketplace will be amply rewarded, particularly as he or she functions in the public arena. This is not to say that such behavior won't result in one being "ripped off" on occasion, or feeling that way. On the average, the collaborator, the co-venturer, will be miles ahead by sharing ideas, power, and the rewards that come with sharing.

IV. When pearls get scarce and expensive, figure out a way to make prune pits fashionable   The effective entrepreneur is someone who can sell you a pet rock and make you smile when you should be stone sober. For example, the community entrepreneur, in a future where energy sources are predicted to be scarce, will undoubtedly be the individual who can recycle everything that penetrates or gets generated within the boundaries of the system (e.g., wind, sun, biomass, garbage, waste of all kinds). These are not new ideas, but the right combination of technology, dedication, commitment, and co-venturing has not yet been redefined in such a way to make the ideas or the investments viable. To return to my first maxim, these ideas are still peripheral to our experience. The challenge is to make them mainstream.

V. The effective entrepreneur doesn't punch a time clock
I've been working on a project in Rhode Island to identify those individuals who are effective in matching individual and community human service needs and resources and to determine why these individuals are more effective at networking needs and resources than their counterparts. Several things stand out. For one thing, these individuals do not separate their professional and private lives. They live integrated holistic experiences that allow them to flow across the boundaries of their everyday existence with relative ease. Entrepreneurs are much the same. They never separate their work time from their play time, and yet they remain vital and creative because they are committed to new ways of defining their universe and the resources at their command.

VI. For entrepreneurs to be successful in the long run, they need cushions to break the short term falls Entrepreneurship is inherently risky. If you plan to build it into the modus operandi of city hall you need to provide protection for those who are charged with the responsibility of undertaking new ventures. Expect short-term setbacks and outright failures. Learn how to pick up the pieces and move forward without undue self or organizational flagellation.

VII. In the long run, the unspoken laws of quid-pro-quoism will determine how successful the public entrepreneur will be In other words, if you haven't figured out what is in it for others to ultimately get involved in what you are about, your chances of success will be drastically minimized. This goes for policymakers who give you license to venture forth; to the community that will ultimately use your products of invention; and to colleagues who provide psychological support along the way.

VIII. Finally, entrepreneurship is antithetical to bureaucracy and largely alien to public governance Whether we want to admit it or not, bureaucracy is the prevailing paradigm of governance and implementation in the public sector. The world the public manager helps create and sustain is largely hierarchical in nature and believes in such things as division of work, unity of direction, centralization, and authority and responsibility vested at the top of the pyramid. Our public institutions, by and large, put restrictions on those who operate within their boundaries; restrict the goods and services these individuals have at their command and how they get allocated; and want to maintain jurisdiction over the interrelationship of form and substance.

Contrarily, the entrepreneur must constantly scan the boundaries of the system and figure ways to poke holes in it. The building of new ideas and resources, which is the main occupation of the entrepreneur, will be seen as haphazard by those who construct their notion of the public domain as orderly and predictable. The manager, in assuming the role of entrepreneur, or in providing others in the organization with the mantle of entrepreneurial acceptance, will need to be cognizant of the risks involved and build into the situation all the support and room to maneuver that is possible.

The eighties promise to be different for the public manager and, in many ways, more difficult and challenging. Resources will not be as readily available as they have been in the past and this circumstance can cause one to naturally hunker down to make a smaller target. It will surprise few that this is not terribly satisfying behavior. The municipal managers who will stand out in the decade ahead are those who are willing to redefine resources, the community, and their roles very differently. They will be those who are willing to take risks, who are imbued with the spirit, knowledge, and skills of the entrepreneur. To these brave souls the eighties belong, and to them the redefinition of public management will fall. Public entrepreneurs, be on with it.

1. Peter Drucker, *Management: Tasks, Responsibilities, Practices* (New York: Harper & Row, 1973), p. 17.

2. Henry Mintzberg, "The Manager's Job: Folklore and Fact," *Harvard Business Review*, July/August 1975, pp. 49-61.

3. C. Wright Mills, *Power, Politics and People* (London: Oxford University Press, 1963), p. 268.

4. Albert Low, *Zen and Creative Management* (Garden City, NY: Anchor Books, 1976), p. 89.

5. *Ibid.*, p. 90.

The New Entrepreneurship

J. Edward Tewes

"Supply side economics," recently the most talked about ideology in Washington, may have some important lessons for management of local government as well as for national policy. In addition to tax cuts and the promise of a balanced federal budget, the Administration has also focused on the role of *incentives* and the importance of entrepreneurship in economic growth. According to "supply-siders," management of the national economy should no longer involve direct intervention to achieve specific results, but rather should be concerned with removing obstacles to incentives for real economic growth.

Economists have long warned public managers that the "perverse" incentives of bureaucracy lead to ever upward growth in government spending and inefficiency. Since the perquisites of government employment are tied to bigger budgets, it is not surprising—we have been lectured—that public managers are motivated to increase their share of the government pie year after year. Unfettered by the discipline of the market, "government services are bound to be inefficient"—or so goes the argument.

In real life, however, we are not concerned with the motivation of faceless "bureaucrats," but of the police chief, the library director, and the other department heads we meet at every staff meeting. As city managers we have a responsibility to our communities, our organizations, and our profession to pay more attention to the system of incentives we have created, or have ignored, and to develop approaches to management which are more consistent with the demands of a changing society and local government environment.

The character of local government in the 1980s is being reshaped

Reprinted with permission from *Public Management*, June 1981. This article is based on concepts presented to the City Manager's Department of the League of California Cities by John E. Dever, city manager, Long Beach, California.

by at least three dramatic forces. Perhaps the most significant is an increasing movement toward individualism and concern for *particular*, rather than community interests. Government by consensus is not only becoming more difficult, it is viewed less and less as a preferred approach to solving problems. Distrust of elected officials, declining participation in political parties, and increased litigation are each symptoms of a movement in public policy toward the attainment of individual rather than group goals. The political manifestation of the "me" generation is an increase in the number of single-issue lobbies and a decrease in the number of voters in elections at all levels.

Larger incomes, more education, and improved communication have led citizens to be less satisfied with national, city, or even group accomplishments or decision making. The mediating role of families, political parties, and even city councils has become less important as individuals become more self-reliant. To managers trained to serve their cities' needs on the basis of community-wide consensus, these changes have only recently become apparent. Yet, they have profound implications for the delivery of municipal services. The challenge of public leadership has been to meet community needs wherever they are within the limited resources available. Now, however, there seems to be much less confidence in the ability of the council or manager to accomplish this *integrating* task. Instead, each citizen wants to decide for himself what services will be provided in his neighborhood, and at what level.

A second factor is the changing nature of city problems themselves. Fewer and fewer managers are as concerned about managing growth as they are with coping with obsolescence. As more cities come to resemble the metropolitan cities of the northeast, managers will be increasingly confronted with communities that are physically deteriorating, losing population, jobs and tax base, and becoming havens for the poor, handicapped, aged, illiterate, and newcomers to our country. The seeming permanence of fiscal stress and the uncertainty of intergovernmental revenues have required not only innovative financing techniques but a new approach to management as well.

Traditionally, city managers have started the annual budget process by spreading the gospel of "cost consciousness" to program managers. If the message failed to take hold, an aggressive budget staff was always prepared to help out. Notwithstanding the efforts of the cost cutters, however, the "perverse" incentives of bureaucracy always seemed to encourage greater spending to meet increasing or newly perceived community needs. Pressure for expansion came not only from program managers themselves but also from elected officials who sought to be responsive to interest groups which were able to articulate their demands for new or increased services.

Even in difficult years the city council was able to balance the budget by adjusting the property tax rate or by levying new or increased taxes. As a result, the basic level of service from one year to the next was essentially "guaranteed." Budget hearings and council decision making revolved around competing proposals for program expansion. Program managers did not need to worry about financing their existing service levels since that was "given." Competition was for a share of the incremental increase in revenues. In such a budget environment, however, there was little reason for anyone to internalize overall city revenue problems, or, indeed, to take seriously the routine predictions of a fiscal crunch.

Now, however, the reality of revenue shortfalls and a declining government pie have changed the way in which departmental and program managers think about their operations. "Cutback" management and program contraction are a reality. Decisions about expenditures can no longer be made independent of decisions about sources of funding. In the past, departments may have competed for a share of a common pool of public tax resources without regard to how revenue was raised. (That was the finance director's problem, or the city manager's.) However, with an ever shrinking amount of available resources and the imposition of often arbitrary spending restrictions, managers are forced to identify offsetting revenues or productivity improvements in order to justify the maintenance of even existing levels of service. Public managers have had to become entrepreneurial in their approach to service delivery, if for no other reason than that entrepreneurship provides the only opportunity to broaden decisionmaking responsibilities when most other factors affecting the budget have had the opposite impact.

Although "privatizing" local services is one option, entrepreneurial thinking means more than just contracting out or relying more on user charges. Indeed, in our case such opportunities are limited since Long Beach's home rule charter discourages outside contracting.

It is the joining of "revenue" consciousness with "cost consciousness" that defines the entrepreneurial approach. Long Beach views local government as a series of service enterprises in which department managers are evaluated and rewarded on the basis of the financial success of the enterprise. By holding managers accountable for *financing* as well as providing services, we have tried to restructure incentives so that success is viewed not in terms of budget size, but on the "fit" between services supplied and services demanded by consumers as measured by fiscal performance. We have tried to make every department responsible for the revenue needed to cover the cost of services provided. Where this is not immediately possible, fixed revenue goals are established to meet a percentage of costs from non-tax sources over an agreed upon number of years. Merit increases depend on meeting these entrepreneurial goals.

For example, the street sweeping operation in Long Beach is not financed from fees for service but from general revenues. Nonetheless, revenues derived from parking violations associated with street sweeping have been "assigned" to that program and establish the amount and level of service which can be financed on a self-sustaining basis. The public works director now has a direct stake in the number of parking fines that are actually paid. As a result, the city now has a much more aggressive effort to collect on parking citations and the collection effort itself has been computerized and transferred to the city from the municipal court which had little incentive to pursue parking violations.

One of the effects of the entrepreneurial approach is increased reliance on marketing principles in analyzing and delivering public services even when pricing is not feasible. For services directly financed by user fees, the market works well in allocating scarce resources and giving signals about customer satisfaction. However, even for traditional, so-called "free" municipal services, marketing techniques can improve effectiveness by focusing on the output or end product and how it is received by the consumer.

The first step is to identify the businesses we are in and the "products" that the city offers. Too often, we take for granted the range and variety of community benefits that city services supply. By forcing program managers to view their operations as outside consumers do, the entrepreneurial approach uncovers new opportunities and exposes old practices to new scrutiny.

When the manager of the public library identifies the various products that are offered, new opportunities for marketing are revealed. The information and research services provided are valuable to local business which are willing to pay for them either individually on a per inquiry basis, or by contributing money as an association or chamber of commerce. The special services provided by the audio-visual section of a library do not differ significantly from those now offered by private companies to rent a film or video cassette. Branch libraries often include unused office space or meeting rooms which can be marketed. The public should expect a return on its investment in real estate. Even the inventory of books and magazines can be marketed with special "rent a book" programs for popular volumes.

Having identified the city's product line, an analysis of "what sells" is also required. Knowing that your firm makes a pretty good ice box doesn't help much if you are in Alaska. In government it is equally important to do some market research. For example, it is possible that a massive effort to expand tennis programs would *misread* the market demand for recreational opportunities which may have shifted from tennis to other racquet sports. Without a market analysis, the city could make a large capital investment, only to learn too late that the market for tennis has been saturated.

Managers must also consider what segment of the market should be targeted. This may be difficult in a profession that has traditionally championed open access and nondiscriminatory services. Nonetheless, the new fiscal realities force us to be both more selective and more effective. For example, the city should not expect to meet *all* the recreational needs of *all* citizens of the community. The city probably cannot compete against private fitness clubs for the self-improvement segment of the recreation market, but it might effectively meet the demand for such leisure time activities as basketball or softball games.

Even when pricing services is not feasible for reasons of equity or politics, an entrepreneurial approach still requires the development of a marketing plan which sets forth the steps needed to disseminate information, gauge consumer response, vary the delivery of programs, and evaluate results. This means selling and competing! Entrepreneurship requires use of sales tools, marketing consultants, and employees with the skills to read market trends and adapt quickly.

Two essential elements of a successful entrepreneurial approach are a system of performance measurement and sophisticated cost accounting. Both provide current feedback on the effectiveness of city services and allow timely adjustments in either level of service or price. Whenever program managers are held truly accountable for both expenditures *and* offsetting revenues they must receive accurate, up-to-date information on fiscal and performance operating results. Although customer satisfaction can be readily determined under a pricing system, it is no less important to measure for more traditional services such as police or fire protection.

Long Beach has experimented with Total Performance Measurement (TPM) as a way of integrating citizen survey data about city services with employee opinions and "hard" data on output. Too often, employees receive feedback only from supervisors and management without any real appreciation for the perceptions of the citizens who receive and pay for local services. Since employees themselves are the most knowledgeable and able to improve performance by reducing costs or increasing quality, TPM seeks to bring information about customer satisfaction to bear where it counts the most—in the work place.

The success of entrepreneurship in the private sector is measured by profit. In the public sector a comparable measure might be the extent to which costs have been met or exceeded by revenues. Such a factor needs to be included in management evaluation and compensation in order to restructure the organization's system of incentives. The successful city of the future must be prepared to compete, by knowing its products, pricing what can be priced, selling, and making a "profit."

The driving force behind the move toward entrepreneurship has been the combination of sluggish revenue growth, a dramatically changing community, and citizen demand for specialized and diversified services at lower cost. The new entrepreneurship means that the city needs to recruit a new breed of managers, support new kinds of training and develop a more flexible and innovative response to measuring community needs and organizational performance.

The Organizational Climate for Innovation

Rosabeth Moss Kanter

Editor's note: The literature on innovation is evidence that entrepreneurial approaches have received more attention in private industry than in the public sector. Although this article focuses on corporate managers and their work, it provides insights for the public manager. The author found, among other things, that innovative managers tend to be visionary, comfortable with change, and persistent. Innovation tends to flourish in organizations where territories overlap and people have contact across functions; information flows freely; numbers of people have excesses in their budgets; many managers are in open-ended positions; and reward systems look to the future, not the past. These findings may suggest ways to encourage innovation in the public sector—or identify some of the factors that make innovation difficult.

When Steve Talbot, an operations manager, began a staff job reporting to the general manager of a product group, he had no line responsibility, no subordinates or budget of his own, and only a vague mandate to "explore options to improve performance."

To do this, Talbot set about collecting resources by bargaining with product-line managers and sales managers. By promising the product-line managers that he would save them having to negotiate with sales to get top priority for their products, he got a budget from them. Then, because he had the money in hand, Talbot got the sales managers to agree to hire one salesperson per product line, with Talbot permitted to do the hiring.

The next area he tackled was field services. Because the people in this area were conservative and tightfisted, Talbot went to his boss to get support for his recommendations about this area.

With the sales and service functions increasing their market share, it was easy for Talbot to get the product-line managers' backing when he pushed for selling a major new product that he had devised. And, to keep his action team functioning and behind him, Talbot made sure that "everyone became a hero" when the senior vice president of engineering asked him to explain his success to corporate officers.

Arthur Drumm, a technical department head of two sections, wanted to develop a new measuring instrument that could dramatically improve the company's product quality. But only Drumm thought this approach would work; those around him were not convinced it was needed or would pay off. After spending months developing data to show that the company needed the instrument, Drumm convinced several of his bosses two levels up to contribute $300,000 to its development. He put together a task force made up of representatives from all the manufacturing sites to advise on the development process and to ensure that the instrument would fit in with operations.

When, early on, one high-level manager opposed the project, Drumm coached two others in preparation for an officer-level meeting at which they were going to present his proposal. And when executives argued about which budget line the money would come from, R&D or engineering, Drumm tried to ease the tension. His persistence netted the company an extremely valuable new technique.

When Doris Randall became the head of a backwater purchasing department, one of three departments in her area, she expected the assignment to advance her career. Understandably, she was disappointed at the poor state of the function she had inherited and looked around for ways to make improvements. She first sought information from users of the department's services and, with this information, got her boss to agree to a first wave of changes. No one in her position had ever had such close contacts with users before, and Randall employed her knowledge to reorganize the unit into a cluster of user-oriented specialties with each staff member concentrating on a particular need.

Once she had the reorganization in place and her function acknowledged as the best purchasing department in the region, Randall wanted to reorganize the other two purchasing departments. Her boss, perhaps out of concern that he would lose his position to Randall if the proposed changes took place, discouraged her. But her credibility was so strong that her boss's boss—who viewed her changes as a model for improvements in other areas—gave Randall the go-ahead to merge the three purchasing departments into one. Greater efficiency, cost savings, and increased user satisfaction resulted.

These three managers are enterprising, innovative, and entrepreneurial middle managers who are part of a group that can play a key role in the United States' return to economic leadership.

If that seems like an overly grand statement, consider the basis for U.S. companies' success in the past innovation in products and advances in management techniques. Then consider the pivotal contribution middle managers make to innovation and change in large organizations. Top leaders' general directives to open a new market, improve quality, or cut costs mean nothing without efficient middle managers just below officer level able to design the systems, carry them out, and redirect their staffs' activities accordingly. Furthermore, because middle managers have their fingers on the pulse of operations, they can also conceive, suggest, and set in motion new ideas that top managers may not have thought of.

The middle managers described here are not extraordinary individuals. They do, however, share a number of characteristics:

1. *Comfort with change.* They are confident that uncertainties will be clarified. They also have foresight and see unmet needs as opportunities.
2. *Clarity of direction.* They select projects carefully and, with their long time horizons, view setbacks as temporary blips in an otherwise straight path to a goal.
3. *Thoroughness.* They prepare well for meetings and are professional in making their presentations. They have insight into organizational politics and a sense of whose support can help them at various junctures.
4. *Participative management style.* They encourage subordinates to put in maximum effort and to be part of the team, promise them a share of the rewards, and deliver on their promises.
5. *Persuasiveness, persistence, and discretion.* They understand that they cannot achieve their ends overnight, so they persevere—using tact—until they do.

What makes it possible for managers to use such skills for the company's benefit? They work in organizations where the culture fosters collaboration and teamwork and where structures encourage people to "do what needs to be done." Moreover, they usually work under top managers who consciously incorporate conditions facilitating innovation and achievement into their companies' structures and operations.

These conclusions come from a study of the major accomplishments of 165 effective middle managers in five leading American corporations (for details on the research, see the box below). I undertook this study to determine managers' contributions to a company's

---

The research project

After a pilot study in which it interviewed 26 effective middle managers from 18 companies, the research team interviewed, in depth, 165 middle managers from five major corporations located across the United States. The 165 were chosen by their companies to participate because of their reputations for effectiveness. We did not want a random sample: we were looking for "the best and the brightest" who could serve as models for others. It turned out, however, that every major function was represented, and roughly in proportion to its importance in the company's success. (For example, there were more innovative sales and marketing managers representing the "market-driven" company and more technical, R&D, and manufacturing managers from the "product-driven" companies.)

During the two-hour interviews, the managers talked about all aspects of a single significant accomplishment, from the glimmering of an idea to the results. We asked the managers to focus on the most significant of a set of four or five of their accomplishments over the previous two years. We also elicited a chronology of the project as well as responses to a set of open-ended questions about the acquisition of power, the handling of roadblocks, and the doling out of rewards. We supplemented the interviews with discussions about current issues in the five companies with our contacts in each company.

The five companies represent a range of types and industries: from rather traditional, slow-moving, mature companies to fast-changing, newer, high-technology companies. We included both service and manufacturing companies that are from different parts of the country and are at different stages in their development. The one thing that all five have in common is an intense interest in the topic of the study. Facing highly competitive markets (for the manufacturing companies a constant since their founding; for the service companies a newer phenomenon), all of these corporations wanted to encourage their middle managers to be more enterprising and innovative.

Our pseudonyms for the companies emphasize a central feature of each:

CHIPCO: manufacturer of computer products

FINCO: insurance and related financial services

MEDCO: manufacturer of large medical equipment

RADCO (for "R&D"): manufacturer of optical products

UTICO: communications utility

overall success as well as the conditions that stimulate innovation and thus push a business beyond a short-term emphasis and allow it to secure a successful future.

Each of the 165 managers studied—all of whom were deemed "effective" by their companies—told the research team about a particular accomplishment; these covered a wide range. Some of the successes, though impressive, clearly were achieved within the boundaries of established company practice. Others, however, involved innovation: introduction of new methods, structures, or products that increased the company's capacity. All in all, 99 of the 165 accomplishments fall within the definition of an innovative effort.

Basic accomplishments differ from innovative ones not only in scope and long-run impact but also in what it takes to achieve them. They are part of the assigned job and require only routine and readily available means to carry them out. Managers reporting this kind of accomplishment said they were just doing their jobs. Little was problematic—they had an assignment to tackle; they were told, or they already knew, how to go about it; they used existing budget or staff; they didn't need to gather or share much information outside of their units; and they encountered little or no opposition. Managers performing such activities don't generate innovations for their companies; they merely accomplish things faster or better that they already know how to do.[1]

In contrast, innovative accomplishments are strikingly entrepreneurial. Moreover, they are sometimes highly problematic and generally involve acquiring and using power and influence. (See the box on pages 26 and 27 for more details on the study's definitions of *basic* and *innovative* accomplishments.)

In this article, I first explore how managers influence their organizations to achieve goals throughout the various stages of a project's life. Next I discuss the managerial styles of the persons studied and the kinds of innovation they brought about. I look finally at the types of companies these entrepreneurial managers worked in and explore what top officers can do to foster a creative environment.

The role of power in enterprise

Because most innovative achievements cut across organizational lines and threaten to disrupt existing arrangements, enterprising managers need tools beyond those that come with the job. Innovations have implications for other functions and areas, and they require data, agreements, and resources of wider scope than routine operations demand. Even R&D managers, who are expected to produce innovations, need more information, support, and resources for major projects than those built into regular R&D functions. They too may need additional data, more money, or agreement from extra-functional officials that the project is necessary. Only hindsight shows that an innovative project was bound to be successful.

Because of the extra resources they require, entrepreneurial managers need to go beyond the limits of their formal positions. For this they need power. In large organizations at least, I have observed that powerlessness "corrupts." That is, lack of power (the capacity to mobilize resources and people to get things done) tends to create managers who are more concerned about guarding their territories than about collaborating with others to benefit the organization. At the same time, when managers hoard potential power and don't invest it in productive action, it atrophies and eventually blocks achievements.

Furthermore, when some people have too much unused power and others too little, problems occur. To produce results, power—like money—needs to circulate. To come up with innovations, managers have to be in areas where power circulates, where it can be grabbed and invested. In this sense, organizational power is transactional: it

---

What is an innovative accomplishment?

We categorized the 165 managers' accomplishments according to their primary impact on the company. Many accomplishments had multiple results or multiple components, but it was the breadth of scope of the accomplishment and its future utility for the company that defined its category. Immediate dollar results were *not* the central issue; rather, organizational "learning" or increased future capacity was the key. Thus, improving revenues by cutting costs while changing nothing else would be categorized differently from improving revenues by designing a new production method; only the latter leaves a lasting trace.

The accomplishments fall into two clusters:

Basic. Done solely within the existing framework and not affecting the company's longer-term capability: 66 of the 165 fall into this category.

Innovative. A new way for the company to use or expand its resources that raises long-term capacity: 99 of the 165 are such achievements.

Basic accomplishments include:

Doing the basic job—simply carrying out adequately a defined assignment within the bounds of one's job (e.g., "fulfilled sales objectives during a reorganization").

Affecting individuals' performance—having an impact on individuals (e.g., "found employee a job in original department after failing to retrain him").

exists as potential until someone makes a bid for it, invests it, and produces results with it.

The overarching condition required for managers to produce innovative achievements is this: they must envision an accomplishment beyond the scope of the job. They cannot alone possess the power to carry their idea out but they must be able to acquire the power they need easily. Thus, creative managers are not empowered simply by a boss or their job; on their own they seek and find the additional strength it takes to carry out major new initiatives. They are the corporate entrepreneurs.

Three commodities are necessary for accumulating productive power—information, resources, and support. Managers might find a portion of these within their purview and pour them into a project; managers with something they believe in will eagerly leverage their own staff and budget and even bootleg resources from their subordinates' budgets. But innovations usually require a manager to search for additional supplies elsewhere in the organization. Depending on

---

Advancing incrementally—achieving a higher level of performance within the basic job (e.g., "met more production schedules in plant than in past").

Innovative accomplishments include:

Effecting a new policy—creating a change of orientation or direction (e.g., "changed price-setting policy in product line with new model showing cost-quality trade-offs").

Finding a new opportunity—developing an entirely new product or opening a new market (e.g., "sold new product program to higher management and developed staffing for it").

Devising a fresh method—introducing a new process, procedure, or technology for continued use (e.g., "designed and implemented new information system for financial results by business sectors").

Designing a new structure—changing the formal structure, reorganizing or introducing a new structure, or forging a different link among units (e.g., "consolidated three offices into one").

While members of the research team occasionally argued about the placement of accomplishments in the subcategories, we were almost unanimous as to whether an accomplishment rated as basic or innovative. Even bringing off a financially significant or flashy increase in performance was considered basic if the accomplishment was well within the manager's assignment and territory, involved no new methods that could be used to repeat the feat elsewhere, opened no opportunities, or had no impact on corporate structure—in other words, reflected little inventiveness. The manager who achieved such a result might have been an excellent manager, but he or she was not an innovative one.

---

how easy the organization makes it to tap sources of power and on how technical the project is, acquiring power can be the most time-consuming and difficult part of the process.

Phases of the accomplishment   A prototypical innovation goes through three phases: project definition (acquisition and application of information to shape a manageable, salable project), coalition building (development of a network of backers who agree to provide resources and support), and action (application of the resources, information, and support to the project and mobilization of an action team). Let us examine each of these steps in more detail.

Defining the project   Before defining a project, managers need to identify the problem. People in an organization may hold many conflicting views about the best method of reaching a goal, and discovering the basis of these conflicting perspectives (while gathering hard data) is critical to a manager's success.

In one case, information circulating freely about the original design of a part was inaccurate. The manager needed to acquire new data to prove that the problem he was about to tackle was not a manufacturing shortcoming but a design flaw. But, as often happens, some people had a stake in the popular view. Even hard-nosed engineers in our study acknowledged that, in the early stages of an entrepreneurial project, managers need political information as much as they do technical data. Without political savvy, say these engineers, no one can get a project beyond the proposal stage.

The culmination of the project definition phase comes when managers sift through the fragments of information from each source and focus on a particular target. Then, despite the fact that managers may initially have been handed a certain area as an assignment, they still have to "sell" the project that evolves. In the innovative efforts I observed, the managers' assignments involved no promises of resources or support required to do anything more than routine activities.

Furthermore, to implement the innovation, a manager has to call on the cooperation of many others besides the boss who assigned the task. Many of these others may be independent actors who are not compelled to cooperate simply because the manager has carved a project out of a general assignment. Even subordinates may not be automatically on board. If they are professionals or managers, they have a number of other tasks and the right to set some of their own priorities; and if they are in a matrix, they may be responsible to other bosses as well.

For example, in her new job as head of a manufacturing planning unit, Heidi Wilson's assignment was to improve the cost efficiency of operations and thereby boost the company's price competitiveness.

Her boss told her she could spend six months "saying nothing and just observing, getting to know what's really going on." One of the first things she noticed was that the flow of goods through the company was organized in an overly complicated, time-consuming, and expensive fashion.

The assignment gave Wilson the mandate to seek information but not to carry out any particular activities. Wilson set about to gather organizational, technical, and political information in order to translate her ambiguous task into a concrete project. She followed goods through the company to determine what the process was and how it could be changed. She sought ideas and impressions from manufacturing line managers, at the same time learning the location of vested interests and where other patches of organizational quicksand lurked. She compiled data, refined her approach, and packaged and repackaged her ideas until she believed she could "prove to people that I knew more about the company than they did."

Wilson's next step was "to do a number of punchy presentations with pictures and graphs and charts." At the presentations, she got two kinds of response: "Gee, we thought there was a problem but we never saw it outlined like this before" and "Aren't there better things to worry about?" To handle the critics, she "simply came back over and over again with information, more information than anyone else had." When she had gathered the data and received the feedback, Wilson was ready to formulate a project and sell it to her boss. Ultimately, her project was approved, and it netted impressive cost savings.

Thus although innovation may begin with an assignment, it is usually one—like Wilson's—that is couched in general statements of results with the means largely unspecified. Occasionally, managers initiate projects themselves; however, initiation seldom occurs in a vacuum. Creative managers listen to a stream of information from superiors and peers and then identify a perceived need. In the early stages of defining a project, managers may spend more time talking with people outside their own functions than with subordinates or bosses inside.

One R&D manager said he had "hung out" with product designers while trying to get a handle on the best way to formulate a new process-development project. Another R&D manager in our survey got the idea for a new production method from a conversation about problems he had with the head of production. He then convinced his boss to let him determine whether a corrective project could be developed.

Building a coalition   Next, entrepreneurial managers need to pull in the resources and support to make the project work. For creative accomplishments, these power-related tools do not come through the vertical chain of command but rather from many areas of the organization.

George Putnam's innovation is typical. Putnam was an assistant department manager for product testing in a company that was about to demonstrate a product at a site that attracted a large number of potential buyers. Putnam heard through the grapevine that a decision was imminent about which model to display. The product managers were each lobbying for their own, and the marketing people also had a favorite. Putnam, who was close to the products, thought that the first-choice model had grave defects and so decided to demonstrate to the marketing staff both what the problems with the first one were and the superiority of another model.

Building on a long-term relationship with the people in corporate quality control and a good alliance with his boss, Putnam sought the tools he needed: the blessing of the vice president of engineering (his boss's boss), special materials for testing from the materials division, a budget from corporate quality control, and staff from his own units to carry out the tests. As Putnam put it, this was all done through one-on-one "horse trading"—showing each manager how much the others were chipping in. Then Putnam met informally with the key marketing staffer to learn what it would take to convince him.

As the test results emerged, Putnam took them to his peers in marketing, engineering, and quality control so they could feed them to their superiors. The accumulated support persuaded the decision makers to adopt Putnam's choice of a model; it later became a strong money-maker. In sum, Putnam had completely stepped out of his usual role to build a consensus that shaped a major policy decision.

Thus the most successful innovations derive from situations where a number of people from a number of areas make contributions. They provide a kind of checks-and-balances system to an activity that is otherwise nonroutine and, therefore, is not subject to the usual controls. By building a coalition before extensive project activity gets under way, the manager also ensures the availability of enough support to keep momentum going and to guarantee implementation.

In one company, the process of lining up peers and stakeholders as early supporters is called "making cheerleaders"; in another, "preselling." Sometimes managers ask peers for "pledges" of money or staff to be collected later if higher management approves the project and provides overall resources.

After garnering peer support, usually managers next seek support at much higher levels. While we found surprisingly few instances of top management directly sponsoring or championing a project, we did find that a general blessing from the top is clearly necessary to convert potential supporters into a solid team. In one case, top officers simply showed up at a meeting where the proposal was being discussed; their presence ensured that other people couldn't use the "pocket veto" power of headquarters as an excuse to table the issue. Also, the very presence of a key executive at such a meeting is often a signal of the proposal's importance to the rest of the organization.

Enterprising managers learn who at the top-executive level has the power to affect their projects (including material resources or vital initial approval power). Then they negotiate for these executives' support, using polished formal presentations. Whereas managers can often sell the project to peers and stakeholders by appealing to these people's self-interests and assuring them they know what they're talking about, managers need to offer top executives more guarantees about both the technical and the political adequacies of projects.

Key executives tend to evaluate a proposal in terms of its salability to *their* constituencies. Sometimes entrepreneurial managers arm top executives with materials or rehearse them for their own presentations to other people (such as members of an executive committee or the board) who have to approve the project.

Most often, since many of the projects that originate at the middle of a company can be supported at that level and will not tap corporate funds, those at high levels in the organization simply provide a general expression of support. However, the attention top management confers on this activity, many of our interviewees told us, makes it possible to sell their own staffs as well as others.

But once in a while, a presentation to top-level officers results in help in obtaining supplies. Sometimes enterprising managers walk away with the promise of a large capital expenditure or assistance getting staff or space. Sometimes a promise of resources is contingent on getting others on board. "If you can raise the money, go ahead with this," is a frequent directive to an enterprising manager.

In one situation, a service manager approached his boss and his boss's boss for a budget for a college recruitment and training program that he had been supporting on his own with funds bootlegged from his staff. The top executives told him they would grant a large budget if he could get his four peers to support the project. Somewhat to their surprise, he came back with this support. He had taken his peers away from the office for three days for a round of negotiation and planning. In cases like this, top management is not so much hedging its bets as using its ability to secure peer support for what might otherwise be risky projects.

With promises of resources and support in hand, enterprising managers can go back to the immediate boss or bosses to make plans for moving ahead. Usually the bosses are simply waiting for this tangible sign of power to continue authorizing the project. But in other cases the bosses are not fully involved and won't be sold until the manager has higher-level support.

Of course, during the coalition-building phase, the network of supporters does not play a passive role; their comments, criticisms, and objectives help shape the project into one that is more likely to succeed. Another result of the coalition-building phase is, then, a set of reality checks that ensures that projects unlikely to succeed will go no farther.

Moving into action   The innovative manager's next step is to mobilize key players to carry out the project. Whether the players are nominal subordinates or a special project group such as a task force, managers forge them into a team. Enterprising managers bring the people involved in the project together, give them briefings and assignments, pump them up for the extra effort needed, seek their ideas and suggestions (both as a way to involve them and to further refine the project), and promise them a share of the rewards. As one manager put it, "It takes more selling than telling." In most of the innovations we observed, the manager couldn't just order subordinates to get involved. Doing something beyond routine work that involves creativity and cooperation requires the full commitment of subordinates; otherwise the project will not succeed.

During the action phase, managers have four central organizational tasks. The technical details of the project and the actual work directed toward project goals are now in the hands of the action team. Managers may contribute ideas or even get involved in hands-on experimentation, but their primary functions are still largely external and organizational, centered around maintaining the boundaries and integrity of the project.

The manager's first task is to *handle interference* or opposition that may jeopardize the project. Entrepreneurial managers encounter strikingly little overt opposition—perhaps because their success at coalition building determines whether a project gets started in the first place. Resistance takes a more passive form: criticism of the plan's details, foot-dragging, late responses to requests, or arguments over allocation of time and resources among projects.

Managers are sometimes surprised that critics keep so quiet up to this point. One manufacturing manager who was gearing up for production of a new item had approached many executives in other areas while making cost estimates, and these executives had appeared positive about his efforts. But later, when he began organizing the manufacturing process itself, he heard objections from these very people.

During this phase, therefore, innovative managers may have to spend as much time in meetings, both formal and one-to-one, as they did to get the project launched. Managers need to prepare thoroughly for these meetings so they can counter skepticism and objections with clear facts, persuasion, and reminders of the benefits that can accrue to managers meeting the project's objectives. In most cases, a clear presentation of facts is enough. But not always: one of our respondents, a high-level champion, had to tell an opponent to back down, that the project was going ahead anyway, and that his carping was annoying.

Whereas managers need to directly counter open challenges and criticism that might result in the flow of power or supplies being cut off, they simply keep other interference outside the boundaries of the project. In effect, the manager defines a protected area for the group's work. He or she goes outside this area to head off critics and to keep people or rules imposed by higher management from disrupting project tasks.

While the team itself is sometimes unaware of the manager's contribution, the manager—like Tom West (head of the now-famous computer-design group at Data General)—patrols the boundaries.[2] Acting as interference filters, managers in my study protected innovative projects by bending rules, transferring funds "illicitly" from one budget line to another, developing special reward or incentive systems that offered bonuses above company pay rates, and ensuring that superiors stayed away unless needed.

The second action-phase task is *maintaining momentum* and continuity. Here interference comes from internal rather than external sources. Foot-dragging or inactivity is a constant danger, especially if the creative effort adds to work loads. In our study, enterprising managers as well as team members complained continually about the tendency for routine activities to take precedence over special projects and to consume limited time.

In addition, it is easier for managers to whip up excitement over a vision at start-up than to keep the goal in people's minds when they face the tedium of the work. Thus, managers' team-building skills are essential. So the project doesn't lose momentum, managers must sustain the enthusiasm of all—from supporters to suppliers—by being persistent and keeping the team aware of supportive authorities who are clearly waiting for results.

One manager, who was involved in a full-time project to develop new and more efficient methods of producing a certain ingredient, maintained momentum by holding daily meetings with the core team, getting together often with operations managers and members of a task force he had formed, putting out weekly status reports, and making frequent presentations to top management. When foot-dragging occurs, many entrepreneurial managers pull in high-level supporters—without compromising the autonomy of the project—to get the team back on board. A letter or a visit from the big boss can remind everyone just how important the project is.

A third task of middle managers in the action phase is to engage in whatever *secondary redesign*—other changes made to support the key change—is necessary to keep the project going. For example, a manager whose team was setting up a computerized information bank held weekly team meetings to define tactics. A fallout of these meetings was a set of new awards and a fresh performance appraisal system for team members and their subordinates.

As necessary, managers introduce new arrangements to conjoin with the core tasks. When it seems that a project is bogging down—that is, when everything possible has been done and no more results are on the horizon—managers often change the structure or approach. Such alterations can cause a redoubling of effort and a renewed attack on the problem. They can also bring the company additional unplanned innovations as a side benefit from the main project.

The fourth task of the action phase, *external communication*, brings the accomplishment full circle. The project begins with gathering information; now it is important to send information out. It is vital to (as several managers put it) "manage the press" so that peers and key supporters have an up-to-date impression of the project and its success. Delivering on promises is also important. As much as possible, innovative managers meet deadlines, deliver early benefits to others, and keep supporters supplied with information. Doing so establishes the credibility of both the project and the manager, even before concrete results can be shown.

Information must be shared with the team and the coalition as well. Good managers periodically remind the team of what they stand to gain from the accomplishment, hold meetings to give feedback and to stimulate pride in the project, and make a point of congratulating each staff member individually. After all, as Steve Talbot (of my first example) said, many people gave this middle manager power because of a promise that everyone would be a hero.

A management style for innovation

Clearly there is a strong association between carrying out an innovative accomplishment and employing a participative-collaborative management style. The managers observed reached success by:

1. Persuading more than ordering, though managers sometimes use pressure as a last resort.
2. Building a team, which entails among other things frequent staff meetings and considerable sharing of information.
3. Seeking inputs from others—that is, asking for ideas about users' needs, soliciting suggestions from subordinates, welcoming peer review, and so forth.
4. Acknowledging others' stake or potential stake in the project—in other words, being politically sensitive.
5. Sharing rewards and recognition willingly.

A collaborative style is also useful when carrying out basic accomplishments; however, in such endeavors it is not required. Managers can bring off many basic accomplishments using a traditional, more autocratic style. Because they're doing what is assigned, they don't need external support; because they have all the tools to do it, they don't need to get anyone else involved (they simply direct subordinates to do what is required). But for innovative accomplishments —seeking funds, staff, or information (political as well as technical) from outside the work unit; attending long meetings and presentations; and requiring "above and beyond" effort from staff—a style that revolves around participation, collaboration, and persuasion is essential.

The participative-collaborative style also helps creative managers reduce risk because it encourages completion of the assignment. Furthermore, others' involvement serves as a check-and-balance on the project, reshaping it to make it more of a sure thing and putting pressure on people to follow through. The few projects in my study that disintegrated did so because the manager failed to build a coalition of supporters and collaborators.

Corporate conditions that encourage enterprise

Just as the manager's strategies to develop and implement innovations followed many different patterns, so also the level of enterprise managers achieved varied strongly across the five companies we studied (see the exhibit on page 36). Managers in newer, high-technology companies have a much higher proportion of innovative accomplishments than managers in other industries. At "CHIPCO," a computer parts manufacturer, 71% of all the things effective managers did were innovative; for "UTICO," a communications utility, the number is 33%; for "FINCO," an insurance company, it is 47%.

This difference in levels of innovative achievement correlates with the extent to which these companies' structures and cultures support middle managers' creativity. Companies producing the most entrepreneurs have cultures that encourage collaboration and teamwork. Moreover, they have complex structures that link people in multiple ways and help them go beyond the confines of their defined jobs to do "what needs to be done."

CHIPCO, which showed the most entrepreneurial activity of any company in our study, is a rapidly growing electronics company with abundant resources. That its culture favors independent action and team effort is communicated quickly and clearly to the newcomer. Sources of support and money are constantly shifting and, as growth occurs, managers rapidly move on to other positions. But even though people frequently express frustration about the shifting approval process, slippage of schedules, and continual entry of new players onto the stage, they don't complain about lost opportunities. For one thing, because coalitions support the various projects, new

	CHIPCO	RADCO	MEDCO	FINCO	UTICO
Percent of effective managers with entrepreneurial accomplishments	71%	69%	67%	47%	33%
Current economic trend	Steadily up	Trend up but currently down	Up	Mixed	Down
Current "change issues"	Change "normal"; constant change in product generations; proliferating staff and units.	Change "normal" in products, technologies; recent changeover to second management generation with new focus.	Reorganized about 3-4 years ago to install matrix; "normal" product technology changes.	Change a "shock"; new top management group from outside reorganizing and trying to add competitive market posture.	Change a "shock"; undergoing reorganization to install matrix and add competitive market posture while reducing staff.
Organization structure	Matrix	Matrix in some areas; product lines act as quasi-divisions.	Matrix in some areas.	Divisional; unitary hierarchy within divisions, some central services.	Functional organization; currently overlaying a matrix of regions and markets.
Information flow	Decentralized	Mixed	Mixed	Centralized	Centralized
	Free	Free	Moderately free	Constricted	Constricted
Communication	Horizontal	Horizontal	Horizontal	Vertical	Vertical
Culture	Clear, consistent; favors individual initiative.	Clear, though in transition from emphasis on invention to emphasis on routinization.	Clear; pride in company, belief that talent will be rewarded.	Idiosyncratic; depends on boss and area.	Clear but top management would like to change it; favors security, maintenance, protection.
Current "emotional" climate	Pride in company, team feeling, some "burn-out."	Uncertainty about changes.	Pride in company, team feeling.	Low trust, high uncertainty.	High certainty, confusion.
Rewards	Abundant. Include visibility, chance to do more challenging work in the future and get bigger budget for projects.	Abundant. Include visibility, chance to do more challenging work in future and get bigger budget for projects.	Moderately abundant. Conventional.	Scarce. Primarily monetary.	Scarce. Promotion, salary freeze; recognition by peers grudging.

Characteristics of the five companies in order of most to least "entrepreneurial."

project managers feel bound to honor their predecessors' financial commitments.

CHIPCO managers have broad job charters to "do the right thing" in a manner of their own choosing. Lateral relationships are more important than vertical ones. Most functions are in a matrix, and some managers have up to four "bosses." Top management expects ideas to bubble up from lower levels. Senior executives then select solutions rather than issue confining directives. In fact, people generally rely on informal face-to-face communication across units to build a consensus. Managers spend a lot of time in meetings; information flows freely, and reputation among peers—instead of formal authority or title—conveys credibility and garners support. Career mobility at CHIPCO is rapid, and people have pride in the company's success.

RADCO, the company with the strongest R&D orientation in the study, has many of CHIPCO's qualities but bears the burden of recent changes. RADCO's once-strong culture and its image as a research institute are in flux and may be eroding. A new top management with new ways of thinking is shifting the orientation of the company, and some people express concern about the lack of clear direction and long-range planning. People's faith in RADCO's strategy of technical superiority has weakened, and its traditional orientation toward innovation is giving way to a concern for routinization and production efficiency. This shift is resulting in conflict and uncertainty. Where once access to the top was easy, now the decentralized matrix structure—with fewer central services—makes it difficult.

As at CHIPCO, lateral relationships are important, though top management's presence is felt more. In the partial matrix, some managers have as many as four "bosses." A middle manager's boss or someone in higher management is likely to give general support to projects as long as peers (within and across functions) get on board. And peers often work decisions up the organization through their own hierarchies.

Procedures at RADCO are both informal and formal: much happens at meetings and presentations and through persuasion, plus the company's long-term employment and well-established working relationships encourage lateral communication. But managers also use task forces and steering committees. Projects often last for years, sustained by the company's image as a leader in treating employees well.

MEDCO manufactures and sells advanced medical equipment, often applying ideas developed elsewhere. Although MEDCO produces a high proportion of innovative accomplishments, it has a greater degree of central planning and routinization than either CHIPCO or RADCO. Despite headquarters' strong role, heads of functions and product managers can vary their approaches. Employers believe that MEDCO's complex matrix system allows autonomy and creates opportunities but is also time wasting because clear accountability is lacking.

Teamwork and competition coexist at MEDCO. Although top management officially encourages teamwork and the matrix produces a tendency for trades and selling to go on within the organization, interdepartmental and interproduct rivalries sometimes get in the way. Rewards, especially promotions, are available; but they often come late and even then are not always clear or consistent. Because many employees have been with MEDCO for a long time, both job mobility and job security are high. Finally, managers see the company as a leader in its approach to management and as a technological follower in all areas but one.

The last two companies in the study, FINCO (insurance) and UTICO (communications), show the lowest proportion of innovative achievements. Many of the completed projects seemed to be successful *despite* the system.

Currently FINCO has an idiosyncratic and inconsistent culture: employees don't have a clear image of the company, its style, or its direction. How managers are treated depends very much on one's boss—one-to-one relationships and private deals carry a great deal of weight. Though the atmosphere of uncertainty creates opportunities for a few, it generally limits risk taking. Moreover, reorganizations, a top-management shake-up, and shuffling of personnel have fostered insecurity and suspicion. It is difficult for managers to get commitment from their subordinates because they question the manager's tenure. Managers spend much time and energy coping with change, reassuring subordinates, and orienting new staff instead of developing future-oriented projects. Still, because the uncertainty creates a vacuum, a few managers in powerful positions (many of whom were brought in to initiate change) do benefit.

Unlike the innovation-producing companies, FINCO features vertical relationships. With little encouragement to collaborate, managers seldom make contact across functions or work in teams. Managers often see formal structures and systems as constraints rather than as supports. Rewards are scarce, and occasionally a manager will break a promise about them. Seeing the company as a follower, not a leader, the managers at FINCO sometimes make unfavorable comparisons between it and other companies in the industry. Furthermore, they resent the fact that FINCO's top management brings in so many executives from outside; they see it as an insult.

UTICO is a very good company in many ways; it is well regarded by its employees and is considered progressive for its industry. However, despite the strong need for UTICO to be more creative and thus more competitive and despite movement toward a matrix structure,

UTICO's middle ranks aren't very innovative. UTICO's culture is changing—from being based on security and maintenance to being based on flexibility and competition—and the atmosphere of uncertainty frustrates achievers. Moreover, UTICO remains very centralized. Top management largely directs searches for new systems and methods through formal mechanisms whose ponderousness sometimes discourages innovation. Tight budgetary constraints make it difficult for middle managers to tap funds; carefully measured duties discourage risk takers; and a lockstep chain of command makes it dangerous for managers to bypass their bosses.

Information flows vertically and sluggishly. Because of limited cooperation among work units, even technical data can be hard to get. Weak-spot management means that problems, not successes, get attention. Jealousy and competition over turf kill praise from peers and sometimes from bosses. Managers' image of the company is mixed: they see it as leading its type of business but behind more modern companies in rate of change.

Organizational supports for creativity

Examination of the differences in organization, culture, and practices in these five companies makes clear the circumstances under which enterprise can flourish. To tackle and solve tricky problems, people need both the opportunities and the incentives to reach beyond their formal jobs and combine organizational resources in new ways.[3] The following create these opportunities:

1. Multiple reporting relationships and overlapping territories. These force middle managers to carve out their own ideas about appropriate action and to sell peers in neighboring areas or more than one boss.
2. A free and somewhat random flow of information. Data flow of this kind prods executives to find ideas in unexpected places and pushes them to combine fragments of information.
3. Many centers of power with some budgetary flexibility. If such centers are easily accessible to middle managers, they will be encouraged to make proposals and acquire resources.
4. A high proportion of managers in loosely defined positions or with ambiguous assignments. Those without subordinates or line responsibilities who are told to "solve problems" must argue for a budget or develop their own constituency.
5. Frequent and smooth cross-functional contact, a tradition of working in teams and sharing credit widely, and emphasis on lateral rather than vertical relationships as a source of resources, information, and support. These circumstances require managers to get peer support for their projects before top officers approve.

6.   A reward system that emphasizes investment in people and projects rather than payment for past services. Such a system encourages executives to move into challenging jobs, gives them budgets to tackle projects, and rewards them after their accomplishments with the chance to take on even bigger projects in the future.

Author's note: I'd like to thank the members of the research team who participated in this study: Karen Belinky, Janis Bowersox, Allan Cohen, Ken Farbstein, Henry Foley, William Fonvielle, Karen Handmaker, Irene Schneller, Barry Stein, David Summers, and Mary Vogel. Ken Farbstein and David Summers made especially important contributions. All individual and company names in the article are pseudonyms.

1.   See my book *Men and Women of the Corporation* (New York: Basic Books, 1977); also see my article "Power Failures in Management Circuits," *Harvard Business Review*, July–August 1979, p. 65.

2.   Tracy Kidder, *The Soul of a New Machine* (Boston: Little, Brown, 1981).

3.   My findings about conditions stimulating managerial innovations are generally consistent with those on technical (R&D) innovation. See James Utterback, "Innovation in Industry," *Science*, February 1974, pp. 620–626; John Kimberly, "Managerial Innovation," *Handbook of Organizational Design*, edited by W. H. Starbuck (New York: Oxford, 1981); and Goodmeasure, Inc., "99 Propositions on Innovation from the Research Literature," *Stimulating Innovation in Middle Management* (Cambridge, Mass., 1982).

PART 2

Rethinking
Public
Services

Rethinking Public Service Delivery

Ted Kolderie

Lou Olsen was talking. He was at a meeting of the task force put together by the Twin Cities Metropolitan Council to look at the need for revenues for regional services. Olsen, the no-nonsense manager of the Metropolitan Transit Commission, was describing the rise in bus operating expenditures.

From the far end of the table came a quiet question from the mayor of Minneapolis, Donald Fraser. "What accounts for those increases?"

Olsen explained that there are many factors. The effort to serve the suburbs in a dispersed, low-density urban region; a peak-hour business operating with a full-time labor force; a labor contract with cost-of-living increases, adjusted quarterly; and the effect of traditional practices and decisions made during public take-over a decade ago—all contributed to the increases.

All Fraser said was, "If we operated like that, we'd be out of business."

The judgment lay heavily in the room. Fraser was saying that this was more than just a funding issue. He continued: "If you want my cooperation, you're going to have to reexamine the fundamentals of that service."

This vignette captures the central policy issue facing local governments. How do they respond to the squeeze between rising costs and stable revenues? More precisely, doesn't their response have to include a major effort to change, in some fundamental sense, the way things are done? Perhaps not everyone would answer yes; perhaps not everyone wants to answer yes.

There are *conventional* policy options to explore before plunging into nontraditional service delivery approaches. Some local jurisdic-

Reprinted with permission from *Public Management*, October 1982.

tions may be able to conceal new taxes. Some central cities may be willing to accept the long-term risks involved in taxing commuters. Other cities may go to the private sector for financial help. Still other local governments may decide to raise revenues by charging user fees, or shifting over monies from other functions or levels of government. You can cut service back, reduce benefit levels and entitlements, or eliminate a service altogether. Much of this is now being done.

If conventional policy options, however, are not feasible or appropriate, local government may wish to explore alternative service delivery approaches. A basic policy decision about alternatives is whether to plunge in or not. This first decision is clearly political. Larry Susskind, the MIT professor directing the Impact 2½ Study in Massachusetts, claims there is no political reward for doing more with less. You may wish to think about the potential for political reward. Where you live maybe there isn't any reward, or maybe there is.

If you decide to use an alternative approach, you need to think it through carefully. This may seem like a minor point. You need to understand well and be committed to an alternative approach. As you find yourself being drawn in, be prepared to do the most difficult thing an individual (or organization) can be asked to do: change his basic way of thinking.

First, you'll need a noncentralist view of the way communities work. Actually, it isn't the service professional, public or private, who ultimately keeps streets clean and safe; it is the way people decide to behave. For example, a city cannot keep city streets clean if people walk along shedding paper. Similarly, doctors cannot keep patients healthy if they are not concerned about nutrition and exercise; teachers cannot educate kids who do not want to learn.

If there are dog bites in the neighborhood, residents may not think it necessary immediately to obtain more or better doctors. They may suggest paying neighborhood kids $5 apiece to round up the stray dogs. Residents may then come to you for the money you didn't need to spend on doctors. Why shouldn't they get it? Most people first think about informal, nonprofessional, low-capital approaches to problems. Governments should, but frequently don't.

Small beginnings are best
The question of scale can also be an important issue. Most alternative service delivery approaches have small beginnings. Many people in government are unaccustomed to solving problems through small scale action. Understandably, they know that it is more expensive for them to rehabilitate one house at a time than a project at a time, or to administer 100 contracts for refuse collection rather than just one comprehensive contract. How will the big job ever get done? If it's a

big job, isn't a big organization needed? So when considering alternative service delivery options, one needs a special attitude to conceive of a big job getting done through a large aggregation of individual, small actions. This is precisely the way much of the progress is being made in energy conservation. America is getting insulated one house at a time.

This leads to an important issue. In using an alternative service delivery approach, government may not clearly be seen "doing something." This may be a problem, especially for elected officials. So what does it mean for government to do something?

Does doing something mean that a local government is providing the service? Or are we talking about government producing the service? There is a fundamental difference in role (confused in much writing and talking by the sloppy use of the word *provider*). Think of it this way.

You provide a college education for your daughter; a university produces it. The federal government provides medical and hospital care for persons over 65; a variety of doctors and hospitals produces it. The city provides clean sidewalks and clean restaurants by requiring their owners to keep them clean, and by penalizing those who do not. In this case, the property owner is the producer.

"Providing" is the function of deciding that something shall be done. Government may act by paying to have something done (or insuring it, subsidizing it, or granting a franchise with a guaranteed rate of return). Or government may simply require of private parties that something be done. In any event, deciding that something should be done is the policy function. It is the essential governmental function.

Having decided to provide a particular service, a governmental unit may or may not then go on to *produce* it. It may turn to some other organization, to some other governmental unit, or to some private entity for the actual *doing*. Going outside does not change the public character of the facility or service: a highway is no less a public road because it is built by a private contractor, nor is a university cafeteria less of a university facility because it is operated by a private food service firm. This distinction is important because in the initial policy discussion about service alternatives there is frequently loose talk about government getting out of something. You need to ask, "Getting out of what? Out of providing the service? Out of producing it? Or out of both?" When people talk about service-shedding, for example, which function are they talking about?

Through contracting, government can get out of production while remaining (as I use the term) the provider. A city can also shed the responsibility for providing—for example, by declining to pay the bill out of public tax revenues. The growing trend of fees and charges, in which the citizens must pay the cost personally, is in a sense a gradual withdrawal from the providing function. This is how the term privatization ought to be used.

Basically, there are two policy decisions involved in arranging for the provision and production of any service (or, as we might say, in the redesign of service arrangements in the local public sector). First, you will want to think about what services to provide, the level of service, and the mechanisms for payment. Second, you will want to think about who actually does the work, how many doers there are going to be, and what they do.

Redesigning public services

As you begin to look at things this way, you will probably see a considerable amount of redesign going on in the service system in your own community, governmental and nongovernmental. Let me give a few examples from the community in which I work:

1. Libraries are charging for the use of meeting rooms, and for service above the minimum guaranteed to all users.
2. The Minneapolis public schools are offering families their choice of school by teaching mode and subject specialties city-wide. They are literally running a regulated-voucher program within the public system.
3. The department of transportation is experimenting with contracts for road maintenance and construction.
4. Employers and employees are increasingly paying doctors a lump sum, up front, to take care of a family's health for a year. The clinic is allowed to keep what it does not spend (usually, what is saved by reducing the use of hospitals).
5. As an alternative to funding the Metropolitan Transit Commission, the Minnesota legislature has allowed suburban cities to decide themselves what kind of transit service they want.
6. Perhaps borrowing from ICMA's *The Essential Community: Local Government in the Year 2000*, the city of St. Paul may soon begin trimming back to a core of essential services, producing for sale other services not needed but wanted by citizens or businesses.

The policy obstacles

Our experience has shown rather clearly some of the policy issues that have to be thought about and worked through. Major policy issues will surface, and every local government and every manager will have to work through them in local terms.

One category of issues needs little elaboration: city employees, including many in management, and public employee unions are troubled by alternative approaches. Some alternatives—contracting, for example—are not inconsistent with the principle of unionization.

There is frequently real discomfort if public services begin to look like a market. People who do not like markets will object when proposals are made to introduce choice and competition. Sometimes the trouble is simply a misunderstanding, an impression that the government is throwing poor people back on their own resources.

You may face another related policy objection—the argument that choice should not be introduced into the public service system (at least not for consumers) because some people do not have the information needed to make good choices. You can do a couple of things with this. You can point out that things have to come in a logical order. There is no way to study the differences between automobiles until there are automobiles. And you can question whether people are really as incapable of choice as this objection suggests. Common experience and savvy are often better than a formal education, and a lot of the poor have pretty good informal networks for information.

The readiness of the community for alternative approaches will be an issue, one way or another. In some communities, the city employees may have an unbreakable lock on service production; in others, some commercial vendor may have a lock on the work. The media may be sympathetic, or may view a proposed change as some kind of rip-off. And perhaps most important, there is the question of alternative producers. Nothing happens unless there are other willing and able parties to assume service delivery (e.g., volunteer, or mutual-help groups, contractors available to bid). When these alternative service producers are not present, they will need to be cultivated. Each community is different. Some will have a fairly substantial ability to implement alternatives, others will not. The ability to redesign and to adapt the service delivery system is a kind of resource—it's almost like having a favorable natural climate. There will be limits to what managers can do, which they will probably have to accept.

If a venture into alternatives seems possible for your community, you will wish to think about how to present it. Is the new approach something you urge be done because it will save money and thereby reduce taxes? Or should it be done because the result will be better for the people? Each case will produce a different reaction. In my experience, a greater risk of ideological polarization comes with the former mode of presentation.

You should also think about how large a leveraging effect might result from the introduction of a service delivery alternative. Some changes are most important in their effect on other people. I suspect that here and there a city manager has bought a used asphalt plant not to operate but to encourage private suppliers to be more careful about their bids. Where I live, the schools moved quickly into programs for gifted children when they saw even a relatively small number of parents moving over to private schools. Producers are extremely aware of changes at the margin, and this sensitivity to competition can have a positive effect. (Remind the evaluators of this when they come to look at what you have done.) Often an alternative launched with great hopes will never grow significantly. This is not because it was a failure, but because it was such a success that the existing system moved quickly to pick up and copy the innovation.

Fears of coming apart

At the heart of experimentation with alternatives is the implication that the traditional model of the local public sector will be coming apart. A city or county will no longer be both provider and producer of a given service to a given population at a given time. The city or county will cease to be the monopoly seller to itself, the monopoly buyer. These functions will separate. For example, the local government may remain a producer but sell services to the community. This is the traditional model of a municipal enterprise and substantially extended. There is some reason to think that city park and recreation departments are moving in this direction, and beginning to resemble city water departments or airports that are fully financed by charges to their users.

Equally important, one unit of local government may become a producer for another unit of government. I am familiar with a suburb where the city government sells police service to the professional hockey club and buys in-house security from Pinkerton's when the high school teams are playing in the city ice arena. It earns $30 an hour, and pays $9.50.

The principal implication of this divorce between buying and selling functions, however, is the growing role of the local government as provider, on the *buyer* side of the market. It will be a real challenge for people trained and experienced in public administration to make this transition. The impulse toward comprehensiveness and uniformity will have to relax. The move into service delivery alternatives is less a matter of redesigning business than a matter of designing opportunities and incentives for alternative producers to create ideas for doing things a better way.

The essential mode of operation for a local government setting out to change the community service system is not active; it is passive. It is not to do things itself as a producer, but to let things be done by others. And this can be the hardest thing in the world for elected officials and managers. So again, it is worth thinking through the policy issues before you begin. And in doing this it is important to think about *what* services to provide and not just *how* to provide them.

Restructuring Service Delivery: The Basic Issue for Government

━━━━━━━━━━━━━━━━━━ James L. Hetland, Jr.

A year ago, deliberating on the Civic Agenda for the '80s in the wake of the 1980 presidential election and speculating on the real meaning of that election, it was apparent that the key for managing the issues of the '80s must be to "enlarge our capacity to adapt." The 1980 elections clearly indicated that citizens desired to have better control over their future—to have a more effective voice in resolving the issues that were plaguing our country—and were asking the federal government to reconsider its role of centralized policy making, and centralized service delivery and financing mechanisms.

Now, reform of the federal system—New Federalism—is reflected in legislation to foster less central government, more local control and better productivity in public services. How are we to adapt to changes that are now apparent through reduced federal budget subsidies and return of responsibility to state and local government and to the private sector?

The dilemma

Unfortunately, many still perceive reform as merely a change in the funding source for public services, with the federal government passing dollar responsibility to the states and the private sector. Many local governmental agencies and social service nonprofit entities that are most affected by the federal budget cuts perceive their problem as merely finding new revenue sources and learning new techniques to secure replacement dollars from the private sector and public foundations.

The issue is not replacement of dollars, but rather a need for basic changes in the way in which services are to be delivered. This is

Reprinted with permission from *National Civic Review*, February 1982. The article is from his address at the 87th National Conference on Government in Pittsburgh, November 15, 1981.

so even if money to permit public services to go on as before were made available. There appears to be a continuing and increasing sense of urgency on the part of the major business corporations and public nonprofit foundations regarding fund availability and the impact of the budget cuts on our service delivery systems. The concern relates in part to the fact that budget cuts currently authorized will amount to $35 billion while total corporate contributions in 1980 were $2.5 billion with approximately the same dollar amount from public foundations. This means that the private sector could double its philanthropic contributions and still meet less than 20 percent of the need if the issue was solely replacement of federal dollars. Even combined with public foundations, the private sector capacity to replace dollars would not exceed 20 percent to 30 percent.

The private sector concern also relates to expectations and perceptions within the public and donee community that cannot be fulfilled if we assume a continuance of the traditional ways in which public services are delivered. Unfortunately, the private sector has no processes in place to determine community priorities, or to effectively encourage nonprofit agency consolidations or mergers, or to assist in setting up mechanisms for resource allocations, or to create new local government policy-making systems.

This dilemma has been compounded because of the serious downturn in the national economy. In addition, the 1981 federal tax law contains incentives for companies that have a profitable year to reduce taxable income. Currently, federal income tax laws permit a business corporation to deduct up to 5 percent of its pre-tax taxable income. For 1982 the amount has been increased to 10 percent. The formula is applied to taxable income, however, not to profitability. As such, provisions designed to increase investment capital through reduction of taxable income in the short run works in opposition to expected increases in charitable or philanthropic giving by the business community.

The current situation may be looked on as a time of major opportunity. It is an unfortunate truism in government that change and innovation occur only when economic conditions prevent continuation of the status quo. The current inability to replace lost state and federal aid payments is a strong motivation toward change. There will continue to be calls for new tax sources, increased tax rates, etc., since governmental and educational professionals, as well as the service recipients, have strong motivations to preserve the status quo, which can be done only through replaced dollars. Our citizenry has awakened, however, like the proverbial sleeping giant, to the realization that our very substantial tax support for public service systems has not produced the expected results.

Accepting the budget cuts as a political response to a public call for change and decentralization, what can we expect to happen? Un-

fortunately, the federal budget cuts were just that and did not provide
new policy decisions relative to public needs and priorities. Local
governments are not told whether such functions as general welfare,
Medicaid, environmental clean-up, interstate transportation, etc.,
are to be federal, state-federal, state-local or local. Clearly, the federal
government must undertake to do some sorting out of functions if
adequate response is to take place at the state and local levels.

During this transition period, certain segments of the population will suffer more than others; mistakes will be made; public un-
happiness will be evident. While these results are unfortunate, they
deal with action to which the federal government is committed, and,
with local, state and private sector efforts to soften the impact, we
will survive the transition. But, what about the long-term question?
How do we establish and coordinate basic changes in service delivery
systems?

In 1980, the Citizens League serving the Twin Cities Area issued
a report entitled "Issues of the '80's." The essential idea was that an
institution's failing behavior can be protested in two ways—people
can stay and talk it out or they can walk away. The first is voice; the
second is exit. Voice can be effective only if a right of exit exists. If
there is no alternative but to stay and talk, basic change will not be
accomplished. Currently, our political system relies on voice—via
elections, referendums, planning commissions. Exit requires alternatives for those who choose not to abandon receiving the service, and
it exists primarily in the non-governmental sectors of our political-
economic system. In government, citizens are encouraged to create
change by remaining and talking. In effect, exit is viewed as disloyal
and voice is viewed as loyal.

What is involved in creating "exit" in governmental services?
Before documenting several possibilities, it is essential that we understand more precisely the existing system. Consider the question
of public accountability through exercise of the ballot. A politician
who perceives a strong citizen demand for change in the way in
which a public service is rendered can campaign on that issue and
promise, if elected, to effect the necessary change. The voters cast
their ballots in favor of that politician and assume that the change
will occur. Does it? In our governmental system we separate the
elected officials from the public agency administrators. Those public
employees who are responsible for delivering the service are insulated
and protected by administrative and civil service rules, and in large
measure they decide when and to what extent modifications will be
made. Clearly, if a department decides to oppose major changes,
nothing will happen, and in all likelihood the administrator will continue in his or her job. Two or four years later the citizen looks to the
politician for accountability and says, "I elected you to create change
in that service system and change has not occurred. I will not vote for

you. I will vote for your opponent and ask him to make the change."
Democracy in action eliminates the incumbent politician, elects a
new knight in shining armor and the voter frustration cycle begins
again.

A second feature is centralized decision making implemented
through tax dollar transfer payments.

A third basic characteristic is a perceived necessity for broad
equality and equal accessibility to public services. Service is to be
universal in the sense of being provided to everyone and standardized
in that the same type or level of service must be provided to all recipients. This political requirement tends to provide levels of service that
are unnecessarily expensive since all must receive a higher level of
service in order to provide an acceptable level to those who really
need it. The alternative is to operate at a minimum level to contain
costs, which may not be sufficient for those who truly need the service.

A fourth characteristic is that most of our public services are
produced by government through publicly employed providers. Generally, governments establish and defend a monopoly position by assertion of their greater accessibility, equality and ethical superiority
compared to the private sector, all essential to protect the public's
interests and to assure better quality services.

A fifth characteristic is separation of those who pay from those
who use the service. We have evolved a system of third-party or indirect financing in which the user of the public service does not incur
direct expense of paying for it. No economic constraints are imposed
on the user to control demand for either the quantity or quality. The
economic effect of providing services without economic limitation or
constraint by the user results in increasingly higher cost, as evidenced by the current difficulties of Medicare and Medicaid.

If we are going to accomplish basic changes in rendition of essential services, attitudinal changes first must occur. If the public-
private partnership is to have meaning, greater credibility must be
accorded between the two partners, and we must recognize that differing management styles can be equally effective. Profit, particularly in the rendition of human services, must be accepted as legitimate if acceptable standards of quality and price are met. Currently,
recommendations for performance improvement in public services
normally occur from the top down, not from the bottom up. Private
sector productivity is beginning to concentrate on the so-called "Z"
type corporation, quality circles and bottom-up planning—a recognition that those who are most directly involved in day-to-day performance of the service are likely to know best what incremental change
can be made to improve quality and/or cost. In the public sector, incremental change occurs from the top down because no incentives
exist for change below and, in fact, road blocks exist in the sense of

policy directives, rules and regulations. These tight constraints are looked on as essential management vehicles to prevent overreaching, fraud and mismanagement in the public delivery systems. Actually, these types of constraints have resulted in paralyzing the system and removing incentives for incremental changes and for experimentation that could prove as valuable in public management as in private.

To encourage change we must acknowledge that experimentation and innovation can result in failure. Failure on the part of public agencies should not be looked on as incompetence, dishonesty or criminal fraud, any more than in the private sector. Public understanding of the need for innovation and experimentation in the rendition of services is as essential in the public as in the private sector. In both instances the public pays the actual cost. In one, through taxes; in the other, through cost of product. When failures are buried in the cost of product, the public does not deem this to be criminal or a matter requiring remedial public action. Public delivery systems must be accorded similar respect.

In rethinking the ways in which service can be provided or obtained, a distinction must be drawn between short- and long-term responses, and between revenue and spending options. Typically, our response to budget deficits has been to concentrate on short-term responses that coincide with the term of office of elected officials. That response is either to seek more money or to reduce expenditures. New money sources may be increased revenues from traditional taxes, new tax sources (e.g., value added tax) or increased private philanthropic contributions to support public programs. Expenditure reductions generally amount to doing less with the same dollar revenues. Neither short-term option results in basic changes, and neither gets at the root causes of budget difficulties.

Long-term responses on the revenue side generally require expanding the national economy to create additional resources. On the expenditure side, the long-term response is to change the way things are done by restructuring the service systems. Since national economy improvements are beyond the control of local public or private entities, if long-term solutions and basic changes are desired, concentration must be on expenditures and on restructuring systems to maintain or improve services with an equal or reduced dollar budget. Restructuring can involve changes in one or all of the following: service, method of payment, users of the services, providers of the service.

In examining services, consideration should be given to alternatives to professional providers. For example, van pools provide transportation service, but without a paid driver. Families can provide care for the elderly or for the very young, without the paid professional services of a social worker, medical nurse or teacher.

In restructuring payment, you can change the money source

from public to private by eliminating government's responsibility but still requiring the service. For example, a city can require solid waste collection and disposal, but impose the responsibility on the home owners rather than having the service provided through the city's sanitation department. Even if tax dollars are used to pay for the service, they can be passed to the users through vouchers or tax credits, and the users then decide who to buy from and how much to pay. This is contrary to our traditional approach of direct appropriation of tax dollars to the service or to the vendors.

Buyers can be restructured by giving decision responsibility to the ultimate user or receiver of the service, encouraging economics through joint purchasing or by parceling the service among several vendors.

It is on the provider or seller side that the basic strategy change to competition and choice is most clear. It requires that we move away from dependence on a single vendor or on government as the only provider. To accomplish this basic change we must return to the concept of choice, of alternatives and of exit. Exit must not be considered a disloyal relationship, but rather the exercise of a free citizen's right to demand that producers of services meet the user's expectations or the service will be purchased elsewhere. This concept is not a reprivatization, nor a call for change from big government to big business, rather it is a reflection of the variety of ways in which choice can be provided in order to create market incentives to the producers of services. Even in those instances in which it is desirable to preserve government service monopolies or exclusive franchises, it is possible to create alternatives and choice for government as purchasers of service or for consumers as users. We must reduce the number of instances in which government is the sole producer, as distinguished from a policy setter or determiner of standards and access, and sometimes as provider of economic resources to allow users to pay for the service. Examples of possible ways to provide alternatives or choice follow.

Alternatives

Restructure government   Determine the most appropriate governmental level to render a service. This is a needed first step, but not a final solution. Reassignment of service functions between the federal, state and local governments must occur for better cost effectiveness in times of limited resources. We have over-expanded and centralized our service systems through the years of affluence, and we now must reassign and restructure to meet new situations occasioned by changing demographics and geographic shifts of population. We must attempt to do more with the same or equal resources. In local government, a return to the concept of full-service units is essential. For many delivery systems, regional or county service will be preferable to maintaining small local delivery systems. In many larger municipalities, however, subdivision into neighborhoods with definition of services and resources to be managed may be desirable.

In so restructuring governments, do not conclude that government also must automatically be the provider of all services. Management and responsibility is not coextensive with being the sole provider. Government can create favorable market conditions for itself, and alternatives available to it and thereby to its citizens, by contracting for services from other governments or from the private sector. This is no reason why a particular service cannot be provided in part by the private sector and in part by government. In so doing, market competition will provide incentives for efficiency and quality. Common examples exist today in solid waste collection, road maintenance, snow removal, etc.

Provide government dollar resources to consumers who purchase service from a variety of public and private providers Common examples exist in higher education, health care and child care. In the health area, Medicare and Medicaid are voucher systems permitting selection of the actual provider by the owner of the card. This is a basic change from the former concept of publicly owned and operated hospitals and publicly employed doctors providing medical services for the needy. Currently, the federal government is considering replacing its Section 8 and Section 202 housing programs with a voucher system to enable renters of low or moderate income, or elderly or handicapped renters, to select housing on a negotiated basis rather than receiving publicly subsidized housing. Child care in many counties is now on a voucher-like system whereby the county will provide aid for a day-care facility selected by the parent.

In education, questions related to tax credits or vouchers are currently major public issues. Public elementary education is the last major human service in which choice by the family is not generally available. It is the best example of a service in which equal access has been deemed so important that government has decided that it can assure equality only by being the provider. In so doing, we may have been confusing education with operational issues involving the school and the teachers. Actually, alternatives do exist at the prekindergarten and post-secondary levels where government support payments reflect a voucher system. In the K-12 school systems, however, alternatives exist only for parents with the economic capacity to move from the public to the private system.

If we are going to improve educational methodology and quality, wouldn't it be wiser to allow the consumers of the service to determine acceptable quality rather than attempting to do so through publicly owned facilities, public employees and public regulation of curriculum, students and teachers? Competition within the public school systems could be created by encouraging entrepreneurial management on a school unit basis by deregulating the methodology of educating. To secure maximum benefits of cost and quality through consumer choice, it is essential that multiple vendors exist so that true choice can be exercised and true competition can be achieved.

Create alternatives by permitting selected use of services or providing differing levels   Policies to allow choices through user fees for public services such as tennis, golf or boating can be expanded to services such as libraries, home security, etc. Since library services are used differently by different people, would it not be possible to reflect this by a policy making services free for those who read or use the material at the library site, but charging a fee for materials taken out? We have adopted differentiated levels in a variety of services in the past, such as toll roads and toll bridges versus public highways and public bridges, single-party or multiple-party telephone service, hospital wards or private rooms, special assessments for those who live closer to public recreational facilities and parks and none for those who are more distant. By recognizing differentiated levels of service and imposing fees structures, individuals may decide how to use available resources and make comparative and selective priority judgments.

We all know that in public transportation the 40-passenger bus is cost effective for trips of three to five miles, but relatively cost ineffective at distances of five to 15 miles from the central business district or from the work station. Alternative transportation systems could involve the use of privately owned taxi cabs, and privately owned and driven vans and car pools. There is no reason why formal public assistance could not go to the private as well as the public providers of the service. After all, public dollars do go into the highway systems and private vehicles drive on them. It may well be, however, that a more appropriate subsidy decision will be to assign responsibility to the private employers through employee fringe benefits. Currently, in Minneapolis, a number of major employers, desiring to reduce the number of cars on the street during rush hour and to avoid parking within the central business district, have agreed to provide a 25 percent subsidy to employees purchasing a monthly bus pass. For those who cannot use bus service, an alternative benefit is provided for van pools or car pools of three or more persons.

Encourage combination of services and multiple or joint use of governmental facilities   Today, there is not a general right to cross service lines between governmental units. Even within a single government, fire and other emergency services are not combined. Perhaps we have reached the stage where technological improvements in communications have eliminated the necessity for fire personnel to remain inactive for 90 percent of the time in order to be available immediately for emergencies. There is no reason to assume that professional firefighters will respond any more quickly or effectively than volunteers are currently doing in reaching the scene of an emergency from diverse locations. No service should be deemed exempt from this type of analysis. In Denmark, a major non-governmental company is providing fire service by contract, as well as emergency tow truck service, rescue service and transportation of the elderly. This company does approximately $150 million worth of business annually; it employs 6,800 people; it owns 3,000 vehicles; it maintains 134 fire stations. It is in direct competition with the local public fire brigades which provide only fire services. The secret to its dollar success is that it has found a way to use the down time of those who are engaged in fire service.

We have a unique opportunity to effect long-term changes if we can release ourselves from traditional mindsets and if we do not become totally consumed with solving short-run problems created by current funding changes. The neighborhood movement, for example, represents a sensible and logical call for change in what are perceived to be ineffective methods of providing basic services. Self-help is merely another method of choice and exit. Decentralization offers an opportunity to improve the effectiveness of the service delivery system by restructuring the ways in which the services are made available, financed and purchased. It is an opportunity to permit local, regional and individual choices, and to respond to the differing needs of our communities and citizens.

Municipal Enterprises: An International Perspective

Eberhard Laux

In Germany local governments are involved in a wide variety of entrepreneurial activity, either on their own or through management. This situation is a product of the constitutional mandate which states that local government (including counties) should provide for the basic needs of its citizens. In the course of history local government activity has broadened to activities which are actually the domain of the private sector. The high demand for municipal investment activity—especially in times of financial constraints—is a most pressing problem.

The various municipal businesses and public corporations play a major role in local government economic and budgetary policy. Due to the indirect but strong ties between municipal business activity and the municipal budget, the former must be solid if the latter is also to be stable.

Profit-making activities

There are various forms of municipal entrepreneurial activity. The core of municipal revenue-generating operations is carried out by market-oriented business endeavors. These include utilities and water supply, local transportation, public municipal banks and municipal housing construction. These market-oriented activities have grown in strength over the past years. Based on the catastrophe of the Great Depression of the late twenties and early thirties, present regulations insure that the quality of management of the enterprise does not endanger municipal budget stability, and that a poor bud-

Reprinted with permission from *Cutback Management: A Trinational Perspective*, edited by George G. Wynne (Washington, D.C.: Council for International Urban Liaison, 1983). The book contains numerous descriptions and case studies from the United States, Japan, and West Germany.

getary situation does not negatively influence the management of the enterprise.

In order to give the public enterprises more management independence, they are given a separate budget status but remain under city council authority, especially in pricing matters. Market-oriented enterprises are profit-making (although the profits remain in the public sector, primarily for investment in the enterprise itself), and are run on private sector economic and accounting principles.

A second major area of municipal revenue-generating activity is public works and public facilities. This area of activity, in contrast to market-oriented enterprises, is under full, formal control of the municipal administration and is accounted for in the budget. Included are sewage and waste disposal, city maintenance, hospitals, theaters, museums, trade fairs, open-air markets, slaughterhouses, sport and recreational centers and old age homes. These facilities and activities collect fees for services, but only at cost covering, not profit-making rates. These, too, are to be run according to business and accounting principles.

The business enterprises, profit-oriented, are designed to provide revenues for the municipality. These revenues are to come from profits to a smaller degree, but, to a larger degree from franchise fees paid to the community for the right to establish a monopoly. Such franchises amount to approximately DM200 million [about $82 million] per year. Revenues from franchise fees are then distributed within the public budget. Those business enterprises which do not realize profits (about one third of all enterprises) are "bailed out" by the budget. The tie between healthy municipal businesses and a solid budget is obvious.

The need for sound business management

Local government economic policy is aimed at insuring that municipal business activity remains healthy. Therefore, all municipal business operations and some public works and facilities must undergo a compulsory, year-end audit (by both private and public accountants) to insure proper business management and accounting. The use of investment and business consulting is also a prominent practice for guiding municipal economic policy. WIBERA, my own firm, is one such organization.

Each major area of municipal business activity is unique. The public utilities command a substantial share of the local energy and water supply market. Regional enterprises usually control energy generation and local governments control distribution. The present problem is a lack of necessary investment capital. Lack of investment capital has often forced the municipalities to bring in larger, non-public investment partners.

Public transportation is both in public and mixed (public-private) hands. This sector has high deficits (DM1,962 million [about

$803 million] in 1980) and a low cost coverage rate (two thirds of costs). An earlier-considered solution was the union of a profitable utility with transportation services: but due to high energy prices following the oil crisis, transportation deficits rose to a level which threatened to be so high as to absorb even the profits of its partners in the utility sector.

Municipal banks and other ventures

Municipal savings banks receive 38.4 percent of the total bank-business volume and 53 percent of the savings volume. The banks are limited to municipally related activities. The municipal savings institutions are run separately from the municipal budget, but are under governmental authority and liability. Bank profits remain in the municipal bank for the creation of capital and reserves. The banks also function as credit institutions for non-profit making municipal facilities and public works.[1]

Of the 3,200 hospitals in the Federal Republic of Germany, about 900 are municipally run. Hospitals are financed mainly by state and federal aid and by statutory health insurance. However, tremendous price increases can no longer be compensated for by health insurance rate increases. A recent survey shows that the federal government pays only 18 percent of its 44 percent share. Municipal governments have been forced to spend DM700 million [about $287 million] in extra revenues for hospitals in 1980. Were hospitals to be run more according to market-oriented principles, and less as controlled municipal enterprises, savings might result.

Local government budgets are strained by low-cost coverage (fee-charging) facilities and services such as theaters, sports and cultural centers. These activities, official entries in the municipal budget, are covered by budget expenditures. As a result they create budget deficits.

Due to the close correlation between solvent municipal businesses and a solid municipal budget, proper business management and a separation between the two budgets are needed. A well run enterprise can indirectly support the municipal budget in that it does *not* present a burden. The business enterprises should generate their own capital for investments as far as possible, and produce franchise-fee revenue so that non-profit enterprises can be covered.

Since fee-charging operations cannot be totally solvent without municipal budgetary assistance, new planning, accounting or management techniques will not be sufficient to stabilize municipal budgets—service limitations and privatization will probably have to follow. However, the first major step is guaranteeing a stable local government budget to insure that the municipal business activity, in all forms, is itself on solid ground.

1. *Editor's note:* In 1981 the municipally chartered savings banks had a combined volume of over $400 billion and provided about $20 billion in infrastructure loans, to their own local authorities.

The Self-Reliant City

David Morris

The two great inventors and entrepreneurs, Henry Ford and Thomas Edison, were contemporaries. One day when Ford visited Edison at his home he found he had to push hard to open the outside gate. Knowing Edison's superb mechanical ability and fetish for perfection, Ford wondered why such an imperfect arrangement was allowed in his own home. Later that evening, he raised the question. Why was the gate so hard to push? Edison's eyes twinkled when he answered. The gate was attached to a pump. Every time a visitor pushed open the gate the pump sent some water to the household tank. Every visitor unwittingly made a modest contribution to the home.

A half century later that story contains a lesson for America's city officials and residents. Thomas Edison made use of a previously ignored resource. Cities must do the same. Beset by shrinking budgets, increased social responsibilities and deteriorating physical plants, cities too must redefine their resource base. The municipal corporation must look to change the nature of its internal balance sheet to maximize the value of the technological, natural and human resources located within its boundaries.

Throughout American history, the role of the municipal corporation has dramatically changed. Before the Revolutionary War cities were primary actors in commerce and trade. By the end of the nineteenth century, theirs had become a minor role, subordinate to the private corporation and the state legislature. After the Second World War cities became responsible for land use planning and the delivery of an array of social services. Now the crisis of our cities requires a new role, one more directly related to the creation of pri-

Reprinted with permission from the October 1982 issue of *Western City* magazine, the official publication of the League of California Cities.

mary wealth. Modern technology provides the means. Shrinking budgets and inflation provide the incentive. A new generation of elected officials provides the opportunity.

New role

This new role has spawned new metaphors—the entrepreneurial city, the city as mine, the city as power plant, the self-reliant city. However varied the slogans, the sentiment is the same. The city is beginning to emphasize production, rather than merely ameliorate the effects of consumption to promote the general welfare.

Consider one commonly overlooked resource: garbage. A city of 100,000 disposes of more than 50,000 tons of solid waste each year. Once separated from the rest of the waste stream, the individual material's value depends in large measure on the extent to which it is processed.

For example, today most cities pay two cents to dispose of a pound of aluminum cans. Even in these depressed times aluminum has a high value. By recycling the cans, the residents of the city receive between 15 and 17 cents a pound while reducing the city's overall garbage bill. Compress the cans to reduce the shipping cost and the value per pound rises to 35 cents. Smelt the cans down into ingots and one can bypass the traditional buyers and sell directly to manufacturers, raising the value even more, to 55 cents per pound. Convert the ingots into a consumer product, such as bicycle handlebars, and the value of the aluminum soars to more than $1 per pound. The self-reliant city captures as much of this additional value as possible for the local economy.

The city of 100,000 also generates 25,000 tons of nutrients annually. These are called human wastes. Currently sewage treatment plants represent a major financial burden to cities and counties. They cost enormous sums to build and just as much to operate. But again, by combining modern science and local political authority, this burden can become an attractive resource.

More than disposal

Hagerstown, Maryland, a city of 37,000 people, has done just this. [In 1980] its sewage system was costing the city almost $1 million a year. This year a new two phase digestion process was installed to double the methane output. Beginning in early 1983 the plant will generate sufficient methane gas to run its entire municipal vehicle fleet, plus its sewage facility. The cost of the automotive fuel will be equivalent to 35 cents a gallon of gasoline. But the methane gas represents only a part of the city's harvest. The sludge is a rich fertilizer.

Hagerstown undertook the long and politically difficult process of mandating industrial pre-treatment plants to eliminate heavy metal contamination of the sludge. Having successfully accomplished this, it has dubbed its sludge Hagonite. It is a commercially viable product but the city isn't selling it because that would not capture the greatest value from the nutrients. Rather, the city has planted 300,000 hybrid poplar trees on 50 acres of municipal land. Seven inches when planted, these trees will be 14 feet tall in two years. At that time they will be harvested, and probably gasified to generate more fuel. The waste products from the gasification or ethanol process is excellent animal feed. The city estimates it will be able to feed 100 cattle and hogs. And, of course, animals produce manure, which in turn produces methane. It is hoped that by 1984 the sewage plant will be generating a million dollars net benefit to the city. It would be hard for a citizen of Hagerstown to call the sewage plant a disposal facility now. It has become a production plant, a gas well and a fertilizer factory.

The self-reliant city views itself as a nation. It analyzes the flow of capital within its borders and evaluates its "balance of payments." It recycles money much as it recycles goods. Every added cycle increases the community's wealth. Businesses are evaluated not only for the services or products they offer but for the way they affect the local economy.

Local investment

The results of these analyses are often surprising. For example, one McDonald's restaurant in a Washington, D.C., neighborhood was found to be exporting out of the area more than two-thirds of its $750,000 monthly gross revenues. Since most of its business was from local residents, one could make a strong case that this enterprise was not benefiting the local economy at all.

Neighborhood investigators in downtown Chicago discovered their community had deposited several millions in local banks, but received back only $150,000 in loans. Of the $35 million the 30,000 residents and businesses of Carbondale, Illinois, and Northampton, Massachusetts, spent on oil, gasoline, natural gas and electricity in 1980, more than $30 million left the economy immediately. As the mayor of Auburn, New York, remarked, "It matters little to us whether a dollar goes to Saudi Arabia or Texas. The effect on the local economy is the same. We are losing control over a substantial part of our resources."

"Plug the Leakages" has become a rallying cry for those demanding local self-reliance. Whether the leakages stem from the lost value of raw materials dumped into landfills, or from branch stores that withdraw the majority of their earnings from the community, or from the wasted potential of retired people who can't find places to offer their time and skills, the result is the same—the loss of valuable resources.

This new way of thinking about cities defies traditional political classifications. It is ideologically neither right nor left. Self-reliant cities minimize government but not necessarily governance. The individual is seen as a producer of wealth and an active participant in the political process of resource management.

Take the cases of Santa Monica and Oceanside. While sharing the coast of southern California, the governing political philosophies of these two cities could not be more different. Both face the problem of rising energy prices that reduce the buying power of local residents and undermine the local economy.

Santa Monica has responded by channeling the capital the city deposits in local banks. A city the size of Santa Monica has tens of millions of dollars on deposit in financial institutions or short term notes at any given time of the year. Recently the city made local banks and savings and loan associations an offer. It would deposit $125,000 of its money in a bank which matched this with $125,000 of its depositors' money for energy conservation loans. The loans would not be subsidized. The city would earn the going interest rate. The bank would earn a healthy return on its loans. But the money would be channeled into a sector of the local economy that would benefit not only individual residents, but the entire city by reducing the outflow of precious capital.

The rapidly growing conservative Republican city of Oceanside faced the same problem. The city has a significant number of retired people. With rising natural gas prices cutting into fixed incomes, the city council investigated the potential for using solar energy to lower hot water bills. Because traditional financial institutions wouldn't provide adequate financing for people to pursue this option, the city council unanimously approved a program to create an alternative method of financing this income and energy saving technology. Homeowners lease solar hot water systems directly from private firms. The city helps to market the system, guarantees them, collects lease payments and reduces red tape associated with permits, building codes and the like. To participate in the program, the private firms must post performance bonds, agree to a consumer complaint process and charge less than a maximum monthly fee. Within 60 days of the commencement of the program, more than $15 million had been committed by private firms for investment in this city of 80,000 people. Oceanside is not only capturing the value of an indigenous resource—the sun—but it is also assuming an aggressive and innovative government role.

Cogeneration

More recently cities have begun to examine the potential for electric generation within their borders. In 1982 a typical city will spend more than $1300 per person for imported energy and almost 50 percent of this will go for electricity. Yet new technologies now make it possible to generate electricity inside the city. Cogeneration, the process of generating heat and electricity in the same process, is more than twice as efficient as a conventional power plant and half again as efficient as a typical commercial boiler. Today utilities must purchase electricity generated on-site at attractive prices, converting the grid system into a giant marketplace.

A new power plant now costs about $5000 per household. A city of 100,000 will pay almost $150 million for a power plant to supply its base load electricity. The very real possibility now exists that much of this investment will be redirected into dispersed, on-site generation facilities. The municipal corporation can play a major role in spurring this redirection of capital.

As the city hall, the household, and the business become producers of wealth and not just consumers of goods, new relationships will probably emerge. For example, in New York City the giant cooperative apartment complex, Starrett City, is no longer coupled to the electric grid system. Natural gas fired power plants generate its hot water, heat and electricity. A few miles away sits a city-owned sewage plant. Starrett City and the city of New York have entered into a contract. A pipeline from the apartment complex will carry hot water to the sewage plant. The hot water will allow the sewage plant to reduce the amount of natural gas needed to warm its digestors. A pipeline from the sewage plant will deliver methane to the apartment complex to operate the power plants.

The relationship between building and sewage plant is changing. Traditionally the building residents flushed the toilet and the human waste moved to the sewage plant, where it was treated and then dumped into the ocean. It was a one-way process. Rising energy prices and modern technology has transformed this into a two-way, symbiotic process. The wastes of one facility become the raw materials of another. The ecologists call this "closing the loop." I call it local self-reliance.

Whatever the terminology, the dynamic is the same. Cities are redefining their resource base. By exercising their political authority and using modern technologies, they are reducing their imports, expanding their on-site production and becoming once again a treasure trove of innovation and experimentation.

Of equal importance, cities are sharing their experiences. The vertical transfer of information from Washington to the hinterlands is being replaced by a horizontal exchange of information from one city to another. As this takes place we find more and more inventiveness coming from the small and medium sized cities. America has always been enchanted with big cities. Indeed, most Americans believe that most Americans live in big cities. They are wrong. Fewer than 10 percent of the population lives in the seven cities with more than one million residents. Almost a third live in the 800 cities with populations of 25,000-100,000. Our small and medium sized cities promise to become a major breeding ground of new ideas, new technologies and new enterprises.

Pricing Policies
and the Economics
of Demand
Management

Norman R. King

California's future [and that of other states] will include some new, different ways of approaching public policy that will make greater use of market systems, pricing, competition, and choice to serve the public.

There are five fundamental conditions in this country today that are bringing about this new age of public administration. The first condition is perhaps the easiest to understand: the very different and fundamental limitations on our resources, both in terms of our government coffers, but also in terms of our finite resources. It's a time to focus on what is enough, as opposed to more; to focus on what is necessary, as opposed to what is good and desirable.

Diminishing returns

We are also beginning to recognize that our entire economy is catching up with the law of diminishing returns. We now face an increasing cost per unit of almost every single resource we consume. You can think about this in terms of timber, food, fish supply, or in terms of one resource that is the perhaps easiest to comprehend: the cost of electricity.

Around 1970, give or take two or three years, for the first time in the last 50 years, electricity began to cost more for each additional kilowatt instead of less. Instead of having a falling cost per unit that encouraged greater consumption, the cost for each additional unit began to rise. That change has affected virtually all finite resources across the board, to the point that we are now beginning to under-

Reprinted with permission from "The Economics of Demand Management" in the October 1982 issue of *Western City* magazine, the official publication of the League of California Cities. This article is based on the author's presentation at the League's Mayors and Council Members' Executive Forum in Monterey, July 1982.

stand that inflation is partly ecological. It is inflation because it costs us more to get the same thing.

For example, we now have the technology to go several thousand feet into the earth to get oil, whereas 40 years ago we couldn't go as deep because the machinery and technology were not there. The point is we are using more energy to get down that deep, and thus, our net payoff is less.

The third fundamental condition is the current trend to over-mortgage our future—to defer costs to future generations. This is taking place in several ways. Cities, partly as a result of Proposition 13, but also as a nationwide trend, have drastically reduced the amount of money used for maintenance of our basic facilities. The percentage of city budgets allocated to maintenance of existing facilities dropped from 29 percent to 15 percent in the period 1965–75 alone.

We see this over-mortgaging in our pension programs, in city as well as other private and government programs. The U.S. military now spends more on retired personnel than on active-duty soldiers. Approximately 30 percent of those who now retire from the military are in their 30's.

We are well aware of our Social Security problems, where costs deferred to the future will come back to us when we have fewer workers to support more retired persons.

Our present unwillingness to pay the cost of reducing major environmental damage—such as is caused by acid rain or toxic waste—is another way in which we are deferring certain costs to future generations, just as it is now all too obvious that past generations have shifted tremendous cost and health burdens to our generation by not handling toxic waste properly. Overdrafting of our water supplies, for instance, may cost us less now, but our grandchildren may well have to pay more for our excesses.

Over-consumption

Fourth, we have created a tax and pricing system, perhaps unintentionally, which has given us all incentives to over-consume. If we stand back and look at the hidden subsidies in our tax system and in our pricing system we find that compared to other countries we encourage more investment in consumables, over-use of energy, over-use of our medical technology and even over-use of free parking.

Donald Shoup of UCLA has done a remarkable paper which suggests that if we converted free parking for employees at downtown locations into a non-taxable transit allowance of equal value, say $25 a month, we would not be increasing the cost to anybody, because in fact it costs that much in many places to furnish free parking. We would be getting rid of the incentives we have in our society to drive alone to work.

These facts help explain why we as a nation are consuming approximately 95 percent of our income, as opposed to countries such as Japan which consumes about 80 percent of its income. The difference, of course, is that all-important amount of investment in capital facilities for future production.

So we have a society which, by encouraging consumption across the board, tends to cause a cycle which is often self-fulfilling. When we have an energy shortage, we rush out and find more money to bring in more energy to solve the problem, but in the process create other problems that require government action. We perpetrate a cycle that will be hard to get out of, and which is caused by the incentives we have in our tax and pricing structure.

Supply oriented

And finally, we have a government which has been very supply oriented. When we have a problem, we tend to define the solution as a new government program supplying an additional resource. If we run out of water, the problem is defined as lack of water, and therefore we need more water. We run out of energy the same way. If we have a problem with disease, the solution is to provide a treatment using more medical technology, as opposed to prevention. As a society, we tend to focus on treating rather than preventing. This "supply management" approach is part of our society and part of our government ethic.

Without changing the importance of supply, we must also look at the alternative: demand management. We must look at that other side of government, at the incentives in this country that encourage us to use more than we really need, and thereby cause basic economic problems. Instead of calling the problem "a lack of . . .," with the solution being "to get more of . . .," we begin to define the problem as too much demand for the government service to start with. If we can reduce that demand, we'll spend less government money on the problem to start with.

Very simplified, this approach emphasizes prevention rather than treatment. In local government we can begin to focus on prevention rather than treatment through our own pricing policies. Fortunately, local government still has a lot of discretion over service pricing in this state.

Let me give you some examples of demand management. Typically, solid waste becomes a problem when we don't have enough money to buy a new dump or a new landfill. The problem, therefore, is defined as not enough money to do something. This is understandable, particularly by the time the problem gets to us.

Demand management

But another way of looking at that same problem is to sit back and say, "Perhaps the problem is that too much is being thrown away;

what can we do about that?" Obviously, many things can be done, not just by local government action but also in broad government policy to give us incentives not to throw away so much. We can close that open ended system that now exists where the manufacturer and consumer have a right to throw away everything without increasing that cost to themselves directly which, of course, only invites us to continue throwing away at a greater rate than our population increase.

Or we could look at energy: the problem is not simply providing enough cheap energy; it's the incentives in our tax and pricing structure that encourage us to use too much energy, to the point that we forgo more economical investments in conservation and put the bulk of our spending into production. We do this even though we know that a very large percentage of our existing energy requirements could be supplied more cheaply through conservation investments if we had the institutional mechanism to accumulate capital for conservation, as opposed to concentrating solely on pipelines, energy plants, and so on.

Unfortunately, what is good for us collectively as a country, as a state, or as a city often flies in the face of what is good for me, the individual. To be a good guy, to put up a solar power plant, for instance, in a home is a good thing to do, but individuals doing that don't necessarily receive all the benefits, because they still pay the same gas and electric bills to build new facilities, even though they have taken some of the burden off the system.

We must begin to make it worthwhile to be a good guy. We want people to be good guys. Those people who don't drive to work alone but drive with somebody; people who don't drink or smoke so much because they're taking care of their personal health; people who put in that second plant in their house through solar or some other energy conservation investment. And yet we have an incentive system that pretty much says to those people they will not reap the full economic benefits of being a good guy.

Let's look at fire service. The problem is not just that we're running out of money for the next fire station with three, four, or five people on a truck and the newest snorkel equipment. Of course we need more money to do that, but we can also ask the question: "Are we really giving the proper incentives to our technology, through our tax system, to see that sprinklers are put in where they should be?"

We know that in many types of new development, especially commercial and increasingly residential, lowering the demand for our fire department's services through a capital investment like a sprinkler system will make the long term cost to us less than the cost of supplying more fire fighters.

We must look to the other side of government, to an incentive system that gives some rewards for being a good guy, that gets us away from subsidizing over-consumption of government resources.

More satisfaction

This is not necessarily what we would call cutback management. We've cut out services that people desire. We've had to make some people unhappy. The promise of demand management is that we actually may be able to increase the satisfaction of our citizens by offering more choices through certain user fees. We will have a less costly government that will increase our citizens' support of how their tax money is being used.

We often look at user fees as a way to get more money. That's important, but fees can also be used to discourage the demand for our services. Fees are not just a way of raising money, but also a way of improving the efficiency of the allocation of our services so that government is less costly in the long run.

We're beginning to apply certain fees to what we would call merit goods. Wilbur Thompson said, "We believe some goals are especially meritorious, like education and libraries. We feel that others might not fully appreciate this truth, so we produce these merit goods at considerable cost but offer them at zero price. Merit goods are a case of the majority playing god and inducing the minority by use of bribes to change their behavior."

As we have given local government more to do, we have almost unthinkingly extended the tradition of free public services to almost every new undertaking. There are certain levels of service that are necessary and, because of equity reasons, should be provided to everyone. But above and beyond that, there are ways to impose user fees to fund those things which are good and desirable as opposed to just necessary. We don't have to provide all our services for free.

Through choice, through variable levels of service, and through the use of pricing to achieve this, we have a chance to provide more efficient government that provides wider public satisfaction at substantially less cost.

One of the greatest problems we have in this country is providing sufficient energy, transportation, water, or other resources at one time, because we all tend to use them at the same time. One way of reducing this peak demand is to apply charges so it costs more to use the service at peak.

The electrical industry is beginning to move toward this, but often to the great dissatisfaction of the consumer. The person who washes clothes at 4 p.m. in the afternoon in July, in Palm Springs, is putting costs on the system that are four or five times as great as the person who washes clothes at 10 o'clock that night or at 10 o'clock in the morning, because at 4 p.m. it costs a lot more money to provide that last increment of power. There are some valid economic reasons, especially in a country that's founded on markets, to say we shouldn't give incentives for people to wash clothes at 4 o'clock in the afternoon, in July, in Palm Springs.

Wrong incentives

Let's look at police. We have a system that tends to focus on punishment. But what if we also looked at economic incentives? An example in Palm Springs occurred with a million dollar grand theft. Our police department spent $15,000 in overtime following up on leads. There were additional costs in the court system, plus the regular police time. The thief was arrested and finally sentenced by the judge to 200 hours of community service work.

Now, most of us will say that's ridiculous, that's not punishment, and I agree. But let's take that one case further. Why should Palm Springs spend $15,000 in overtime, plus thousands elsewhere to see the criminal in this case invest into society 200 hours of her work? The incentives are all confused.

Arizona recently passed a racketeering law that says if you are convicted of selling, say, two ounces of heroin, the state will come back at you for $150,000 in a civil suit seeking to recover the cost that went into the investigation of getting to that point in the judicial system. Perhaps that has opportunities for us. At least it begins to straighten out this crazy incentive system that now pervades our criminal justice system.

For a last example, take our local library. Palm Springs has an excellent public library, as do many, if not most, California cities. Despite having to close two branches in the past four years, leaving one main library and one small minor branch, readership is going up and demand for our library services is escalating. We are, in fact, creating our own demand because we have a very good librarian and a very good staff. By doing a better job, our services become more popular. If we did a poor job the demand would go down.

So what do we want to do? Where are our incentives in this situation? It all comes home, of course, when we get that request for an additional librarian. Readership has gone up, books have gone up, people are coming to the library, so we need more help. If the city council approves a new librarian, we encourage the demand for our services, and we cause those who are not interested in libraries to pay more money to satisfy others who are. If we deny the librarian, we're making a decision to reduce the popularity or our services. The suggestion is simply that there are opportunities in our local governmental services, library included, to attach some fees that would then allow the service to become more convenient, to improve its diversity, to improve the services offered to citizens, and not require an increased contribution from the general fund.

What is needed is a reuniting of economics with political science and with public administration. Proposition 13 may have ostensibly been a vote against high property taxes and waste in government, but it should also be seen as part of a broader revolution reacting to our present political economy, an economy which by encouraging excessive consumption of government services and other resources is tottering on bankruptcy.

We now have the opportunity to make our governments better, to use the market mechanisms of price, choice, and competition, and above all to facilitate a reduction in the demand for our services.

Using Fees and Charges to Adjust Demand

Harry P. Hatry

Definition and rationale

Users of a service can be charged a fee based on the amount of their use of the government-supplied activity, thus putting the financial burden on users of the activity. This article is not concerned with the use of fees and charges for the sake of raising revenues, but rather with their use for adjusting the amount of service demanded by individual citizens or private organizations and, thus, affecting the cost of services. The use of fees and charges has been increasing in recent years, especially in areas affected by state fiscal containment efforts.[1] The major purpose of those fees, however, has been to raise revenues.

The rationale of this approach is that the persons who use a particular service should pay for it, in accordance with their amount of use. This should cause people to consider the service's cost to them and cause them to adjust their demand for the service in proportion to the value they set on that service. This, then, more closely approximates the business principle of being able to sell to citizens only those services citizens want. When fees are charged, many citizens can be expected to reduce their use of the service from the level of use when the service represented no added cost to them (which occurs if an activity is funded out of general revenues). The use of general revenues, such as the property tax, drives up the demand for, and consumption of, services since there is no added cost to the consumer and thus no incentive to conserve.

An additional advantage of fees and charges is that they give

This article is taken from *Alternative Service Delivery Approaches Involving Increased Use of the Private Sector*, by Harry P. Hatry, published by the Greater Washington Research Center, Washington, D.C., 1983. That publication covers contracting out, franchises, grants and subsidies, vouchers, use of volunteers, self-help, and other alternative approaches to service delivery and reduction of demand.

better signals to government managers about the needed size of public facilities. For example, if large numbers of citizens are using a service when the charge for the service is close to the cost of producing it, then it is more likely to be appropriate to add additional facilities.

Fees and charges are applicable to a specific service to the extent that usage by individual customers can be distinguished and charges can be related to individual uses.

The key to the ability to use fees and charges is that specific beneficiaries receive the service, and that service can be divided among them without a substantial number of "free riders" who escape the charges but nevertheless receive benefits. Another way of expressing this is that the service should be "private" rather than "collective," that is, there are specific identifiable users, and those not paying for the time can be excluded from the benefits. Fees and charges are, thus, potentially applicable to services such as those listed in Exhibit 1.

Charges can be used to ration demand only if the client controls the demand. Charges such as monthly garbage collection charges and assessments per front foot for street sweeping, cleaning, and street repairs are not demand-affecting charges. These are primarily revenue-raising devices. Once someone moves into a house, the charge for that lot no longer rations demand; subsequently, the cost to the household does not vary, regardless of how much waste or wear is generated by the household. The front lot charge can, however, conceivably affect house-purchase decisions.

Governments can develop fees and charges based not only on quantity of use, but also on the timing of that use (to encourage off-peak usage and thus reduce expensive capacity requirements, as with

---

Exhibit 1: Potential services for fees and charges

Police services
Fire services
Emergency ambulance services
Solid waste collection
Solid waste disposal
Street repair, traffic engineering/street lighting
Buses/public transit
Water and sewer
Recreation programs
Parks
Libraries
Human services to low-income families
Inspections (building, housing, food, etc.)
Support services (vehicle and building maintenance, EDP, etc.)

transportation and water). Fees and charges can conceptually take into account other cost-generating characteristics of the services, such as location; for example, larger fees can be charged for water and sewer connections located in sparsely settled parts of the community where the costs of capital facilities and maintenance are expected to be higher. Such charging arrangements would tend to encourage the private sector to request services in less costly areas of the community (and at less costly times of the day). Another example used in some cities, such as Fort Worth, Texas, is to give citizens a choice between levels of service, for example, different fees for different levels of garbage collection, backdoor or curbside.

Finally, a drawback to switching from taxes to fees and charges is that the latter are not deductible for residents who itemize their deductions for federal income tax purposes.

Examples

Classic examples of fees and charges occur for special recreational activities (such as golf courses, tennis courts, and swimming pools) and for water use. In the latter case, the charge depends on metering the use of the water supply by individual customers. For recreational activities involving open parks, entrance fees have seldom (if ever) been charged at the local level. Nor have entrance fees been used for libraries. Services of police and fire departments tend to be collective, though in recent years proposals for fees and charges for some activities have been proposed, such as charging for calls made or charging for false alarms (fire or police).

Local governments have increasingly charged developers for the costs of new infrastructure generated by their projects. For example, in Corvallis, Oregon, housing developers now must meet much of the cost of extending the city's water system before they build.[2] To the extent that such charges ration demand, they are relevant to the discussion here. For example, Snohomish County, Washington (337,000), has different developer road charges, depending on the expected congestion level and expected road costs. This approach can encourage developers to build in less costly areas.[3]

Exhibit 2 shows a list of recent applications of fees and charges. This list does not cover all activities for which they have been proposed or used.

Evaluation

Cost of government service   The purpose of the fees and charges discussed here is to reduce service cost by reducing the amount of demand and consumption that would occur without added costs to citizens for using the service. Thus far, however, the author has not found specific studies that provide empirical evidence for the extent to which, after the introduction of fees and charges, service costs have actually declined. Many examples should exist, particularly for recent years, from which useful evidence could be obtained.

Administrative billing and collection costs for fees and charges can be considerable. For example, for charges based on the amount of water used, the agency must purchase, install, and maintain meters at each customer's location, as well as provide for reading the meters, billing, and collection. In some cases, however, these administrative costs may be relatively small, as in water supply. Little documented information on the administrative cost of switching to fees and charges exists.

Cost to citizens   Theoretically, reduced use of a service should lead to lower tax bills. Consumers' actual cost for the service then depends on the amount they use (and are charged for). In actual practice, since fees and charges are most often used as a revenue-raising de-

---

Exhibit 2: Types of fees, charges, and licenses

Police protection
  special patrol service fees
  parking fees and charges
  fees for fingerprints, copies
  payments for extra police
    service at stadiums, theaters,
    circuses
Transportation
  subway and bus fares
  bridge tolls
  landing and departure fees
  hangar rentals
  concession rentals
  parking meter receipts
Health and hospitals
  inoculation charges
  x-ray charges
  hospital charges, including per
    diem rates and service
    charges
  ambulance charges
  concession rentals
Education
  charges for books
  charges for gymnasium
    uniforms or special
    equipment
  concession rentals
Recreation

greens fees
parking charges
concession rentals
admission fees or charges
permit charges for tennis
  courts, etc.
charges for specific recreation
  services
picnic stove fees
stadium gate tickets
stadium club fees
park development charges
Sanitation
  domestic and commercial trash
    collection fees
  industrial waste charges
Sewerage
  sewerage system fees
Other public utility operations
  water meter permits
  water services charges
  electricity rates
  telephone booth rentals
Housing, neighborhood and
commercial development
  street tree fees
  tract map filing fees
  street-lighting installations
  convention center revenues

vice, citizens could actually end up paying more—both the old tax and added charges.

A major concern with fees and charges is that they are not deductible for federal income tax purposes, as are property and sales taxes. Thus, for those households that itemize their deductions the switch to fees and charges is likely to mean increased taxes. The result would be increased net cost to those households unless cost savings due to lower use of the service were enough to offset this federal tax increase.

Choice to clients   With fees and charges, the individual potential customer is faced with more choices, now that the customer has to pay for usage. The customer now has the opportunity to make less use of a service rather than paying a bill whose size is independent of the amount of use.

event charges	lumber dealer
scoreboard fees	pawnbrokers
hall and meeting room leases	plumbers—first class
concessions	plumbers—second class
Commodity sales	pest eradicator
salvage materials	poultry dealer
sales of maps	produce dealer—itinerant
sales of codes	pushcart
Licenses and fees	rooming house and hotel
advertising vehicle	secondhand dealer
amusements (ferris wheels, etc.)	secondhand auto dealer
billiard and pool	sign inspection
bowling alley	solicitation
circus and carnival	shooting gallery
coal dealers	taxi
commercial combustion	taxi transfer license
dances	taxi driver
dog tags	theaters
duplicate dog tags	trees—Christmas
electrician—first class	vending—coin
electrician—second class	vault cleaners
film storage	sound truck
foot peddler	refuse hauler
hucksters and itinerant	land fill
peddlers	sightseeing bus
heating equipment contractors	wrecking license
junk dealer	
loading zone permit	

Source: Selma J. Mushkin and Charles L. Vehorn, "User Fees and Charges,"
Governmental Finance (November 1977), p. 48.

Quality and effectiveness of the service   Though fees and charges do not directly affect service quality, the customer has the opportunity to express concern over quality through nonuse. If an agency finds revenues dropping, it has the opportunity to find out why and to determine whether customers are reducing use because of poor quality or for some other reasons.

Distributional effects   This is probably the central concern for communities considering fees and charges. At first glance, it would appear that fees and charges generally would adversely affect low-income families. For example, the fees and charges for use of drinking water would likely absorb a higher proportion of those families' income than it would for middle- and upper-income families. But, as noted above, higher-income families that itemize deductions may also resist fees and charges because of the federal tax implications. A few studies have been done on the distributional effects of various user charges.[4] Fixed-rate charges (for example, a fixed sum per month) are likely to be regressive, whereas charges based on amount of use or the timing and locational characteristics of use may not be regressive, or at least may be less regressive. The argument is that high-income people tend to live in larger homes, at lower density, and at more distant locations and so have higher costs of services; if the charges are constructed properly, they will have higher user charges. With fixed-rate user charges that are primarily for revenue-raising purposes and not really part of privatization proposals, low-income people could, however, end up paying more than the cost of serving them, since their use may be less frequent and less costly.[5]

Staying power and potential for service disruption   Fees and charges are not likely to cause service disruption since the delivery is still being undertaken by the governmental agency. Once fees and charges have been introduced, they are likely to remain in effect for at least a number of years. If the charges are readily relatable to the amount of use and readily understood by the public, they are likely to remain.

Feasibility   Fees and charges to affect demand are not feasible for collective services. For other services, legal issues may require review of each individual case. Fees from developers to cover costs of related new infrastructure have raised legal problems. If a local government can show a "reasonable" relationship between the cost of the service and the charge, these charges probably will pass the legal test.[6]

A recent ACIR survey provides evidence of the current salability of fees and charges. A nationwide survey found 55 percent of the respondents felt that "charges for specific services" was the best way for local governments to raise needed additional revenues.[7] And in a

December 1981 survey, 45 percent of responding local governments reported no opposition to increases in fees and charges.[8]

Overall potential impact   Not enough empirical evidence exists to determine whether the introduction of fees and charges would lead to significantly reduced costs to the government and customers. Governments can probably increase fees and charges more readily than general taxes. Since they are presumably based on actual costs, increases should be easier to justify to the public.

The overall advantage to the government may not be reductions in actual local expenditures, but rather the degree to which expenditures can be directly related to revenues and the ability to be more sensitive to demand. However, without well-constructed fees and charges (related to important cost-affecting variables), charges can easily become regressive.

Author's note: The paper by Paul B. Downing, "User Charges and Service Fees: An Information Bulletin for the Urban Consortium," U.S. Department of Housing and Urban Development, Office of Policy Development and Research, 1981, has been very useful in preparing this chapter.

1. For example, while total revenues for cities and counties increased at an annual rate of 9.6% between FY 1977 and FY 1981, revenues from charges increased at the annual rate of 13.9% (derived from figures from Table 1 of *City Government Finances in 1980-81*, GF81 No. 4, and *County Government Finances in 1980-81*, GF81 No. 8, both U.S. Bureau of the Census reports, December 1982). A December 1981 survey by the Advisory Commission on Intergovernmental Relations and the Municipal Finance Officers Association found that 77.5 percent of the 307 responding cities reported increased use of user charges over the period 1980-1982; 25.1 percent re-

ported increased use of special assessments, ACIR, February 10, 1982.

2. Frazier and Lewis, *German Marshall Fund Transatlantic Perspective*, July 1981.

3. Michael Fix, "The Impact of Regulation on Housing Costs: Snohomish County Case Study," The Urban Institute, February 1982 draft.

4. Downing, "User Charges and Service Fees."

5. Fees and charges may be less fair to apartment dwellers living in apartments that provide privately for services such as waste collection. Apartment dwellers may pay through their rent both for property taxes and the private service (unless the government has adjusted the taxes accordingly).

6. Downing, p. 55.

7. "1981 Changing Public Attitudes on Governments and Taxes," S-10, Advisory Commission on Intergovernmental Relations, Washington, D.C., 1982.

8. Data from ACIR-MFOA, December 1981 survey, February 10, 1982.

Data on User Charges and Fees

In addition to their use to regulate demand, fees are of course used to raise revenues. To determine the extent to which cities rely on user charges and fees, the International City Management Association surveyed 2,497 cities in 1981. It found that revenues from user charges had increased during the past decade at a faster rate (176%) than tax revenues (107%). By FY 1980, charges amounted to 31.6% of city tax revenues.

Cities with medium-sized and small populations tended to rely more on charges and utility revenue than did cities with larger populations. The sum of charges and utility revenue in FY 1980 amounted to 49.5% of tax revenue for the six cities having populations of 1 million or more, while the percentage for cities of 100,000 to 199,999 was 92.5%. The ratio for cities under 50,000 was 123.6%.

As cities have searched for additional sources of revenue in recent years, they have imposed new charges for such services as special police patrols, outside fire calls, recreational activities, and some health services.

The tables on the following pages show the percentages of cities imposing service charges, cities adding charges since July 1978, and cities in which charges defray 50% or more of service costs.

Tables from: Maurice Criz, *The Role of User Charges and Fees in City Finance*, Urban Data Service Reports, Vol. 14 No. 6 (Washington, D.C.: International City Management Association, June 1982).

Table 1 *Percent of cities imposing service charges, by population group*

Type of service	All cities reporting % reporting service	All cities reporting % with charge[1]	250,000 and over % with charge[1]	100,000-249,999 % with charge[1]	50,000-99,999 % with charge[1]	25,000-49,999 % with charge[1]	10,000-24,999 % with charge[1]
Public safety							
Special police patrols	43	23	24	28	26	26	19
Police service at private events	45	69	56	71	66	77	66
Outside fire calls	52	40	36	39	36	41	40
Building, electrical, and plumbing inspection	90	88	96	97	91	88	84
Zoning and engineering services	79	75	81	89	79	80	67
Sewage and sanitation services							
Residential sewerage	74	91	93	99	90	93	90
Commercial and industrial sewerage	70	92	93	97	89	92	92
Residential refuse collection	62	55	42	56	61	61	52
Commercial and industrial refuse collection	39	72	71	76	72	76	70
Refuse disposal, use of landfills, and incineration	42	61	89	72	60	60	55
Recreation facilities and cultural activities							
Swimming pools or beaches	66	85	70	86	88	86	85
Golf courses	26	98	100	100	99	100	93
Tennis courts	74	30	60	45	38	26	24
Skating rinks	20	40	75	52	60	36	30
Recreation and hobby classes	67	78	67	83	81	79	76
Picnic grounds	74	16	38	24	20	13	12
Ball fields	82	31	58	49	37	33	24
Museums, zoos, and galleries	19	29	72	38	28	12	13
Concerts and plays	23	38	45	51	49	37	27
Convention halls	17	94	97	100	95	93	89

Table 1 (continued)

Type of service	All cities reporting		250,000 and over	100,000-249,999	50,000-99,999	25,000-49,999	10,000-24,999
	% reporting service	% with charge[1]	% with charge[1]	% with charge[1]	% with charge[1]	% with charge[1]	% with charge[1]
Health services							
Medical laboratory services	8	50	68	42	32	56	50
X-ray services	6	41	59	36	33	100	100
Outpatient clinics	10	56	74	66	47	46	40
Nonemergency ambulance service	13	58	83	92	71	67	46
Emergency medical service	35	45	62	53	54	41	40
Nursing homes	4	78	82	100	76	0	100
Parking							
On-street meters	35	100	100	100	100	100	100
Off-street lots and garages	50	66	98	82	80	69	52

Note: 0=0.5%

[1] The base of the percentage is the number of cities that reported providing the particular service.

Table 2　Cities adding user charges since July 1978: percent of respondents by population

Type of service	All cities reporting	250,000 and over	100,000-249,999	50,000-99,999	25,000-49,999	10,000-24,999
Public safety						
Special police patrols	33	29	25	28	33	34
Police service at private events	16	28	15	14	10	19
Outside fire calls	25	31	18	21	25	27
Building, electrical, and plumbing inspection	4	0	4	6	4	4
Zoning and engineering services	10	6	5	7	7	14
Sewerage and sanitation services						
Residential sewerage	7	3	6	9	6	6
Commercial and industrial sewerage	6	5	5	9	5	5
Residential refuse collection	16	5	10	15	11	19
Commercial and industrial refuse collection	10	19	6	13	7	12
Refuse disposal, use of landfills, and incineration	17	8	19	21	13	20
Recreation facilities and cultural activities						
Swimming pools or beaches	9	15	3	10	7	9
Golf courses	4	0	0	3	4	6
Tennis courts	26	23	20	25	26	27
Skating rinks	20	11	15	13	16	29
Recreation and hobby classes	10	19	4	7	5	14
Picnic grounds	26	31	23	29	24	25
Ball fields	24	25	17	26	23	26
Museums, zoos, and galleries	21	13	22	24	22	27
Concerts and plays	26	27	27	26	21	29
Convention halls	12	6	7	11	12	10

Table 2 (continued)

Type of service	All cities reporting	250,000 and over	100,000-249,999	50,000-99,999	25,000-49,999	10,000-24,999
Health services						
Medical laboratory services	13	8	9	21	33	0
X-ray services	17	8	16	19	0	0
Outpatient clinics	20	18	12	35	25	0
Nonemergency ambulance service	23	2	30	20	15	27
Emergency medical service	23	20	24	30	18	24
Nursing homes	0	7	0	0	0	0
Parking						
On-street meters	0	0	0	0	3	0
Off-street lots and garages	16	11	10	15	13	17

Note: 0 = less than 0.5%

Table 3   Cities in which charges defray 50% or more of the costs of services: percent of respondents by population group

Type of service	All cities reporting	250,000 and over	100,000-249,999	50,000-99,999	25,000-49,999	10,000-24,999
Public safety						
Special police patrols	15	9	20	15	16	11
Police service at private events	54	28	59	46	64	47
Outside fire calls	18	19	21	21	17	15
Building, electrical, and plumbing inspection	51	73	71	57	53	44
Zoning and engineering services	27	37	37	27	25	25
Sewerage and sanitation services						
Residential sewerage	79	84	89	75	81	77
Commercial and industrial sewerage	69	81	86	65	74	64
Residential refuse collection	44	30	50	45	52	41
Commercial and industrial refuse collection	49	59	63	45	56	44
Refuse disposal, use of landfills, and incineration	34	50	45	34	34	28
Recreation facilities and cultural activities						
Swimming pools or beaches	31	17	22	30	30	35
Golf courses	77	79	87	80	84	69
Tennis courts	10	16	10	13	10	8
Skating rinks	17	22	25	19	16	10
Recreation and hobby classes	42	17	44	43	43	42
Picnic grounds	3	12	1	0	4	3
Ball fields	10	17	9	12	11	7
Museums, zoos, and galleries	0	10	5	5	0	0
Concerts and plays	13	14	33	17	11	12
Convention halls	29	30	46	32	24	20

Table 3 (continued)

Type of service	All cities reporting	250,000 and over	100,000-249,999	50,000-99,999	25,000-49,999	10,000-24,999
Health services						
Medical laboratory services	0	18	0	0	0	0
X-ray services	0	14	0	0	0	0
Outpatient clinics	10	11	16	6	0	0
Nonemergency ambulance service	16	25	10	10	15	13
Emergency medical service	9	22	5	6	13	6
Nursing homes	50	40	78	60	0	0
Parking						
On-street meters	74	83	88	82	78	64
Off-street lots and garages	48	72	75	63	52	32

Note: 0 = less than 0.5%

Marketing for Public Managers

James A. Goodrich

In the words of a popular introductory text on the subject, marketing can be defined as "human activity directed at satisfying needs and wants through exchange processes."[1] Note that this definition covers a very wide range of activities, well beyond those that occur between buyers and sellers of a product. That this definition of marketing has broadened to cover nonbusiness applications is itself a sign of the times, as marketing is increasingly viewed in more "generic" terms.

Philip Kotler has outlined steps in this process by which marketing, originally conceived of as a business subject mainly concerned with market transactions between producer and consumer, came to apply to virtually all contacts any organization has with all of its different "publics."[2] We can define marketing management generically then as being concerned with the effective management by an organization of its exchange relationships with various target markets and publics. When viewed in this way, there seems little reason to believe that marketing know-how could not be potentially applied to orchestrating exchange processes in all types of organizations.

The idea that marketing concepts, technology and ideas can be useful for the public sector has been suggested for several years, especially by community leaders and those who want to see a more "businesslike" approach to managing government. Most such suggestions have gone unheeded, however, and it is clear that there are relatively few public sector marketing applications to date.

It is particularly ironic that, as marketers have become more concerned with defining their activities more broadly than those di-

This article is based on a presentation at the 44th annual conference of the American Society for Public Administration, New York, New York, April 18, 1983. Published with permission of the author.

rected at enhancing business profits, there is still such a lack of marketing "consciousness" among public executives. In the business world marketing is seen as increasingly crucial to management strategy. In spite of resistance, eventually a marketing orientation came to be viewed as essential even for service industries in the private sector. By contrast, administrators in government agencies typically do not think of themselves as needing a marketing approach to meet their organizational objectives.

In part this divergence between business and government is due to inevitable differences in the public organizational environment, which can be seen to limit or provide disincentives to marketing development. In addition, the notion of marketing is not an easy one for public sector executives to understand. In spite of the widespread definition of marketing in more "generic" terms, relatively few public administrators have much familiarity with marketing concepts or ideas. Recently I spoke before a group of 15 city managers with over 300 years' experience among them, and only one had ever had a marketing course. This is not surprising—while marketing is a required subject in all accredited business school curriculums, there are very few public administration programs (except those in combined schools with business administration) where marketing courses are even offered, much less required.

Overall there is very little evidence that marketing has moved substantially into the mainstream of public sector management thinking or concerns. As Lovelock and Weinberg conclude in their excellent review of public and nonprofit marketing advances, "When one looks at the record of marketing in a non-business managerial context ... the picture appears cloudy and the results have been mixed."[3] In the face of growing recognition that marketing techniques provide a useful perspective and powerful new tools for tackling a wide range of public problems, marketing has been noticeably absent in the management of nonbusiness organizations. It is also apparent that, even though marketing techniques are now more widely discussed and disseminated among practitioners in some fields (e.g., health care, energy conservation, transportation planning), most governments and public agencies do not have marketing departments or programs; nor are they hiring marketing people.

This unfortunate state of affairs arises more from ignorance than contempt, I believe, although marketing has been viewed by some public officials with a jaundiced eye. The group of city managers mentioned above, for example, showed a remarkable upsurge of interest in discussing the subject when they realized that they were *already* engaged in many "marketing" activities, though they did not recognize them as such. Public managers make marketing decisions every time they: (1) establish a new location for some public facility; (2) decide to offer a new service or modify an existing product; (3) choose to eliminate or add a program; (4) start charging fees or change prices for services; (5) develop and publish a brochure; or (6) hold a press conference.

These are just a few instances where public managers engage in marketing type activities, more or less consciously and in ways more or less related to overall management purposes. Unfortunately in the public sector managers usually do these things without the benefit of marketing skills and know-how, even though these are all areas where marketing ideas can potentially be very useful.

Since there are numerous areas where marketing can help in public problem solving, there seem to be no inherent reasons why marketing must remain on the "fringes" of public administration. Indeed, development of a marketing perspective has the potential to make government agencies more responsive to the people they serve. To take advantage of marketing insights, though, we must integrate marketing more directly with public management planning and policy making—in short, develop an overall marketing orientation within government itself.

Need for a marketing orientation

Because public organizations are all essentially in the business of providing some public service, it is interesting to look at them in terms of a marketing orientation as compared to other management philosophies that might guide them in service provision. We can visualize these along a continuum of contrasting possibilities, from more internally focused to more outward looking, as suggested here:

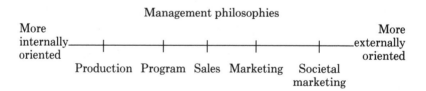

Production orientation   Many public agencies are characterized by a *production* orientation. Their major emphasis is on running a smooth operation at all costs. The management focus is on pursuing efficiency in production and distribution, even if client needs must sometimes be squeezed a little to fit into organizational service categories. Examples of this kind of an orientation are all too common. The assumption of most employment agencies and county hospital emergency rooms seems to be that customers must meet their operating standards and needs even if this means standing in long lines or waiting hours for service. Bus drivers speed by waiting passengers in order to meet their timetables, and the attitude of most people behind the Department of Motor Vehicles windows seems to be that their agency would run perfectly well if they could be left alone without all these disorganized customers clogging up operations.[4]

Program orientation   Other government organizations have more of a *program* orientation. They are strongly committed to putting out products or services which agency professionals feel will be good for the public. However, their tendency is to continue producing the same service in about the same way even in the face of clientele changes, competition or other environmental shifts. Thus the U.S. Postal Service continues to offer basically the same line of services and products, even as it loses more customers to private carriers and runs up large operating deficits. City parks and recreation programs often remain basically unchanged year after year (though the fees rise), while private swim and tennis clubs take more and more of their customers. Local museums and libraries continue to feature the same kinds of art works and books (which they have decided the public should be interested in) even as their attendance declines.

Sales orientation   At the next point on the continuum, a *sales* orientation reflects management assumptions that there is at least some need to pay more attention to the agency's environment, in order to stimulate the interest of potential clients/customers in the organization of its services. We see evidence of this orientation when the U.S. Army increases its budget for advertising and gives more extensive training sessions for its recruiters in the field. In recent years economic development agencies have begun to use tax dollars to promote certain communities and to attract business to areas in order to expand local job opportunities and to improve local tax bases. Social service agencies seek to design better brochures and ad campaigns trying to induce more volunteers to help with their programs.

Marketing orientation   By contrast, a *marketing* orientation emerges as a concern for the changing needs of clients or customers and involves setting up organizational practices to constantly improve services in order to help meet these needs. The focus of attention is not on production, programs, or selling the agency services, but on determining the needs of target markets in light of the organization mission and objectives. Ideally, this consumer orientation will prevail throughout the agency, with employees characterized by a sensitive, caring attitude in working for the client as well as for their boss.

Societal marketing orientation   More recently, many marketers have come to define their roles in ways that go beyond this traditional marketing conception, which ignores social costs and sidesteps
conflicts that may exist between consumer wants and societal welfare. They suggest the need to take account of these longer-run public
concerns and future needs in terms of a concept of "societal marketing." In this orientation, management tasks are defined in broader
terms:

The key tasks of the organization are to determine the needs, wants and
interests of target markets and to adapt the organization to delivering the
desired satisfactions . . . in a way that preserves or enhances the consumer's *and the society's* well-being.[5]

Here at the right of the continuum is a definition of marketing
management philosophy that is not only generic but directly relevant
to public administrators, who must rationalize their activities in
terms of serving the public interest. Certainly regulatory activities of
government as well as direct services provision could readily be included in this "societal marketing" concept, which is concerned with
overall public welfare and the quality of life. At the same time, this
array of management philosophies is helpful in defining the marketing orientation more broadly and avoiding the normal tendency to
equate marketing with advertising or public relations.

Selling vs. marketing public services

Marketing is commonly identified with advertising. In this sense,
government has gone into business in a big way. The growth of government advertising budgets in recent years has been nothing short
of amazing. In 1970 the U.S. Government was not even on the list of
the 100 largest national advertisers; by 1975 federal agencies totaled
more than $100 million in paid media advertising. In 1981 the U.S.
Government ranked 26th among leading national advertisers, with
its annual expenditures of $189 million ranking slightly behind Coca-
Cola and Chrysler Corporation and ahead of such industry giants as
Unilever, Anheuser-Busch, Gillette and General Electric.[6]
Even these totals are conservative, for they do not include the
estimated $100 million spent annually by state and local govern-
ments, and these figures include only paid advertising expenditures.
Public agencies and programs receive free public service ads in far
more significant amounts. It was estimated in 1980, for example,
that governments and nonprofit agencies together received over $2
billion worth of donated broadcast time and print space—as much as
the total amount spent by the top 10 advertisers combined.[7]
In terms of the points described on the continuum, however, this
activity usually represents a focus on *selling* rather than *marketing*.
The differences are important. The marketing conception focuses on

the needs of the client or service user, while the selling concept emphasizes the needs of the producer. Marketing basically seeks to "find needs and fill them" rather than to "create programs and sell them." Whereas a selling orientation starts with an existing organization and its "products," then focuses on stimulating demand or attracting resources for them, a marketing orientation begins with agency goals and "target markets," then plans its programs and activities in order to best respond to and satisfy these needs.

The public sector parallels the private sector in that most products or services start off with somebody's bright ideas, followed by a "sell job." The difference is that much less attention is systematically paid to customer needs and requirements on the public side. Politicians themselves are "sold" to the public through carefully orchestrated, media-blitz campaigns.[8] After elections, political leaders continue to take a "sales oriented" view toward citizens, with little research into what the public wants or needs and lots of selling to get people to accept what chief executives and other politicians view as their "program." All too often public administrators (as professionals with a mainly programmatic orientation) spend their time figuring out how to "sell" their agency or its services rather than planning how to respond to client needs. This producer orientation has many disastrous consequences—including low-cost housing projects which must be destroyed since people don't want to live in them, bus lines without many riders, and public events with low attendance and lots of vacant seats.

Of course, there is nothing inherently wrong with promoting public "products." Certainly advertising can help to put people in touch with services they need and reach out to potential "target markets" previously untouched or untapped. Managers in the public sector are involved in selling much of the time—whether convincing farmers to use new technologies, people to stop smoking or drivers to observe speed limits—and they probably need to pay more explicit attention to their "sales force" and to promotional techniques.[9]

The basic problem lies with the logic of the sales (as opposed to marketing) concept. Public organizations often tend to increase their selling efforts rather than change their agency or its services to make them more attractive. Thus, even as the U.S. Army succeeds in getting more recruits, limited changes in its organization staffing, training and compensation practices mean it continues to lose more people at reenlistment time or at mid-career levels.[10] Social service agencies line up more volunteers but find they drop out in ever greater numbers due to difficulties in fitting into agency schedules, lack of adequate training or a feeling that they are relegated to relatively meaningless tasks. County Welfare Departments succeed in attracting more potential foster parents, only to find them frustrated by departmental red tape which makes them wait months for a child, or states that they must build a fence and modify their homes to comply with regulations.

Organizations in the public sector are now repeating some historic patterns that occurred with the introduction of marketing into different areas of business. Like their private sector counterparts, public managers are likely to view marketing ideas as controversial, and even as they come to adopt marketing practices in their agencies, to define marketing too narrowly at first. Many have gone along for years as victims of what Levitt called "marketing myopia," just like those business executives who thought they were in a secure position and could concentrate on more efficient production and advertising, instead of considering changes in the business environment which would affect demand for their products.[11] It is also likely that public administrators will parallel their business counterparts in the early stages of marketing thinking, viewing marketing primarily as promotional.

Typically organizations become interested in marketing when significant shifts occur in their environment. If revenues or resources decline, if more competition appears, or if new and different client needs emerge, organizations become more receptive to marketing efforts. It is not unexpected, then, to find increasing numbers of public administrators looking for ways to survive in these perilous times of tax referendums, budget cuts and fiscal austerity, exploring marketing possibilities with some interest. What is different for them now is that economic circumstances are changing, political winds are shifting, and their environment is much more "turbulent" and uncertain.

In this context—with a number of different agencies often competing for scarce resources and a limited amount of taxpayer dollars to go around—they are looking to see what marketing has to offer them. However, most of these administrators tend to view marketing as useful in a very limited way—namely, as "better public relations." They see marketing in terms of a need to "explain" their agency and its services to a hostile or uninformed citizenry and to build support for their programs as essential (or at least more so than those of competing agencies) in the face of potential budget cuts.

The problem with this limited perspective is that it has a tendency to backfire. There is already a great deal of public concern about using tax dollars to plug government services. It is this type of concern that leads President Reagan, himself a former movie actor, to go on record against the making of films in order to publicize and explain government programs. In this view, marketing is often seen as an administrative "overhead" activity which is ancillary or, at least, not essential to the provision of public services. If marketing is defined simply as advertising and PR it becomes more vulnerable to cutbacks. The considerable outcry about the huge advertising budget of the armed forces is just one example of this. These kinds of expenditures are likely targets for critics of defense spending, as are other government advertising expenditures for critics of their programs.

Ironically government agencies may "regress" from a sales orientation to more of a production orientation in the near future. As marketing becomes identified with the *promotion* of government services, it seems out of touch with the times, especially when governments have fewer services and less to fund them with. A major emphasis today is "productivity." To most public administrators, this seems to mean focusing on producing existing services more efficiently, rather than strategic planning about which services to offer in the face of changing demands and resource limitations.[12]

The worst problem with defining marketing so narrowly, however, is the failure to develop overall organizational strategies built around different elements of the marketing "mix." These are generally classified as the "four P's": *product, price, place, promotion.*[13]

All four of these variables are critically related to strategic planning in an organization and must be considered in deciding what particular blend of marketing activities the organization uses to attain its objectives, to reach and to serve its clients or "target markets."

An emphasis on promotion to the exclusion of the other three variables obviously limits the usefulness of marketing applications in the public sector. For example, an extensive marketing analysis of government anti-litter campaigns revealed that they mainly emphasized advertising approaches, with ads urging people not to litter and asking them to pick up litter when they run across it. For various reasons (e.g., low issue salience, low public involvement, low cost-benefit ratio to individuals picking up litter) these anti-littering ad campaigns tended to have only slight short-run impact, and none had much long-run force in changing people's behavior.[14] Yet the impact of these anti-litter efforts could be significantly enhanced by giving more attention to the other three P's. Local governments could put in more public refuse containers (product) in each crowded location (place) found to have high concentrations of litter. Also fines (price) and other sanctions could be enforced more severely on persons caught littering.

Even where marketing information exists, it may not be effectively used by public officials who are unaccustomed to dealing with marketing concepts. Although the reintroduction of the $2 bill was the subject of an extensive marketing research study commissioned by the Federal Reserve Board, it appears that the Fed made little use of these data when making strategic decisions to introduce this particular "product."

They basically limited their efforts to a very low-level PR campaign, ignoring survey results which suggested significant distribution problems due to negative attitudes of banks, retailers, and other cash handlers.[15]

In sum, several negative consequences may result from confusing marketing with a sales orientation or defining marketing merely as advertising. Probably the ad campaigns themselves will be less effective, and there will be a tendency to view marketing activities as "overhead" expenses which are subject to cuts or can even be dispensed with altogether in the face of budget constraints. Also there will be a tendency for public managers to view marketing as perhaps a necessary tool for some specific purposes (e.g., attracting more volunteers for a program) but not necessarily as a fundamental concept underlying management strategy and decision making.

The promise of marketing

As noted, while public agencies are implicitly concerned with the major issues and variables dealt with in marketing, there is little explicit consideration of these by public managers in terms of an overall marketing perspective. Marketing is fundamentally concerned with identifying and preparing to meet the needs of target markets (e.g., potential or existing users, customers, recruits, clients). In contrast to more programmatic, "producer" orientations, these consumer needs are the basic beginning point, the linchpin for marketing management strategy and decision making. This kind of orientation could be useful for improving public organizations' exchange relationships in at least four ways:

1. Improved policy planning, through selection of better policy designs and more effective implementation
2. Improved satisfaction of target market and better matching of client needs to services
3. Improved efficiency in service delivery resulting from better communication, packaging, distribution and so forth
4. Improved attraction of resources and public support with more positive image of government agencies and programs.

The promise of marketing for the public sector seems almost unlimited, provided marketing concepts are well understood by public managers and a consumer orientation can be developed within public agencies. For example, when developing a new program or service, a number of questions need to be studied very carefully. Among them are:

1. Who are the potential users of these products/services?
2. Which of their needs will this program help fulfill, and how?
3. What alternative programs could be developed to meet these needs?
4. How is this service or program to be distinguished from others already available?
5. What strategy and tactics will be required to launch the program and have it adopted by intended users?

Marketing techniques could be helpful in finding answers to all these questions. Indeed, all these are central concerns for business marketers, where relatively sophisticated marketing skills have been developed. However, they typically are not brought in as part of a systematic marketing orientation in the public sector. One has only to contrast the extensive and careful marketing research accompanying product development or modification in business organizations with the very superficial "needs assessments" performed in connection with public programs to see the difference here. This is a real problem. While many factors contribute to the failure of government policies from a marketing perspective, one factor stands out—public programs are often planned, developed and implemented without an adequate understanding of how the intended "target markets" will use or accept the new product or services being offered.

We can also learn a lot from business marketers about the importance of rapid feedback and its uses in planning out and adjusting programs over time. Typically the evaluation component which is tacked on to most public sector initiatives asks a fairly narrow set of questions related to whether the program achieved its goals. By contrast, marketers are typically less interested in the question "Did it work?" than in the question "Why did it work or not work?" Normally the evaluation process in the public sector tries to answer the first question in ways that are relatively cumbersome, after the fact, and quite often useless to the program itself, as well as to future efforts or groups working in similar areas of concern.

Marketing research tries to answer the second question in a number of relatively more sophisticated ways. First, by carefully researching consumer behavior and pretesting the product, program or service as part of the design stage; then by setting up a model of the process by which people will accept this design and carefully monitoring that process over time. In this way, there is still some possibility of modifying the program if it seems less than successful. Douglas Solomon offers an example of how this could be done for a fire prevention program.

Students in elementary schools are presented a series of filmed messages about fire prevention, they are given brochures to bring home to their parents and are asked to talk to them about what they learned, they are also taught a special Smokey the Bear song that they are asked to sing to remind their parents the next time they visit a forest or wildlife preserve with them. Based on this simple model, a series of "guideposts" could be set up to monitor the process. Simple research techniques can be used to monitor whether the booklets are passed out, whether they ever reach the home, whether children understand the message and have the relevant skills to talk to their parents, whether they learn the Smokey the Bear song, whether they sing the song upon visiting the forest, and so on. If a campaign monitored in this way fails, it will be fairly easy to understand the reasons for failure and correct them in subsequent efforts.[17]

Utilizing marketing research techniques in this way is obviously important as an initial activity in the marketing of a program or a service. Such techniques can also be used by a city or other governmental jurisdiction to determine public attitudes toward proposed changes in the provision and delivery of goods and services. Marketing research is a rational, representative approach to getting public input. Careful study of consumer behavior can help in getting timely, relevant information to public managers in order to improve the match between services provided and consumer needs.

Another very important area where marketing can contribute to public sector management is in highlighting the importance of public image. Organizations that serve the people must have a vital concern in understanding how their "publics"—defined as any group that has an interest in or impact on the organization—view them and their programs or services. In government we have a special concern in seeing to it that these images enhance rather than impede service delivery. This process of improving an organization's image involves careful planning and is not simply a matter of improving public relations. As Kotler suggests,

An organization does not acquire a favorable public image simply through public relations . . . Its image is a function of its *deeds* and its *communications*. Good deeds without good words, or good words without good deeds, are not enough. A strong favorable image comes about when the organization creates real satisfaction for its clients and lets others know about this.[18]

For marketing to be successful, a marketing orientation—defined as outward-looking, customer-oriented attitudes and behavior—must prevail at all levels throughout the organization. This is because everything about an agency and the way it operates is significant in terms of its image. The manner in which the lowliest receptionist answers the telephone, or the helpfulness of agency employees in solving client problems means a great deal in defining the organization's outlook and its public reputation. Obviously a truly responsive organization can only be created through hard work.

Not only must a great deal of time and effort go into the systematic study of consumer needs, preferences and satisfactions, but the organization must carefully act on this information and constantly work to improve its services in order to meet customer needs better. Careful recruitment, selection and training of employees is necessary to get across the idea that they are working for the customer first (rather than just their immediate superior within the organization). Developing the teamwork necessary to meet the needs of specified

target markets will not occur by accident. It involves carefully orchestrated efforts throughout public organizations using personnel
policies and customer relations methods built on a true commitment
to a marketing orientation.

Once having developed a marketing orientation, the public executive and agency administrators can turn their attention to a wide
variety of possible marketing applications. There is a small but growing literature which suggests the relatively wide scope and range of
these applications, as well as numerous examples of ways marketing
can help public managers with particular tasks. Marketing can help
in making product mix decisions, such as the number and level of
services offered at a county hospital or even a municipal zoo.[19] In
other cases, marketing provides assistance in planning the location
of public services and dealing with scheduling problems.[20] While the
detailing of such applications is beyond the scope of this article, it is
worthwhile to note that these examples range from overall planning
of a program, campaign or service to specific decisions about a particular type of activity or prices to be charged. One recent study even
applies product life cycle theory to the handling of books in local public libraries.[21]

Of course, the promise of marketing for the public sector will be
fully realized only to the extent that it is understood, organized and
used properly. This means we need to go beyond a narrow definition
equating marketing activities with advertising or selling. The more
we define marketing in this way, the more likely it is to be considered
as "overhead" activity which wastes taxpayer dollars, rather than as
essential to improving public services delivery in order to meet community needs. Such a definition of marketing also tends to limit our
consideration of marketing management tools to a relatively narrow
range of applications.

Public managers need to learn what their counterparts in the
private sector have already found out—that no amount of promotional activities will rescue a program or service that is not needed,
has a poor image, or is not appropriate to people's needs. No amount
of "marketing" in this sense will salvage a poor product like the Susan B. Anthony dollar, or Amtrak's long-haul trains, just as it is unlikely that more advertising will rescue some unpopular local government agencies and programs from budget cuts or even oblivion. We
need to deal with all four "P's" in the marketing "mix" to improve
service efficiency, or even to supplement the selling of ideas as in
energy conservation, anti-litter or family planning ad campaigns.
Above all, we need to integrate the whole range of marketing concepts into public management concerns and educate ourselves about
the broader connection between marketing and strategic planning, if

these concepts are to help public agencies become more responsive to changes in their environment.

The challenge to marketers

It has been over 30 years since Wiebe introduced the idea of using marketing for the public sector in asking the question, "Why can't you sell brotherhood like you sell soap?"[22] During this time, the field of marketing has expanded dramatically and gone through tremendous changes, breaking into new areas of industry and even previously untouched arenas (e.g., law, accounting and medicine). However, much of this expansion and the explosion of new marketing ideas and technology has passed right by the public sector. In this sense, penetration of the government "market" is a significant challenge to marketers.

To successfully meet this challenge, we must perhaps first understand some of the differences between business and government organizations. There are a number of reasons why it is difficult to sell brotherhood like soap. Marketing concepts cannot be lifted without alteration from business situations to public sector programs. For example, a great deal of effort is expended by business marketers in "segmenting" markets and focusing on certain target audiences with the most potential. A government agency often cannot be satisfied with a certain share of the overall market, but must continue to try and extend services to all possible clients or constituents. It cannot practice market segmentation by focusing its attention on certain categories of clients which it could serve best or most efficiently—to do so would be politically fatal as well as legally indefensible.

In other situations the public sector introduces a focus on new or different market segments than those typically studied by the business marketer. The most important public for many government agencies is often key legislators or committees which review agency activities and have the power of the purse. This may be the most important "target market" the organization must appeal to in structuring or organizing its activities. Also, private business programs can more easily ignore marketing to less profitable segments of the population, while public sector programs are often specifically designed to serve these hardest-to-reach segments.[23]

This is not to suggest that marketing ideas cannot be useful here. Many of the same variables (e.g., product adaptation, communications designs, cost and distribution considerations) are involved. However, it is true that we have less knowledge about marketing applications and operations in these areas. Achieving success in orchestrating public organization exchange processes will not be easy, because it directs attention to a whole new set of concerns and requires a different research agenda. Here is a major reason why the public sector represents new challenges for marketers. Some areas which are just beginning to be explored within the marketing field are already of major concern to public sector managers.

The whole concept of "demarketing" is a good example of this. While most marketing experts are in the business of encouraging and building up demand for an organization's products or services, a major task of public managers in these times of scarcity is often to stretch their meager resources, trying to make sure that there is enough left of the shrinking pie to give all their clients some amount, however reduced. They are not trying to attract customers for their programs. In some other cases (e.g., energy or water conservation, HMO office visits, or 911 emergency calls) the aim is to dampen public demand or limit usage to only "essential" customers and activities as a matter of public policy. Demarketing—the use of marketing strategies to reduce demand or channel it to appropriate uses—can be helpful here.

While demarketing has been described conceptually in marketing terminology, it has yet to be refined in practice and applied to a wide variety of situations.[24] This is mainly because there are so few instances in the private sector where it proves necessary to demarket. The public sector provides an abundance of examples of demarketing opportunities where demand is too great. Indeed, to public administrators charged with reconciling demands for more and better services with the facts of economic downturns and budget-cutting initiatives, this function of marketing as "demand management" can hardly be overlooked.[25]

In relating marketing to the management concerns in government today, we should be realistic and not expect too much. While there are some indicators that marketing ideas are indeed "generic" and can usefully be applied to public administration, we lack experience in applying them in nonbusiness situations. There is a need to define more carefully the key differences in public organization decision processes and public agency task environments. Also we will have to develop a new research focus in areas that until now have not been central concerns for business marketers. Ultimately, an increase in the number of successful public sector marketing applications will require the reeducation of government executives as well as the demonstration of ways that marketing can help them in their specific context with management tasks. This process, part of the "marketing of marketing itself," involves the development of familiarity with marketing terms and concepts, and increasing the awareness of public managers concerning the scope and diversity of the marketing field.[26]

The challenge to public managers

To public managers, the challenge of marketing is both more straightforward and more compelling. It is clear that we need to make more use of marketing resources. In this country and throughout the world there exists a wealth of know-how and ideas—in marketing research, advertising, distribution—which need not be limited to commercial and industrial applications. In many instances these resources are already being used as marketing activities have been legitimized in government budgets and legislation, and some success stories have already been noted. In the long run, the need to develop in-house capabilities and expertise will require more people trained in marketing within government itself. The tendency has been to use outside consulting firms to supplement public sector personnel, but there is a need to hire and develop our own marketing people if we are to build knowledge about the actual range of specific public sector applications and develop deeper insights into marketing as a strategic planning tool.

The challenge goes beyond using marketing expertise or hiring marketing people, however. Public managers need to integrate marketing with other management tasks. Too often, marketing is regarded as a set of techniques, useful for specific purposes such as advertising or services utilization planning, yet still viewed as an appendage, somewhat removed from the central management concerns of the organization or government unit. The successful application of marketing skills in the public sector will require more than this— more than just better marketing research or consumer analysis— however useful these are to identify public needs and to pre-test decision alternatives. It will require a commitment to a marketing orientation—a way of thinking that is fundamentally based on meeting the needs of the customer, the ultimate user or beneficiary of government services.

In the public sector we have yet to realize the depth of this commitment, or what it can mean for our organizations. To illustrate, I recently gave a marketing presentation in Anaheim, where Disneyland is located. We entered into a discussion of the declining image of government today and what could be done about it. As part of this discussion, state and local officials present were asked to compare their personnel policies and customer relations to those of Walt Disney Enterprises.

In the Disney organization, even the lowliest ticket-takers at their theme parks are put through 32 hours of instruction before they go "onstage" (their term) to serve the public. During this training period, they are introduced to every aspect of the business and are socialized to the "Disney way" of serving the customer. (Contrast this to the baptism under fire we all too often expect of public employees.) In order to respond to consumer questions, there is a special switchboard number with operators standing by to answer any question Disney staffers cannot answer.

As Red Pope observes in his famous piece on "Mickey Mouse

Marketing," the organizational commitment to customer and employee satisfaction does not end there. At Disney Enterprises, every person wears a name tag with just his or her first name on it, regardless of rank or title. This is part of the "family feeling" that Disney advocates and creates a sense of unity among the employees. Special company publications publicize the activities of Disney people, featuring employment and other opportunities within the organization. There is a computerized car pool service with free vans and a separate recreational facility for employee use. In a week-long program called "cross-utilization," top management (VP levels on down) give up their desks and take jobs assigned to them selling hot dogs, parking cars, or others "designed to give management a better 'hands on' view of how the guests need to be served and, at the same time . . . [get] a better understanding of what the cast member must go through to properly serve the guests."[27] At the end of the week these managers must write a report on their activities.

The point of such a comparison should be clear by now—in the public sector we are concerned about improving our image but often unwilling to make this kind of organizational commitment supporting a consumer orientation. Even though we realize that government agencies may be under more public scrutiny than private companies, we take too little time to prepare our employees to serve the public. Yet putting customer relations and employee relations as top priorities is critical to making the marketing orientation a part of any organization. Certainly there is a great deal of effort and resources involved, but the payoffs are substantial. When a community's citizens or an agency's clientele are happy with the service as well as the product, and are met with enthusiastic and knowledgeable personnel who are eager to help out, it is likely that the credibility of the organization will rise and so will the level of their support for its activities. Only when public sector employees know that their employer has a solid concern and interest in their job satisfaction, and is working to make meaningful programs to demonstrate that interest, will their performance begin to measure up to "customer-oriented" standards.

There are, of course, many different levels of "customer-centeredness" in business organizations; not all are run like Disney. Yet this kind of commitment, concern and responsiveness is increasingly viewed as crucial to success, and seems to be exemplified in those enterprises judged to be "the best" in their domains.[28] We may not soon see the day that government units get consumer ratings to compete with Delta Airlines or IBM, but in these days of declining budget revenues and increased critical evaluation by the public, customer impressions may be recognized as increasingly important. Citizen perceptions of public officials or an agency are often based on a relatively small number of contacts or experiences. Whether these have been satisfactory or unsatisfactory may be very significant in terms of their attitudes and support.

Here we can see marketing ideas and democratic ideals converge —both are concerned with developing responsive, adaptive public organizations to meet people's needs. To the extent that it is concerned with developing strategies to meet these citizen needs, marketing already is—or should be—in the "mainstream" of public administrative thinking. For public officials, the call to bring in a "new" marketing management orientation can be visualized in terms of a return to (or a fresh look at) a tradition of public service in the public's interest. To suggest that we move beyond a program or a producer orientation and define public management roles in terms of "meeting people's needs" rather than "selling existing programs" is critically important. For marketing to be more than promotion or propaganda it must be used to meet the needs of agency "publics" and ultimately of the larger society.

In business we have seen many times that the failure of a firm to market effectively can undermine service efficiency and eventually can do great harm to the organization itself as its image declines and public confidence in its products is eroded. We need to take this lesson to heart. In the public sector, marketing holds forth the possibility of enhancing the image and effectiveness of public organizations (and public administrators) even as it seeks to make government "of, by and for the people" a more workable concept. The challenge to public managers is to take the plunge and commit the necessary energy and resources to make these marketing ideas pay off.

1. Philip Kotler, *Principles of Marketing* (Englewood Cliffs, N.J.: Prentice-Hall, 1980), p. 10.
2. Philip Kotler, "A Generic Concept of Marketing," *Journal of Marketing* 36 (April 1972), pp. 46-54.
3. Christopher H. Lovelock and Charles B. Weinberg, "Public and Nonprofit Marketing Comes of Age," in Lovelock and Weinberg (eds.) *Readings in Public and Nonprofit Marketing* (Palo Alto, Calif.: Scientific Press, 1978), p. 12. This article summarizes a wide variety of nonbusiness marketing developments and contains an extensive list of references.
4. A humorous discussion of the consequences of such an operations orientation is Patrick Ryan's "Get Rid of the People and the System Runs Fine" in Lovelock and Weinberg (eds.) *op. cit.*, pp. 23-24.
5. Kotler, *Principles, op. cit.*, p. 25 (emphasis added).
6. "100 Leading National Advertisers," *Advertising Age* (September 9, 1982). This figure includes two "quasi-public" government enterprises, the U.S. Postal Service and Amtrak.
7. The Advertising Council of America, "Public Service Messages: Volunteer Advertising," pamphlet, n.d.
8. See, for example, Joseph McGinnes, *The Selling of the President* (New York: Trident Press, 1969).
9. An excellent discussion of these subjects is found in Philip Kotler, *Marketing for Nonprofit Organizations*, 2nd edition (Englewood Cliffs, N.J.: Prentice-Hall, 1982). See chapters

15, "Sales Force Decisions," and 16, "Advertising and Sales Promotion Decisions."

10. For a discussion of the army's recruiting and retention problems, see Congressional Budget Office (CBO), *Costs of Manning the Active-Duty Military* (May 1980), especially pp. 5–11; and CBO, *Resources for Defense: A Review of Key Issues for Fiscal Years 1982-1986* (January 1981), pp. 85–94. Both of these analyses emphasize problems in the straight pay bonus system as a means to improve retention, in the absence of changing the organizational climate and overall personnel practices of the army.

11. Theodore Levitt, "Marketing Myopia," *Harvard Business Review* (July–August 1960).

12. This is not to suggest that more productivity is not a good idea; indeed, since government (and the whole service sector) is highly labor intensive, one of the main needs is to find ways to increase productivity. However, a narrow productivity emphasis is probably a mistake, if it means simply concentrating on doing the same old things more efficiently. We should put equal emphasis on making public organizations more responsive and adaptive to changing environmental situations as well as on making people in them more productive.

13. This classification of variables in the marketing mix is attributed to E. Jerome McCarthy. See his *Basic Marketing: A Managerial Approach*, 6th edition (Homewood, Ill.: Irwin, 1978), p. 39.

14. Michael L. Rothschild, "Marketing Communications in Nonbusiness Situations or Why It's So Hard to Sell Brotherhood like Soap," *Journal of Marketing* (Spring 1979), pp. 11–20.

15. Intercollegiate Case Clearing House, "Department of the Treasury: Reissue of the $2 Bill," 9-576-102 (Boston, 1975). See also Michael M. Amspaugh, "Americans Continue to Ignore the $2 Bill," in Lovelock and

Weinberg (eds.) *op. cit.*, pp. 221–222.

16. See Ben M. Enis, *et al.*, "Public Policy Development: A Marketing Perspective," in Lovelock and Weinberg (eds.), *op. cit.*, pp. 33–36, for a discussion of marketing uses in public policy development and implementation.

17. Douglas Solomon, "A Social Marketing Perspective on Campaigns," in R. Rice and W. Paisley, *Public Communication Campaigns* (Beverly Hills, Calif.: Sage Publications, 1981), p. 288.

18. Kotler, *Nonprofit, op. cit.*, p. 56.

19. See William Flexner and Eric Berkowitz, "Marketing Research in Health Services Planning: A Model" and Carol Kovach, "A Hungry Problem for Zoos: in Search of New Prey," in P. Kotler, O. C. Ferrell and C. Lamb, *Cases and Readings for Marketing for Nonprofit Organizations* (Englewood Cliffs, N.J.: Prentice-Hall, 1983), pp. 112–126 and pp. 201–209.

20. See Charles Lamb and John Crompton, "Distributing Public Services: A Strategic Approach," in *ibid.*, pp. 210–221, and Christopher Lovelock, "A Market Segmentation Approach to Transit Planning, Modeling and Management," in Lovelock and Weinberg, *op. cit.*, pp. 101–110.

21. John Crompton and Sharon Bonk, "An Empirical Investigation of the Appropriateness of the Product Life Cycle to Municipal Library Services," in Kotler, Ferrell and Lamb, *op. cit.*, pp. 169–177.

22. G. D. Weibe, "Merchandising Commodities and Citizenship on Television," *Public Opinion Quarterly* (Winter 1951–52), pp. 679–691, especially p. 679.

23. This may be why it is proving more difficult to "sell" the poor on *free* weatherization programs, for example, than to sell middle class homeowners on zero-interest *loans* for this purpose.

24. See also Philip Kotler and Sidney J. Levy, "Demarketing, Yes Demarketing," *Harvard Business Review* (November–December 1971), pp.

74–80, for further discussion.

25. Kotler describes the basic tasks of marketing management in broad terms as "demand management." This definition recognizes the fact that marketers are concerned not only with the creation and expansion of demand but with its possible modification or even its reduction. Marketing management tasks can be described as related to "regulating the level, timing and character of demand for a product, service, place or idea." See Philip Kotler, "The Major Tasks of Marketing Management," *Journal of Marketing* (Octo-

ber 1973), pp. 42–49; quote from p. 48.

26. Lovelock and Weinberg, *op. cit.*, p. 12.

27. N. W. (Red) Pope, "Mickey Mouse Marketing" and "More Mickey Mouse Marketing," in Kotler, Ferrell and Lamb, *op. cit.*, pp. 18–27, especially p. 26.

28. See, for example, the discussion in Thomas Peters and Robert Waterman, *In Search of Excellence: Lessons from America's Best Run Companies* (New York: Harper and Row, 1982), Chapter 6.

Marketing Strategies for Local Government

J. Scott McBride

There is a growing interest in the whole area of marketing the services of local municipalities, although actual involvement in marketing may be just beginning. As a start, it is important to develop a greater understanding of how marketing might play a role in local government, because marketing is going to be more important in the 1980s than perhaps ever before.

When I was first asked whether our firm would consider offering marketing consulting services to local municipalities, I wasn't sure of the need for them. I really wasn't sure how marketing might fit into a local government context. But after becoming more familiar with local government, I am persuaded that marketing may in fact have a more important role in communities than ever before. In particular it may provide the way to generate new revenues. It also may be a complement to the whole notion of cutback management, because when an organization is faced with a reduction in resources, it has two opportunities: (1) to reduce expenditures to be consistent with the resources available; and (2) to employ some of those resources to multiply revenue.

I would suggest that local municipalities ought to be doing both those things—cutting back if necessary but also considering the use of some resources to more effectively market the services they already have and in turn improve services and increase revenue.

The following is a discussion of what is called the marketing mix, a fancy title for the elements that make up an overall marketing program. Each element will be described briefly and related to the local government context.

This article is based on a presentation at the 67th annual conference of the International City Management Association, Anaheim, California, September 23, 1981. Published with permission of the author.

Marketing strategy

The first element in the marketing program is the development of a marketing strategy and plan.

Long-range objectives An interesting thing we find when we work for client organizations and begin to develop marketing strategies and plans is that it opens up the whole corporate strategy area, because if an organization is going to develop a marketing plan it ought to support and help implement the organization's overall objectives. Often as we start to write the marketing plan we find that there are few if any well-articulated corporate goals and objectives. So be forewarned that if you start writing marketing plans it may well raise issues about the longer-range goals and objectives for the municipality.

The local role as service provider A second issue that arises as you consider marketing and its applications to government is the role of the local government in providing services. Is the local government simply a court of last resort providing only those services that the private sector cannot or will not provide? Or is its role to provide not only those necessary services but perhaps others that maybe the private sector would provide but the city elects to provide instead, either because it can deliver better service or because there is a financial incentive the city keeps for itself? The whole issue of service provision is going to be raised as local managers develop marketing plans.

Specific marketing objectives The next issue that will come up are specific marketing objectives. The obvious one of course is to increase revenues, and certainly that's a worthy objective. But there may be even more important ones, such as increasing and broadening citizen participation, utilization of parks, recreational facilities, libraries, and so on. In broadening that participation you might not only increase revenues but also substantially increase the involvement of citizens in local government.

Another objective may be to improve the overall quality of services that are rendered. For example, in some cities with an unusually high incidence of fire or damage to property, it might make sense to develop a surveillance system that corporations and individuals might pay for to provide greater protection and in turn perhaps reduce insurance premiums for fire protection and the like, and thereby enhance the services that are already available.

Or might there be some unmet need in the community? I've observed recently that airline service seems to be reduced into many small and medium-sized communities. That may put some pressure on local airports in these cities, and there may be an unmet need that the city should be responsive to—perhaps providing some sort of support and assistance in financing to continue the service. These are examples of the variety of objectives a local government may seek to accomplish through its marketing program.

Leverage areas   In developing a marketing plan, it is useful to quickly identify what we call the leverage areas within the organization. Many activities go on in any organization, but the old 80-20 rule that 20 percent of the activity produces 80 percent of the results often applies. For example, a local government may have a great number of user service fees, but many of them may provide a very small amount of revenue. An early step in marketing efforts is to find the one or two that provide a significant amount of revenue and concentrate on them. Don't be concerned with the areas that provide very small amounts of revenue unless you can make a significant change. (See the later discussion of pricing.)

Focus on performance measurement   Finally, the marketing process should help a local government focus on performance measurement rather than on cost or resource constraints. In other words, a good marketing program ought to have built into it certain predetermined performance measures in terms of revenue, net surplus generated, or the like. And as long as those objectives are met, the government should continue to pursue them and continue to apply resources to achieving even greater results from its marketing program.

Markets

Local governments often are not accustomed to thinking of citizens as market groups, but they are the market for local services. Some markets tend to be universal in that everyone uses a service, such as police, fire, sanitation, or streets. Other markets tend to be discretionary or voluntary—people who use libraries, golf courses, swimming pools, or airports, for example.

In that latter area there may well be many markets within a local community where new services could be provided or where existing services could be improved. The first step is to profile or identify those kinds of markets. The traditional way of doing it is demographically through the use of census data on income, education level, sex, and so on. More recently, marketers are talking about something called psychographics. The concept behind psychographics is that within a marketplace people who use a good or service frequently share common values and exhibit some common behaviors. For example, it is possible that the old 80-20 rule applies to the utilization of library services—that 80 percent of the utilization is by 20 percent of the users. It is also possible that the 20 percent tend to be parents and the school-age children of parents who place a high value on education and are prepared to spend considerable amounts of money to enhance the educational development of their children. If so, perhaps with current technologies there is an opportunity to provide a computer tie-in for such families through home computers, so they could directly access information in the library and in so doing enhance services that are already available and also generate additional revenues.

Finally then, after you have identified markets and profiled them in terms of demographic and psychographic characteristics, you begin the process of identifying their needs. Marketers talk about defining needs in terms of *user benefits* as opposed to what are called *product features*. For example, a speaker's podium could be described as brown, two feet high, and made out of wood. The user, however, is essentially uninterested in that. The user cares about its height and whether it will hold his or her notes in a convenient position. The *benefit* is the fact that it is of a particular height, regardless of its features. This distinction is important as you develop services for a market.

Product or service design

The third area is product design, or service design in the case of a local government. Begin by looking at existing products and services. Almost invariably local governments are surprised by the number of products and services that they really offer. They have never taken the time to list them all. Some products and services may be intangible but have a very real value. In your own municipality you might want to break them into those for which there is universal utilization—those that all citizens use—and those for which there is discretionary demand. The latter group may offer some real opportunities for increasing demand and increasing the revenues produced from such services.

After identifying the services the government provides, look at the design options that may be available. For example, can you improve the quality of an existing service? (An illustration would be a computer tie-in with the library, suggested earlier.) Can you reduce the cost of providing that service through some technological innovation without markedly reducing quality? Can you change the form in which the service is currently offered? If it is now offered through print media can it be electronic, for example? Or can you create new products? The development of municipal fire insurance as a way to help pay some of the costs of fire services is a good example of a new product.

Pricing

The fourth area is pricing. In the local government marketplace, price setting is often somewhat random, sometimes influenced by political or other decisions. That may be an appropriate way to set prices of certain services, but a somewhat more analytical approach may be to base prices on the cost structure associated with that product or service. In some cases that is easier to establish than in others. The third approach that local governments should consider for some services is a market-based approach—looking at the customer's perception of the value of a service and establishing the price that way. For example, if the community has several privately run golf courses that charge $10 for a round of 18 holes and the municipal course is charging $4, there is already an established perceived value in the eye of the customer. Therefore, even though it may cost only $4 to deliver that service, the customer's perception is that it's worth $10, and the local government ought to consider charging $10.

Another consideration is what marketers call the "price elasticity of demand," which simply refers to the fact that demand may change as price changes. With some products a little variation in pricing changes the demand significantly, pushing it down. With other products, a change in price hardly affects demand at all. For example, the demand for construction permits probably won't be significantly affected by the charge, at least within a range of pricing. On the other hand, the price charged for a 12-year-old to swim in the municipal pool might significantly affect the utilization of the pool. So it is important to look at *who* bears the charge. Generally organizations and corporations are less price-sensitive than are individuals. So if a service is being paid for by an individual, the government ought to be a lot more sensitive in setting prices. If it is being paid for by an organization or an institution, very often they are buying it because they need the product or service, not so much because of its price.

Promotion and advertising

A fifth part of an overall marketing program is promotion and advertising. Pages could be devoted this subject, but here are just a few observations. There are some real possibilities to develop partnerships and nontraditional approaches in the area of promoting and advertising municipal services. For example, local officials could approach local advertising agencies or local corporations that have marketing departments to see whether they would be interested in contributing their creative resources to developing materials and information about local public services.

At the national level the Advertising Council is the vehicle by which many major national agencies contribute their time and creative energies to worthwhile causes, but the same kind of model can apply at the local level. These organizations would love the opportunity to have that kind of visibility. They can be encouraged to think about creating verbal and visual identities for cities—the "I Love

New York" campaign—things of that type that get people involved and excited about the city and its services.

The media also can become involved. The traditional media for communicating information about services include television, radio, and newspapers. But what about nontraditional media? As a person whose children have not yet entered the school system, I find that my most frequent contacts with local government employees are with refuse people, with whom I have contact a couple of times a week. In the three years we have lived in our community they have never asked me anything about the service they were delivering—whether I liked it or not, whether I had any ideas about improving it—nor have they ever talked to me about any other services that the city offers. Yet I have more person-to-person contact with these individuals than with anyone else in the local government right now.

Perhaps individuals like these offer an opportunity to gain information about services as well as to distribute information to people in the community. Local retail businesses and banks also may provide useful outlets for information on services. Rolling stock and capital equipment can be used in effect as billboards to get messages across. These nontraditional means of delivering the message need to be considered.

Service delivery

The final part of developing a marketing program is delivery of the service itself, the distribution of service to the ultimate user. Often the marketing process is perceived as ending at the point of sale. That can be dangerous, because if you've made the sale and then the product is poorly delivered, that can really sour the whole experience. There's an expression in marketing that the last experience customers have is the first one they remember. So it is important that a service not only be delivered in a way that is commensurate with the quality you have promised but that the delivery reinforce that sale. The best customer for the purchase of another service is someone who has already bought from you. A lot can be done when the service is actually delivered at the golf course, the library, the refuse service, or whatever, to enhance the interest in the use of additional city services in the future.

Finally, the point of service delivery is the point where the local government ought to be getting information to evaluate and assess its marketing efforts. That's where that refuse person ought to be asking me what I think about their service, what alternatives might be available, whether I would be willing to assist them by taking my trash to a more convenient place for pickup. But nobody is asking me those kinds of questions, so there is no opportunity to feed that evaluation back into the city.

Those are the six primary elements of what the marketing profession calls the marketing mix—the development of a strategy and plan, the identification of the primary markets the local government is trying to reach, the design of products and services, the effective pricing of them to maximize financial return, promotion and advertising (which are particularly amenable to nontraditional approaches), and the delivery of the service.

PART 3

Entrepreneurs in Action

Public Transportation in the 1980s: An Era of Change

Paula R. Valente

Dire prognoses about the future of public transportation are commonplace today in reaction to the impending loss of federal operating assistance and the cutback in aid for capital projects. The assumption is that public transportation cannot survive without massive government subsidies—in particular, federal subsidies. The assumption is true only if policymakers continue to hold transit hostage to traditional, rigid notions of what public transit service is and how it should be provided.

Encouraging signs of change and innovation are evident, and give reason for optimism about the long-term survival and revitalization of public transportation. Public and private sector entrepreneurs in a number of communities are challenging established patterns of service and operation, and are cooperating to reshape local transportation systems.

In an effort to reduce congestion and improve mobility in the large, multi-complex Tysons Corner Mall in Fairfax County, Virginia, a group of businessmen and developers formed a voluntary association (Tysons Transportation Association) and initiated a twin program of vanpooling and shuttle bus service for employees and visitors to the mall. Members of the association assess themselves an annual fee, which raises approximately $100,000 per year to cover the costs of the program.

The city of Bellevue, Washington, and Seattle METRO recently concluded a unique service agreement, which could serve as a model for other suburban communities seeking ways to integrate public transit and community redevelopment efforts. The METRO/Bellevue Transit Service Agreement links increases in the level of transit service from METRO to changes in Bellevue's land use patterns.

Reprinted with permission from *Public Management*, July 1982.

Bellevue can claim up to 10,000 additional hours of service from METRO over a two-year period in exchange for increases in its downtown employment density and reduction in its parking supply. In addition, Bellevue's downtown business association is funding construction of a pedestrian walk in downtown Bellevue, which is a central piece of Bellevue's redevelopment and transit plans.

A group of real estate developers in Dallas, Texas, is proposing to finance the construction of a $357 million light-rail line to connect a low income area east of downtown Dallas with approximately 390,000 jobs in four major employment areas, and to link downtown Dallas with the Dallas-Fort Worth Airport. As one of the proponents of the plan explained: "The development community in Dallas understands the importance of transit, of moving people about in the community. . . . Something had to be done to capture the imagination of the people of Dallas."[1]

The Tidewater Transportation District Commission (TTDC) in Norfolk, Virginia, has been experimenting successfully for several years with different service delivery mechanisms, in an effort to improve service and reduce costs. To reduce the high cost of providing commuter bus service, TTDC sponsors a vanpooling program, which carries about 2,000 commuters per day to and from work. TTDC buys and maintains the vans and tests and insures the drivers, and then leases the vans for one year to groups of commuters. Through the leases, the transit agency recoups 100 percent of the capital, maintenance, and insurance costs, as well as a portion of administrative expenses. In addition to the vanpooling program, TTDC contracts with private taxi operators to provide door-to-door demand-responsive service in low density areas, where bus service is uneconomical, and during evening hours, when bus ridership is low. TTDC also leases vehicles to private operators and groups, who provide service to various client groups. These leasing arrangements not only cover TTDC costs but also include a 20 percent profit margin for the transit agency.

In several cities across the United States taxi service is successfully substituting for or complementing bus service. Although shared-ride taxi service is licensed in only a tiny fraction of U.S. communities, it holds enormous potential for addressing community transportation needs.

1. The city of Phoenix, Arizona, contracts with a private taxi company to provide taxi service instead of bus service on Sundays. Although the city subsidizes fares, it is saving approximately $600,000 per year by eliminating Sunday bus service.
2. Last year Santa Fe, New Mexico, initiated public transit service, relying solely on three private taxi operators to pro-

vide shared-ride taxi service to the general public. Through the use of vouchers distributed to the public, the city pays for a portion of the cost of each trip.

3.   In California, more than 50 publicly supported community transit services are operated by taxi firms under contract to public agencies.

Jitneys—small-capacity vehicles privately owned and operated—are now cruising the streets of San Diego and Indianapolis. Jitneys were a popular form of public transportation in the United States in the early 1900s, but by 1930 had been banned in virtually all U.S. cities because of the competition they gave to trolley car service.

Employer-sponsored vanpools are gaining in popularity throughout the country as a commuting alternative. Currently there are about 12,000 employer-sponsored vanpools. The National Association of Van Pool Operators (NAVPO), however, predicts as many as 100,000 by 1985. Vanpools are one of the most cost-effective methods of commuting. Congressional Budget Office figures put the average cost per passenger mile for a 10-mile, one-way commuting trip in a large metropolitan area at 5.7¢ for a 10-member vanpool, compared to 23.1¢ for a bus and 29.7¢ to 36.1¢ for rail transit.[2]

Although these kinds of initiatives are still more the exception than the rule, they do point to a new era for public transportation. The 1980s will witness a major restructuring of local transportation systems, in terms of the types of services offered, who provides them, and who pays for them. The changes are inevitable. The immediate catalyst is the impending loss of federal funds; but the pressure to reassess transportation services, how they are delivered and how they are financed, has been building for years, fueled by steadily increasing operating costs (in the period, 1973-1979, transit operating costs nationwide rose from $2.5 billion to $5.5 billion),[3] skyrocketing deficits, and changes in demand which traditional transit systems have failed to address. If public transportation is to survive as a viable municipal service, it will require a major reorientation in how local governments define this service, and their role in its provision and financing.

The irony of the current situation is that for decades, the general public quietly but effectively has been conveying its dissatisfaction with public transportation services: the vast majority simply do not use them. Public transit ridership began to decline in 1950 and dropped a total of 62 percent in 20 years.[4] Although transit ridership increased during the 1970s, when both federal subsidies and national concern over gasoline shortages and environmental pollution were at their peak, public transit still serves only about 3 percent of the population on a daily basis.[5]

What is the reason for transit's dismal performance? Does disuse of services indicate a lack of need for public transportation, or a more fundamental problem with how systems are structured and the kind of service provided? Much evidence suggests the latter reason is the cause.

Although the structure of American society has changed radically in the past 50 years, concepts about public transportation and methods of delivering services have remained very much the same. As a public service it continues to be tightly regulated by state and local governments, which restrict the types of service provided and who is allowed to provide them. This regulatory environment has restricted competition and created a highly centralized, monopolistic system of service. The primary form of public transportation continues to be bus service, operated over fixed routes, on a fixed schedule, and provided by a single public agency or private company through an exclusive franchise from the local jurisdiction.

This mode of service was effective in the early 1900s, when few people owned cars, most lived along densely populated urban corridors, and businesses, jobs, and retail stores were located in centralized areas of a city or town. But times have changed. Cities and communities of 1982 bear little resemblance—in physical structure, economic activity, social composition, and lifestyle of inhabitants— to their counterparts in 1930. American society today is much more affluent, mobile, and dispersed. We are a society of suburbanites rather than urban dwellers. Cities no longer are the sole centers of economic and commercial activity in a region, nor necessarily the primary residential centers. Families typically own two or more cars. The majority of married women work outside the home, and a much greater percentage of all women are working fulltime. More people reach retirement age today healthy and self-supporting. We are a much less homogenous society in terms of social patterns, habits, and economic activity; and as demographic and economic patterns change, so, too, do people's travel patterns and transportation needs.

These are the realities affecting public transportation which all levels of government and the transit industry have ignored for years. When ridership declined severely in the 1950s and 1960s and scores of private bus companies ceased operation, the response was federal government aid to resurrect failed transit systems. Beginning in 1964 with the passage of the Urban Mass Transportation Act and throughout the 1970s, Washington made available billions of dollars to local governments to restore, upgrade, and expand public transportation systems. During the period 1973 to 1980, $13 billion in federal money was spent to buy more than 25,000 buses and rail cars.[6] The annual federal subsidy for transit operating costs grew from $300 million in 1974 to $1.5 billion in 1981. Nationwide federal operating subsidies now fund an average 17.5 percent of transit system deficits.[7] For smaller systems the level is much higher. Data from a recent ICMA survey of small urban and rural transportation systems reveal that on average 36.1 percent of their operating funds come from federal sources.

State and local governments also are heavily subsidizing public transportation costs. ICMA's survey found that local government sources on average provide 41.5 percent of transit operating funds; state sources account for an average of 37.5 percent.

Yet, despite the massive infusion of federal, state, and local dollars, public transportation is meeting only a minuscule portion of total motorized travel needs in the United States. More than 90 percent of motorized trips are made by private automobile rather than by public transportation. Demand for public transit remains concentrated during certain hours of the day (i.e., morning and evening rush hours) and in the nation's largest urban centers.

Although the statistics about transit usage paint an accurate picture of the present dilemma, they belie the real needs for public transportation services that exist in both urban and rural areas. In every community, groups of transit-dependent people exist—people whose age, health, income level, or lack of a car necessitate reliance on some form of public transportation. Rural and small urban areas, in particular, contain some of the largest concentrations of these groups.

In large urban areas public transportation serves not only a social function, in terms of providing mobility for transit-dependent people, but also economic and environmental ones. A good transportation network, including public transit service, is essential to economic health, development, business, and retail activity. And anybody who lives in a large urban area knows well the problems of traffic congestion, pollution, and high parking costs. Public transportation plays a critical role in coping with these problems.

Current public transportation services clearly have been missing the mark in responding to transportation needs. While the phaseout of federal operating assistance poses the immediate threat for local transit systems, the more fundamental threat lies in transit's continued inability to capture and maintain a significant portion of the transportation market. The policy change at the federal level raises anew critical questions about the goals and objectives of public transportation. As competition for funds becomes more intense at the local level, clarity about what purposes public transportation serves, which groups need transportation services, who within the public and private sectors is best equipped to provide service, and how to structure a transportation system to accommodate a variety of needs in a cost-effective, efficient manner, becomes of paramount importance.

No one solution to transit's current crisis exists, but perhaps that's the key point. For too long a one-dimensional view of public transportation services has stymied creative, responsive approaches to transportation problems. If solutions exist, they will be found through freeing our collective imagination, to recognize and utilize resources that may already be at hand, and to try new approaches where old ones have failed. Innovative, flexible, less costly methods of delivering services can be found, and both the public and private sectors need to be involved in providing and funding these services. Perhaps the key to the dilemma lies in the idea of a transportation mix—putting together an array of services, providers, and funding sources to create responsive, affordable community transportation systems. Creating such systems is the challenge and opportunity of public transportation in the 1980s.

1. Clint Page, "Business-Backed Transit Plan Stirs Dallas," *Nation's Cities Weekly*, April 5, 1982.

2. Gabriel Roth and George G. Wynne, *Free Enterprise Urban Transportation*, Council for International Urban Liaison, Transaction Books, New Brunswick, New Jersey, May 1982.

3. Neal R. Peirce and Carol Steinbach, "Cuts in Transit Aid May Hurt But Could Have a Silver Lining," *National Journal*, May 4, 1981.

4. Michael A. Kemp, A Proposal to the East-West Gateway Coordinating Council (St. Louis, Missouri) by the Transportation Studies Program, The Urban Institute, 1981.

5. The Knoxville Transportation Brokerage Project, Final Report—Volume 1, U.S. Department of Transportation, Washington, D.C., November 1978.

6. Arthur E. Wiese, "Reaganomics Spelling Trouble for Transit," *Mass Transit* 8 (October 1981).

7. *Transit Fact Book 1981* (Washington, D.C.: American Public Transit Association, 1981).

Citysteading: Use of Surplus Municipal Property

Arthur E. Pizzano

Necessity may be the mother of invention, but "survival is the father of imagination." This phrase surely captures the realities and challenges which local governments will continue to face during an era of diminishing federal financial resources and general local belt-tightening.

Accordingly, economic development professionals and planners involved in improving the community economic base are well advised not to rely solely on tax incentives, sophisticated loan programs, and assorted federal largesse. Alternatively, a basic understanding of the intrinsic workings of the local marketplace must be combined with the imaginative use of local resources, persistence, style, and an effective, professional and aggressive marketing program. The more traditional tools can be used to fill in the gaps, where needed. Most importantly, existing businesses must be given a helping hand at the same time as you attempt to attract new commercial and industrial investment to your community.

East Orange [New Jersey] anticipated the shift in federal policy, that has now become coined "Reaganomics," several years ago. The city initiated a unique and targeted program which disposes of "surplus" municipal property in order to bolster its tax base. The program has had the secondary positive effect of keeping the city out of the real estate management business.

In the late 1970's, East Orange, a city of 90,000 people housed in 3.9 square miles, found itself faced with a rather typical urban dichotomy: a totally built-up city, with little or no vacant land on which to expand its ratable base, while it attempted to effectively respond to increasing resident service demands in an inflationary economy. The city has no appreciable industrial base, having served

Reprinted with permission from *New Jersey Municipalities*, May 1982.

as an affluent residential enclave of New York and Newark up to the middle of this century. Its principal nonresidential base was created in the 1960's, when it became a regional office center.

Irony

The parallel scenario is one of irony rather than dichotomy: several properties were coming into the possession of the city—by gifts, deed, or outright default (the latter as a direct result of an all-out tax foreclosure program instituted under Mayor Thomas H. Cooke, Jr., who took office during this same period). Thus, while the city had virtually no land on which to expand its potential economic base, the very foundation of its existing base was beginning to crumble. Hundreds of properties had been foreclosed upon by the city (or abandoned by their former owners) for a variety of reasons. Physical or economic obsolescence of structures and an almost confiscatory local tax rate (within a state relying predominately on real estate tax revenues) may generally be considered major factors leading to this property abandonment syndrome.

While the tax foreclosure process has affected all aspects of the real estate market within East Orange, I shall review that area of the economy which initially prompted such drastic action by the city administration—several large commercial property owners who, in continuing to leverage their investments and pull existing equity out of their properties during a "soft" rental market, increasingly found themselves financially disheveled and unwilling, or unable, to redeem properties with large tax arrearages. These accumulated arrearages were having the profound effect of transferring an increasing share of the city tax burden to the small commercial property owners as well as to the residential homeowner, which, in turn, was wreaking havoc in that segment of the real estate market as well.

The city recognized that the extreme tax arrearages on major commercial office structures were negative early warning indicators. Officials further reasoned that private management bore much of the responsibility for excessive vacancy rates in an otherwise sound, modern regional office subcenter, for which the city had made a place for itself some 10 years prior. The rumor mill, of course, lays blame on the city's poor image, perceived crime rate, and assorted social ills. This has become the standard litany of those who prosper by creating instability, toward the purpose of filling the next wave of suburban office construction in the outer ring of older metropolitan areas. East Orange's geographic position, on the other hand, can be viewed as first tier, inner ring, inasmuch as it lies directly adjacent to the core city of Newark and just 12 miles from New York City.

Unfortunately, the rumors circulated long and loud enough so that the doomsdayers were able to instill their effected agenda on several commercial office tenants. The rest is history! The great migration wave began and built up steam during the freewheeling 1970's when suburban construction competition was at its peak. Vacancies occurred, tax appeals were filed, and tax payments initially lagged on some large properties and eventually ceased on a few. Abandonment would follow on the heels of poor management, and private marketing was a word not even being uttered. It was even suspected that potential tenants for these East Orange properties had been steered to competitive space outside of the city where return on investment was virtually assured. In short, until an aggressive stance was taken by the city administration and all the stops were taken out of the property foreclosure process in an objective manner, the properties could be milked and the losses written off against higher yield investments out of the city.

Real estate commission established

In 1978-79, Mayor Cooke and the East Orange City Council established the City Real Estate Commission, whose function has been to formally review and advise the administration on all matters concerning city-owned real estate, principally in the areas of tax payment plans, interim management of commercial and residential properties assumed by the city due to foreclosure, and ultimately, to establish an auction disposition program by which these same properties would be put back into productive use as well as onto the tax rolls. Shortly thereafter, the city's Economic Development Department was established as a full-time professional activity of city government in order to respond to the city's dwindling economic base.

The department initially was viewed as a means to closing out the city's longstanding urban renewal activity, most notably the 12-acre Brick Church Center Project, which, for years had been mired in red tape and serious underfunding. A $7.8 million settlement grant was received during the waning years of the Carter Administration and the Department took on, as its first order of business, the completion of site assembly and land clearance. It also concentrated heavily on the retention of eligible business relocatees and has been successful in keeping over 80% of the remaining renewal area claimants within the city. Most of these have moved to formerly vacant structures around the periphery of the renewal area. As to the project disposition phase of the project, it was becoming increasingly clear that any attempt to attract new construction activity was bound to flounder while excessive vacancy rates in several existing relatively modern facilities persisted. The city, in fact, had just taken title to one of the largest office buildings in town, and the rumor mill ran on.

Therein lay the element of survival which spawned an imaginative and unique effort to combine the liability of city owned commercial property with marketing savvy, resulting in new found assets which, in turn, are used to encourage new construction and financing activity.

Case studies

Case 1: American International Group Insurance Company

During the late 1960's, East Orange was known as a regional insurance center, being considered second only to Hartford, Connecticut, in the number of regional office locations within its borders. This fact was a source of pride and image for the city. However, the dependence on a single-service industry also proved to be a matter of great economic exposure as well. One by one, the larger companies moved to lush corporate facilities which were being developed further from the core, where not only status, but growth, could be nurtured and accommodated. These facilities were not only the so called "back office" paper machines which generated substantial local clerical or technical employment, but were front office "blue chip" corporate facilities to which the city had formerly pointed with confidence. Today, East Orange retains several of these same facilities, but the initial exodus sparked a substantial enough retreat to impact directly the loss of firms in such support areas as law, accounting, and even retail sales. But, as the saying goes, "What goes around, comes around!"

In late 1979, the city received title to a major office facility on Evergreen Place, East Orange's principal commercial center. Evergreen Place developed during the 1960's in response to a new interstate highway being constructed adjacent to its eastbound exit ramp, in hopes of intercepting the professional commuter population residing to the west en route to completing their daily journey to the urban concentration in the city of Newark further to the east. In addition, commuters from both northern and southern New Jersey could easily exit the Garden State Parkway at its interchange with the Interstate. Secondly, the early planners saw the potential for the Brick Church Redevelopment Area one block away from Evergreen Place, inasmuch as it was served by a major railroad facility which was but a ten-minute ride to the then proposed World Trade Center in New York. Thirdly, Evergreen Place was to be the spine which linked the Redevelopment Area at the north end of the street to the Central Avenue shopping district (known as the Fifth Avenue of New Jersey in its heyday) which lies at its southern extremity.

With these inherent locational assets in mind, it may be difficult to comprehend why a 138,000 square foot, modern, eight-story office facility and parking deck would be allowed to be foreclosed on by its owners, other than for poor internal management. Whatever the reasons, while the city attempted to institute a stop-gap building management program to keep those few tenants still on the premises reasonably happy, it proceeded to auction the building at a minimum upset price of $750,000, a figure almost twice the back tax arrearage that had been due, in anticipation of attracting investors who would have the ability and desire to turn the building around. The initial price had been set partly recognizing the tremendous investment that would have to be made by the new owner to reverse years of deferred maintenance, and partly out of concern by the city to insure a swift sale and, thus, get a tremendous management problem off its hands.

A highly professional ad was placed in the real estate sections of the *New York Times* and *Wall Street Journal*, patterned after standard commercial advertising. Pre-inspection sessions were arranged for prospective bidders and a detailed list of conditions of sale was prepared, which included the fact that the auction price could not be used against the city in the event of a future tax appeal.

The city's expectations were more than realized when the American International Group (AIG) Insurance Company successfully bid at public auction in early 1980. AIG is the largest insurance-brokerage firm in the United States and had been looking for modern, attractive, strategically located, back-office space for its regional data processing unit. It owns and utilizes several large office complexes in New York's Wall Street financial district. The company has financed both the acquisition and several million dollars of structural improvements and equipment installations in the building through its own internal means. There has been *no* tax abatement, *no* UDAG, and *no* industrial revenue bonding due to the favorable initial terms of sale. This is not to say that East Orange has not, or does not, take advantage of these tools where necessary. It is only to relate that liabilities can be made into assets with professionalism, dedication, persistence, and timing. In summary, the city now has a fully tax-paying structure, a prestigious name to add to its corporate roster, hundreds of new "back-office" clerical and technical jobs to service its resident population, and a new faith among its business community. It has also secured the amount of its former tax liability loss along with a handsome profit which enabled it to immediately reduce the 1980 tax burden to its citizens by $750,000. The ultimate irony is that AIG's new presence represents the largest single insurance firm that East Orange has ever had, inclusive of its blue-chip days.

Case 2: Wayne Coffee Company   The city's urban renewal strategy has concentrated not only upon the assemblage of property required to attract a large scale private instrument, but also upon the physical rehabilitation of the immediate area surrounding the downtown core in which the renewal area is housed. An immediate example of this latter strategy has been the renovation of what was a former abandoned supermarket within the city. This former liability is now the home of The Wayne Coffee Company of East Orange. Wayne Coffee Company has been a prospering business within the city for some 40 years, and is involved in the processing, grinding and packaging of coffee and tea to the restaurant trade. Following a sequence of events in which the company was contemplating moving out of East Orange and into a nearby suburb, the city's Economic Development Office approached the principals of the company relative to their possible interest in remaining in the city and in purchasing a boarded up, former supermarket, inasmuch as the inventory of available industrial space was in short supply. The facility that we had in mind was rather typical of older supermarket structures which range from 10,000 to 20,000 square feet in size. These buildings have all but been abandoned by the major retail food chains in favor of higher volume stores. The subject 20,000 square foot structure has been foreclosed upon by the city, who had attempted to auction it on three previously unsuccessful occasions. Given the matter of timing, which cannot be overstressed, the Wayne Coffee Company indicated that it would, indeed, be interested in the acquisition of this vacant eyesore, which is immediately on the fringe of the renewal area, particularly given the fact that the Federal Urban Renewal Program would provide valuable relocation assistance to help bring the facility into operable condition. Subsequently, Wayne Coffee purchased the facility, via public auction, at a price of $50,000, is totally gutting and renovating the entire building (as well as its three adjacent satellite stores which were part of the package) and is retaining, and adding to, those jobs, which were to be lost, along with provision of an annual tax revenue of over $25,000 a year to the city. The dramatic change to what was an eyesore, into what is now becoming an attractive and functional facility, has been a cause of optimism in the immediate neighborhood. It is also providing a sense of pride for both the community at large and for the Wayne Coffee Company. It must be noted that the professional input of the city's relocation staff, coupled with a sense of commitment and trust on behalf of the Wayne Coffee Company, has been essential to the success of this project despite various hurdles of defects in title, variance proceedings, awarding of construction bids, etc. This project was successful in coupling federal dollars with local initiative and it imaginatively applies adaptive reuse principles through the replacement of a functionally obsolete retail space with a modern one-story industrial plant.

Case 3: Vogel Insurance Company and Center for Growth and Reconciliation   During early 1980, the Economic Development Department was approached by the William S. Vogel Insurance Company, a member of the East Orange business community for approximately ten years, relative to the city's assistance in finding a buyer for its existing office, which consisted of a converted frame dwelling. Detrimental to finding a potential commercial user for the property was a lack of available off-street parking. The Vogel Agency expressed a need to expand its existing space in order to accommodate its entry into the area of data processing, which would require

updated and larger facilities. Its expressed initial intention was to
seek greener pastures in suburbia, despite its self-proclaimed need for
accessibility.

As has been mentioned, the city operates an ongoing Urban Renewal Program, which entails the relocation of various businesses
from an area undergoing government land assemblage. This program
has, as a primary local goal, the retention of existing businesses from
within the urban renewal area, to relocation facilities elsewhere in
the city. The Center for Growth and Reconciliation, maintaining offices within the renewal area, was in the process of locating suitable
facilities for its own use, and the Vogel facility appeared to be well
suited to its needs. However, the lack of parking was a serious drawback to implementing the relocation package. Fortunately, an adjacent piece of city-owned vacant land, on which there had formerly
been an abandoned home, prior to its demolition by the city, was
placed on public auction and purchased by the Vogel Agency. The
resultant land had the capacity to serve the Center's needs and both
the facility and parking area were subsequently purchased by the relocation claimant.

The side benefit that has accrued from this transaction has been
even more dramatic. The Vogel Agency, both out of confidence from
the rapport developed with the city, as well as from the measurable
perspective of cash flow, was able to use the proceeds from the sale by
the relocation claimant to purchase a major office facility. This facility, interestingly enough, had been vacant for almost two years, and
was being held by a bank as mortgagee in possession, to the bank's
extreme dismay. It was perfect, however, to accommodate Vogel's
projected growth. The new East Orange Vogel Insurance headquarters has been totally renovated without benefit of federal or state
subsidy and is now fully occupied. William S. Vogel has since become
one of the city's principal boosters, having even appeared as a business testimonial in East Orange's full color marketing film, "Pride in
the Past—Faith in the Future."

Summary

Economic development planning literature is replete with various incentives which have been used in order to attract commercial and
industrial growth. It runs the gamut from low interest loans and
grants, tax abatement formulas, and the creation of local development companies to the utilization of various manpower training programs. The equally important variable; i.e., the provision of suitable
land and/or building facilities required to accommodate this growth
is generally assumed or ignored in these discussions. It has been our
experience that the immediate availability of facilities is a primary
consideration, particularly relative to negotiations with businesses
currently located within the community who are contemplating ex-

pansion or updating of facilities. It is also our contention that the retention of these businesses results in far greater immediate results than do attempts to lure outside businesses into a community. This is not to minimize the active role to be played by planners and economic development professionals in attracting new business, as shown in the AIG example, but only to recognize the short-term capability to deal with outside, built-in perceptions of crime, taxes, and cost of land. These perceptions are generally not as heart-felt by existing local business concerns who have prospered within the confines of the community. It cannot be overemphasized, however, that the immediate provision of available land and buildings at a competitive price is essential in order to present realistic alternatives to a business concern who is contemplating a move out of the community. In most cases, these businesses are well aware of the locational advantages of a centralized location and of the cost effectiveness of remaining and expanding rather than moving. The lack of available land or buildings may obviate the ability to exercise this latter option, however.

The traditional vehicle for effectuating land transfers between a community and a business concern has been through the Urban Renewal Program, which has been closed out at the federal level. It is evident, however, from the foregoing discussion that alternative techniques are available to municipalities to assemble and/or convey buildings and property to private concerns for productive use. Knowledge of the new federal laws relative to rehabilitation tax credits will then be invaluable to upgrading high percent rehab to purchase price projects.

The foregoing case studies represent only three projects out of over a dozen documented success stories that have utilized this element of East Orange's overall economic development program in just over two years' time. Of course, local administrative support is an essential ingredient in garnering all of the resources available to the city behind any real estate disposition strategy.

The ancillary issues relative to both the problem of surplus municipal property and its potential uses are two. First, municipalities generally do not have the staff expertise or budgets required for effective real estate property management and, as such, it behooves municipal administrators to make surplus property available to private individuals or corporations as early as is feasible, subsequent to its ownership by the municipality. The prolonged maintenance of vacant lots, as well as the management of tax foreclosed residential or commercial structures, cannot be permitted to contribute to the decline of adjacent property values as a result of further deterioration of municipally owned property directly. Secondly, from the perspective of municipal budgeting, the proceeds from the sale of surplus municipal property can be used to adjust the local tax rate during the year of the sale. East Orange has found that it has been able to effectively utilize its auction proceeds toward that end. Of course, the effect of putting properties themselves back on the tax rolls is of prime consideration as well.

Municipalities should carefully review properties currently under their ownership and move expeditiously to take action against those properties which are in the midst of going into serious disinvestment. Prior to award of final judgment, a carefully executed auction strategy should be put in place. This process should dispose of those properties for which there is no immediate use by the public sector. There may be instances where property is better off being held in a land bank or perhaps coupled with an existing municipal facility if the need warrants. But generally speaking, the sale of excess municipal property can generate both fiscal relief as well as strengthened tax base. Aside from the creation of a logical process, which is available to those practitioners involved in the business of marketing a community, the remaining vital ingredient to a successful program includes ongoing discourse between those involved in real estate disposition and those in the market to purchase real estate. A thorough knowledge of the community and an imaginative pursuit of alternative uses of surplus municipal property can yield tangible local assets from what were former municipal liabilities.

The Portsmouth Energy Recovery Plant

———————————————— Calvin A. Canney

In 1973, the city of Portsmouth entered into a long-term contract with a landfill operator outside the city boundaries to handle the disposal of solid waste. This was necessary because we were unable to find a suitable location within the city limits which could receive state approval. After using this facility for a few years, we became concerned about the apparent short length of time that the landfill would be able to continue to receive our solid waste and what alternatives were available once it had been filled to capacity.

Examining alternatives

In 1977, we began to examine alternatives. They included locating another landfill even farther away from the city boundaries, the possibility of contracting out for refuse pick-up as well as disposal and allowing a private contractor to solve the problem of what to do with the waste once he collected it, or converting the materials to some other use by reprocessing it.

After discussing these possibilities with a number of engineering firms and contractors, we decided that landfilling the material would not be a long-term solution. It might get us into more difficulties with leachate and other adverse consequences common to this method of disposal. It also became evident that we would have to have a user for the end product if we were going to convert solid waste for some other use.

Initially, we discussed the possibility of converting a furnace at one of the generating plants of the Public Service Company of New Hampshire for burning this material. Unfortunately, it was not compatible with the method of operation in existence at that time and the company did not see this as a realistic option for generating electricity.

While discussing these options with a number of students in a graduating class at Pease Air Force Base, it became evident that the air base had a large central heating plant which burned #6 fuel oil and was used to heat the entire base, both the operations and housing. With this large user within the city limits, it seemed reasonable to pursue the idea of burning the waste material to produce steam and sell it to the Air Force.

A solution

In 1977, the private landfill contractor decided to do a feasibility study, as he was interested in taking our waste material on a long-term basis and selling the end product, heat, to the air base. The engineering study was accomplished in about six months, and when it was completed, the feasibility of this process was evident. However, the amount of money involved in the construction of the facility was beyond the capability of the contractor at that time. As a result, the city decided to undertake the financing of the construction of the refuse-to-energy plant and contract directly with the Air Force for the sale of steam.

A committee was appointed by the city council comprised of the mayor, the assistant mayor, one other member of the city council, the city engineer, the director of public works, the finance director, and the city manager to investigate the feasibility of the project, to develop a request for proposals, and to determine what interest there was in the private sector to build such a facility as well as the cost. This committee authorized the hiring of a consultant, Ross Hofmann, to assist in the wording of the contract between the city and the successful bidder and also to assist in the negotiation of a contract with the Air Force for the sale of steam. In addition, after the contract was signed for the construction of the facility, Mr. Hofmann reviewed all plans and acted as a clerk of the works for the city of Portsmouth on the construction project.

Contracting

In putting together the materials for the RFP, the city used a preliminary design report done by Wright-Pierce Engineers for the private contractor in 1978. We also used much of the material developed for the Auburn, Maine, project. The Wright-Pierce report indicated that a 200-ton-per-day energy recovery solid waste incinerator could be coupled with the Pease Air Force Base central heating plant to supply much of the heat demand. They proposed four 50-ton-per-day modular incinerators of the starved air type and indicated construction costs of approximately 5.5 million dollars in 1979.

A request for proposals that outlined the scope of the facility was prepared and two equipment suppliers responded. Both proposed to supply the equipment and construct the buildings and mechanicals by joint venture with another firm. After a review of the proposals and a visit by the members of the council committee to a number of facilities, the committee voted to negotiate further with Consumat Systems, Inc., and to enter into a contract for the design, construction, and operation of a 200-ton-per-day facility.

These negotiations took approximately one year to reach final contractual form, and the city entered into a contract with Global Development Engineering Company, Inc., and Consumat Systems, Inc., on November 14, 1980. The amount of the contract was to be $5,846,000. As adjusted later, with various fees, land lease costs, and consultant fees, the total cost became $6,270,000.

While the city was putting together the RFP and soliciting proposals, we also began negotiations with the Air Force in order to establish a contract for the sale of steam and a contract for the location and construction of the facility on the base. A 3.6-acre site was selected for the plant approximately 1,200 feet from the base's central heating plant. The non-electric energy for the base is supplied by high-temperature (325 degrees F. and higher) water pumped through several miles of pipe to the various base buildings from this location.

Negotiations continued with the Air Force for approximately another year, and by late December 1980 the city felt that it had an agreement in principle with Pease Air Force Base for the energy purchase. The pricing formula was tied into the price of fossil fuel. In mid-February, SAC headquarters rejected this, stating that there was nothing in the Air Force service contract procurement regulations permitting a contract pricing formula to be tied into the cost of alternate fuel.

Negotiations were renewed immediately with the understanding that they would develop a set of contract regulations for the purchase of energy from such a facility. The result is the first such contract in Air Force history. The most important point is that the purchased energy is tied into the cost of fossil fuel. The Air Force guarantees to pay for all purchased energy based on its current cost of producing similar heat from fossil fuel as set by the Defense Stock Fund. The city guarantees to supply a minimum hourly quantity of heat each hour of the year, the quantity varying with seasonal conditions, with the Air Force guaranteeing to purchase this same amount.

In general, the Air Force agreed to guarantee to purchase from the city a minimum of 236,000 MBTUs of steam per year for 10 years, the cost of the steam to be charged at the rate of 90 percent of the stock fund price of the fossil fuel it displaces, which could be either oil or gas. All revenues generated from the plant including steam sales, tipping fees, and future revenues from any other source would be used to pay off the bond issue and the operation and repair of the facility. If any money was left after that, the balance would be accrued 60 percent to the Air Force and 40 percent to the city of Portsmouth. In addition, the final contract provided that the Air Force guarantee that if the base closed during the life of the contract they would pay to the city an amount equal to the outstanding balance of the bond issue or capital costs of the facility. The benefits to be derived from that contract seem to be favorable for both the city and the Air Force. The city had solved its problem of what to do with solid waste for a minimum of 10 years and the Air Force was able to purchase its much-needed energy at a savings, reducing its dependence on foreign oil.

The major ingredients in our analysis of this total operation involved two components: transportation and disposal. When the present landfill runs out, the city would have to transport to a new site in some other community. A number of studies done by various consulting firms indicated the costs for Portsmouth to use another facility in 1983 would range from $15 to $20 per ton plus transportation. It was our feeling that the transportation costs would increase more rapidly than the disposal fee because of inflation and higher fuel costs. Therefore, we should try to dispose of the material as close to the city limits as possible. The major advantage of using Pease Air Force Base was that there were no transportation costs. We estimated this would save a minimum of $6 to $7 per ton in 1983.

Once the contract had been signed with Consumat, the construction work started and proceeded quite rapidly to completion. The city obtained a 20-year lease on the land from the air base at a cost of $12,800 per year.

Technical data

The basic system consists of four 50-ton-per-day Consumat starved air furnaces which are connected to boilers converting water to steam. This steam is then moved under pressure to a heat exchanger at the central heating plant of the air base. The air base has a large hot-water heating system which provides not only building heat but also industrial hot water used throughout the base in what is probably equivalent to the demand of a community of 15,000 people. This hot water is pumped at the rate of 2,000 gallons per minute throughout the entire air base piping system. As the water enters the central heating plant, it goes through our heat exchanger, where the steam that we delivered raises the temperature of the water in the heat exchanger from approximately 260 degrees to 320 degrees. This differential in heat is the energy which is sold to the air base.

During the six months of winter, the refuse-to-energy plant, which produces approximately 45,000 pounds of steam per hour, is unable to meet the demand of the air base, and the Air Force central heat plant supplements that heat. During the six summer months, the facility exceeds the low demand of the air base. They use approximately 40 percent of the energy produced at the plant in the summer. The excess energy is vented in the form of steam into the atmosphere.

The city of Portsmouth contributes approximately 400 tons per week of solid waste to this facility, and the rest comes by way of contracts with 10 other communities or organizations. There is a standard tipping fee of $7.50 per ton of raw material coming over the scale to the plant, and this tipping fee is guaranteed for 10 years. The 10-year contracts were signed with these communities to ensure that there would always be a supply of waste available at the plant. The goal was a minimum of 190 tons per day of waste in the winter months, but not more than 250 tons per day on a regular basis during the summer months. Safety valve contracts were let with commercial haulers at the same rate. These provide waste over each weekend and additional commercial waste in the winter months to prevent a drop-off in steam production. All communities signed a contract with a minimum amount of tonnage they would deliver on an average week, and if they do not deliver that minimum they are penalized for the loss of revenue from our inability to produce steam. The 10-year contracts negotiated with the communities require all of them to meet certain standards, and all material is delivered to the base in entirely enclosed drip-proof vehicles. All vehicles have to pass inspection and receive special passes to allow them to come on the base. The Air Force reserves the right to restrict any vehicles or transportation on the base at any time.

Financial data

Annual operating and maintenance costs are established under a first-year budget, subject to audit by both the city and the Defense Department, to be adjusted after one year, if necessary. The bonds were issued for construction at a ten-year maximum life. The total revenues are estimated to be sufficient to pay off all capital, financing, operating, and maintenance costs of the facility over the first 10 years of operation.

After the construction contracts, the Air Force service contract, and the various waste tipping contracts were signed, initial cash flow to the project became necessary. Financing was begun by bank borrowing. After bond counsel packaging of an in-house-prepared prospectus, the bonds were sold in one day, on February 4, 1982, and at a rate of 10.4 percent.

Between February 15 and March 1982, test protocols were written for the plant. All testing took place during the trial operation period. The first tests were for air quality. U.S. Environmental Protection Agency Method Five was used: 0.08 grains per standard cubic foot of dry flue gas corrected to 12 percent carbon dioxide is the standard for New Hampshire. The second test was on burning capacity.

The plant had to burn at least 200 tons per day for 10 days running. Third was steam production, which at 200 tons per day had to exceed 45,000 pounds per hour at 200 psig.

The air quality tests exceeded standards by more than 25 percent. After correction to 12 percent carbon dioxide, the furnaces all met 0.08 grains per standard cubic foot of particulate emissions. The testing for non-particulate emissions was equally impressive, with all ratings far below the state standards.

From July 1 to 11, the Air Force prepared for the shutdown of its boilers to go on-line from the energy produced solely by the city's plant. The transition took place smoothly on July 12, with the energy plant supplying all the hot water for the base.

In the original plans for the facility, the city had intended to add a cogeneration unit which would allow the generation of electricity

---

Vital statistics: Portsmouth energy recovery plant

The city of Portsmouth began construction of a resource recovery facility on August 11, 1981, which became operational July 1, 1982. The facility contains four 50-ton-per-day starved air modular units which operate 24 hours a day, 7 days a week and will annually produce 250,000 MBTU of steam energy at about 300 pounds pressure. The steam goes through a heat exchanger at the central heating plant of Pease Air Force Base, where it heats high-temperature hot water for space heating and processing. It is anticipated that in 1983 the steam will also be used to produce up to 700 KWH of electricity through cogeneration.

The city has a contract with Consumat Systems, Inc., for up to 10 years for the operation of the plant, a 10-year warranty on the production of steam, a 10-year contract for the purchase of steam, 10-year contracts for the supply of solid waste from surrounding communities, and a 10-year tipping fee of $7.50 per ton. The cost to the Air Force for the steam is based on 90 percent of the cost of oil-produced steam.

The four 50-ton-per-day units burn a minimum of 170 tons of waste per day from Portsmouth, Pease Air Force Base, Portsmouth Naval Shipyard, and other local communities. Wastes are delivered to the plant by both private and municipal haulers.

The cost of the facility was approximately $6,270,000, which was financed through general obligation municipal bonds. Special legislation was introduced in order to allow the city to extend its general obligation bond capacity to cover the funding of this project.

The first year's operating budget including debt service and maintenance reserve is $2,079,000.

For the period from August 1, 1982, through November 30, 1982, the Portsmouth energy recovery plant had processed 22,169 tons of waste, which produced 72,334 thousand pounds of steam, while Pease Air Force Base purchased 64,554 MBTUs of energy.

through turbines using the excess steam which was available when the Air Force was not using the full production. It was anticipated that the city would get into this operation about the third year after construction. The present plan is to accelerate this in order to be into cogeneration in year two because of the change in the financial components over the last two years. When this facility was designed and the contracts were entered into (1980), all of the income from the production of steam or energy from the facility was based on the price of oil. As everybody is well aware, the price of oil has not risen, and therefore the income of the facility has not lived up to its expected level. With the present rate of income, the city would be in a deficit position for approximately three or four years while it is in the process of paying off the capital debt on the facility. In order to correct that situation we are anticipating moving into cogeneration immediately to increase the income level. The city has completed the preliminary studies on cogeneration and the system is very compatible for this purpose. It is estimated that the payback on the investment in cogeneration would be approximately three years.

The Entrepreneurial Municipal Strategy

———————— B. Gale Wilson and Donald D. Brown

In 1981, the state of California selected the city of Fairfield as one of
its four most fiscally sound cities. This designation was especially
gratifying to the city in light of the fact that, historically, the city's
per capita revenues from traditional primary sources (sales tax and
property tax) have been about one-half the statewide average. How,
then, did Fairfield achieve this apparent success? This article reviews some of the history and background of the city and the progress made in achieving the goals of fiscal independence and balanced
growth.

Fairfield is a city of 62,000 population lying midway between,
and a part of, the major metropolitan areas of San Francisco and
Sacramento. The city achieved a degree of success over the past 10 to
15 years in making significant progress toward some goals that were,
in earlier days, only a dream. In 1950, the city had only 3,000 permanent residents and only one primary source of economic stability:
Travis Air Force Base. The air force base population has varied over
the past 10 years from 10,000 to 15,000 military personnel and de-
pendents.

While the air force base has been a very stable and positive economic influence, it presented the city with a unique challenge. This
challenge was the reality that reliance on a single economic base
makes the city and its citizens vulnerable to influences beyond local
control. As a result, the city council and management team established a general goal of achieving a more balanced and therefore more
economically self-reliant community.

Development plan

Part of the process of working toward this goal involved taking a look
at where the city was heading and where it would end up if the nor-

Reprinted with permission from *Public Management*, April 1983.

mal market forces were allowed to operate without direct city action. A close look was taken at the city's location in relation to the Sacramento-San Francisco corridor, in terms of how to take the best advantage of this location in the years to come. And, finally, specific opportunities for changing and enhancing the competitive market forces that would be affecting the future of Fairfield were reviewed.

As an initial planning effort, the city took steps to confirm and consolidate the ultimate sphere of influence (extraterritorial planning area) to provide the needed control over the area around the city that would be subject to future urban development pressures. A part of this consolidation was, of course, developing general plan policies to designate the patterns of land use that could best make use of development opportunities. The planning framework, subject to minor alterations in subsequent years, was thereby established and approved by the city council, the county board of supervisors, and the California Local Agency Formation Commission, which is empowered by law to oversee municipal annexations.

The next stage was to develop specific strategies by which the city could become directly involved in the actions necessary to bring about the ultimate goals. It was understood early on that if the city was to be more of a master of its own destiny, an active and somewhat unconventional role in real estate development would be needed. "Unconventional" applies because the entrepreneurial activities the city became involved in, while common to the private sector, were still viewed with suspicion and reluctance by most public practitioners and elected officials. What follows is a brief recap of some of the most prominent successes in the continuing effort to achieve the city's overall goal of economic balance and self-reliance.

Real estate initiatives

One of the early efforts involved the city's taking a direct hand in convincing Southern Pacific Railroad to undertake the development of an industrial park. The 600 acres in question were on the outskirts of the city near Travis Air Force Base. A Southern Pacific mainline track bisected the property. To avoid the property's falling into the eager hands of residential subdividers, a hasty meeting with Southern Pacific was called by city management. Both parties readily agreed that industrial park usage would be in the best interest of both the company and the city. The city had a three-day option on the property but lacked sufficient funds to complete the purchase. The price was attractive enough that even the railroad giant astounded everyone by "moving faster than a jet plane." The firm picked up the option from the city and purchased the property with the city's blessing. Further cooperation between the city and the railroad resulted in multimillion-dollar assessment districts to install streets and utilities to the industrial park, which now houses plants of Ball Metal Containers, Robbins-Meyers, Owens Illinois, Clorox, Michelin

Tires, Frito Lay, and others. That example of public-private cooperation was repeated in less dramatic fashion many times over the years to come. It was positive planning and positive follow-through to implement community goals.

A 1-million-square-foot regional shopping center with five major department stores is now nearing completion in the city. This project is an example of the city's entering into a direct partnership role with the private sector to achieve a better result. The developer of the project initially approached the city to develop a small shopping center with one major anchor store. City staff felt that, while it might be somewhat premature economically, this location adjacent to the main connector freeway between Sacramento and San Francisco could certainly one day support a major commercial facility. Discussions and negotiations were held with the developer to determine what it would take to make such a major center proceed sooner than if the market were the sole determinant of project implementation. As a result of these discussions, the city assumed some new roles: those of landowner, developer, and equity partner.

The first step was the acquisition of the land which would eventually house a five-major-store shopping center. When the opportunity presented itself, the city also bought the 54 acres surrounding the mall. This adjacent property was mostly vacant except for an obsolete elementary school that was poorly located for current and forecasted school attendance demands. The city sold off sections of the mall property as development occurred for a substantial direct profit, resulting in an ability to finance needed offsite improvements. These improvements included major roadway and traffic directional improvements and a complete redesign and construction of a freeway interchange. The developer also agreed to assist in offsite improvements to the tune of $400,000 per year for 25 years, beginning in 1981.

At the time that negotiations with the mall developer were proceeding (1978), Proposition 13 passed, resulting in a significant reduction of forecasted city property tax revenues that were earmarked to offset some of the development costs. It was at this point that the city requested and gained an equity position in the net cash flow of the leasable space from the mall developer. A percentage share ranging from 10 to 17 percent of the net cash flow in perpetuity was a direct trade-off for the reduced revenues resulting from Proposition 13. Proceeds from refinancing are also deemed to be "net cash flow." Thus, the city's interests are protected from future inflation and new financing, and the developer has an attractive development opportunity. Major problems were solved by public-private cooperation, with both parties benefiting.

As part of the overall project, including the acquisition of the surrounding land, the city demolished the obsolete elementary school and built a much-improved replacement in a location that addressed the school district's current and future attendance needs. The 54 acres surrounding the mall are being sold off at attractive prices for individual commercial and office uses that are consistent with the newly adopted planning and design guidelines.

The biggest single manufacturing plant to locate in the city has been the Anheuser-Busch brewery. The city financed $12 million of water and $50 million of sewer improvements not only to secure the Anheuser-Busch facility but to guarantee a long-term capacity for other prospective users. Part of the ability to finance these major improvements was tied to convincing Anheuser-Busch to prepay substantial capacity fees in advance of the city's long-term expansion plan.

The company was willing to do this partly because the city could show a consistent policy of pay-as-you-go for all new development. "Pay-as-you-go" translates into relatively high connection fees for water and sewer and high development fees for parks, schools, and general services. (The January 1, 1983, total fee payable to the city for a new three-bedroom single-family home is $9,205.) These fees reflect the real cost of gaining access to capital facilities and service levels provided by the city and are recognized by most developers as a reasonable trade-off for the opportunity to participate in orderly and predictable growth of the real estate market. Since economic laws of supply and demand determine home prices in a metropolitan area, these costs are not necessarily passed on to homebuyers. In fact, a recent study by the Association of Bay Area Governments pointed in the opposite direction, i.e., those cities with the highest development fees had the region's lowest housing costs.

Another example of the city's aggressive role in solving physical and developmental problems is the current construction of a state highway bypass. This bypass will solve flooding problems and will open up new manufacturing properties in addition to relocating heavy through-traffic from the city's old downtown main street. After years of begging the state for the construction of this important roadway, the city, using California's redevelopment law, undertook the construction of the multimillion-dollar project. To do so, the city must pay a majority of the construction costs.

California redevelopment law provides for the capture of incremental property taxes that accrue from all the new assessed value (tax increment) in the project area. This added property tax revenue must go to repay the debt of the redevelopment area—in this case, the debt is owed to the city and is repayable with interest as new revenues are realized. Three new manufacturing users, with a fourth to begin in the late spring of 1983, have already located in this area. The private sector's commitment to this project came when the major industrial landowners in the area agreed to a $15 million assessment district to finance the needed roadway, landscaping, drainage, sewer, and water improvements that will turn this marginal land into a high quality business and industrial park. The new industrial area will house plants realistically capable of adding 15,000 new jobs to the community by the early 1990s. Again, the city's identifying and solving major developmental planning obstacles—in this case, flooding and traffic circulation—when combined with a significant private sector commitment yields long-term benefits to both.

Energy initiatives

A more recent, but potentially very significant, area of city involvement is alternate energy development. Public-private cooperation is a key element in addressing what may well be the single most critical issue facing the long-term development of the city: the ability to call on a reliable and reasonably priced source of energy. Two major efforts using different technologies are planned for initial construction in 1983 or soon thereafter.

Following three years of studies and review, it was concluded that the hills lying along the city's southwestern boundary are the site of a reliable and economically viable source of wind energy. With the advice of wind energy specialists, the city realized early on that such a project was only marginally viable if undertaken as a city owned and operated project. However, when private investors assume an ownership role, access is gained to substantial state and federal tax credits. The city therefore elected to work with a private group toward the construction of what could eventually be 125 megawatts of renewable power at a cost of about $300 million for 32 Boeing wind turbines. The city's roles in this project have been to undertake some of the initial technical studies, to locate and work with a private wind energy developer, to negotiate leases for wind rights from private property owners, and to act as the overall lead agency for environmental review of the project. The city stands to gain revenues from the wind rights as well as the property tax accruing from these very expensive wind machines. Eventually, once the private sector investment returns have been maximized, the city has the potential to acquire the machines for a long-term renewable energy and/or revenue source.

The second area of energy development is cogeneration: the ability to burn one source of fuel to achieve two byproducts—electricity and waste heat in the form of steam. Bids have been awarded for a city-owned 775 kilowatt facility at the Fairfield Civic Center for the generation of electricity for the city hall, public safety building, community center, and additional planned buildings. In addition to electricity, the power plant will produce waste heat to power the building's heating and cooling systems. Financed through the sale of revenue bonds, this project will yield a positive cash flow to the city in the fifth year of operation. The cash flow from that point through

---

Getting their trees' worth

Years ago I noticed in our community that although we had about
25,000 trees, they were not well trained. Some seemed to jump out into
the way of oncoming cars. We used to apologize for such behavior, but
there were accidents invariably. At first we said, that's too bad when a
motorist runs into a tree, and then we started to send them bills. A tree
has value. What's a tree worth? Well, we worked with the National
Shade Tree Conference and came up with a formula. We ascribed a
value to every kind and size of tree, and when a motorist hits a tree in
our community he gets a bill. And the insurance companies pay it.
Sometimes it will go up into the hundreds and thousands of dollars for
a tree. Motorists have insurance for that purpose, so why shouldn't
they pay for damaging city trees?

That's a little thing, but it's an example of an attitude on the part
of public administrators in developing revenue sources and looking out
for the interest of the community.

Source: B. Gale Wilson, "A New Portfolio for the City Manager,"
Western City, March 1982, p. 14.

---

the useful life of the generator (approximately 30 years) will result in
significant cost savings and added revenues to the city.

At least two larger cogeneration plants that would serve private
commercial and industrial users are in the initial planning stages.
Anheuser-Busch is a major user of steam, one of the products of cogeneration. The availability of additional steam is a key ingredient in
Anheuser-Busch's ability to move ahead on a major plant expansion.
The city would very much like to see this expansion because it will
increase the real estate tax base and generate new jobs—both primary city goals. The city is optimistic that two major cogeneration
facilities will be constructed during the next three to five years. In
addition to the financial advantages for the city, these projects will
be an attraction to manufacturing and commercial developers who
are increasingly looking for reliable and competitively priced electricity.

Public benefits

The city has taken a direct role in a number of other activities in the
pursuit of an economically balanced and fiscally sound urban environment. These include utilizing current and future fee revenues
from new development to market long-term financing to complete a
major network of neighborhood parks. Eight new neighborhood
parks were constructed and brought on-line during the 1981-1983 fiscal years. The added revenues from the shopping center provided financing for a senior citizens center in the existing civic center. A new

post office building, secured by a long-term lease, was constructed for the U.S. Postal Service by the city. To meet the demand for low- and moderate-income housing and to stimulate a moribund housing construction industry, two separate bond issues, totaling $46 million, have been sold. They provide first-time homebuyers an opportunity to purchase new or resale housing in the city. The city received the development fees from the construction of these homes when housing construction elsewhere was practically at a standstill. Private developers were able to build and market new housing units through below-market long-term financing.

While it could be argued that some of the above results would have occurred without the city's direct intervention, there is little question that they would not have taken place as quickly nor would they have fit in as smoothly with the city's overall land use strategies. A general theme that has developed in the philosophy of the city council and the city management team has been to stay ahead of the game. That is, if you wait until the pressure is on, it is likely your options will be fewer, your costs higher, and your land use less integrated. The city's proactive position has paid off handsomely: 14 industrial parks with a broadened revenue base, and high job generation. It didn't just happen. The city took control of the driver's seat and made it happen. That is turning out to be a win/win situation. When the private sector makes money, the public sector wins too.

The Lakewood Corporate Management Program

Gary R. McDonnell and Gordon E. Von Stroh

The Lakewood Corporate Management Program is based on the premise that local government must change to meet the modern needs of those it serves, within acceptable time frames, using newly restricted resources. More important, it is based on the premise that government must operate with business management principles and techniques that are known and understood by all parties involved in the public/private transactions taking place. Lakewood managers are participating in this program, designed not only to improve their business style but also to create a hard dollar return to Lakewood.

Background

The city of Lakewood, Colorado, has long been an innovative developer of management models. Being a young, growing city, it has had the opportunity over the years to adapt to the needs of its constituency without having to change management traditions drastically.

Lakewood is still a new city. Incorporated in 1969 as the largest (92,500) new city in the history of the United States, Lakewood has been able to design programs and management models on a "first-time" basis, learning from the mistakes and successes of other municipalities while pursuing "state-of-the-art" systems that properly serve the needs of the area's residents at the time. In subsequent years, the Lakewood organization has made service and management adjustments with a minimum of trauma as municipal growth, economic forces, and the changing desires of citizens have dictated.

Trauma, in a management sense, however, does take place even in the best-managed organizations when they are faced with change. Lakewood, while highly adaptive, certainly is no exception.

For a number of years, municipal government in Lakewood enjoyed the relatively high-flying "fat days" of ample funding, adequate staffing, and high performance capabilities. As in most cities, little attention was paid to the potential of hard times ahead.

Then came the so-called "black days" of the mid-1970s: The oil embargo and rapidly rising gasoline prices struck a severe blow to the mobility of citizens; accelerating interest rates made it impossible for many young families to purchase homes and greatly increased the cost of credit to consumers. Security in the job market became a personal concern for the first time in years because of the rising rate of bankruptcies in firms of all sizes.

As a result of these and other pressures on the taxpaying public, there appeared to be only one major course of action for citizens to take. Cut back! Proposition 13 was passed in California, and similar forms of tax revolt took place throughout the country, giving a clear mandate to government in general and local government in particular that massive changes are needed in future governmental management programs.

Previously, Lakewood's adjustments to changing trends had been undertaken within the generally accepted realm of "doing it the government way." Soon it became apparent that the "government way" would need to be changed as Lakewood found traditional public management processes and procedures somewhat "long in tooth" and not necessarily productive in accomplishing community needs in a timely way. Lakewood needed to depart from tradition.

While major changes have taken place nationally for better municipal productivity and greater, more meaningful, citizen involvement, most local governmental organizations can still be classified as "reactive" (waiting for someone else to identify needs and then moving to address those needs) rather than "proactive" (recognizing, understanding, and preparing in advance for changes and trends yet to come).

Citizens, the private sector, and local government (for that matter, government in general) have long been at odds with one another due to their different management backgrounds and bases. The average citizen and business concern may be characterized as action-oriented, while government has remained "reactive," bureaucratic, and enamored of a "do it by the manual" approach.

Lakewood's Corporate Management Program is designed to change this approach, making government more proactive in preparing for future changes and trends. City administrator William E. Kirchhoff and other members of the management team have long felt that the next few decades will necessitate a radical change in the philosophical approach to managing local government. In fact, that trend is emerging now.

The program

Representatives from the Lakewood management team have been working with the faculty of the University of Denver, College of Business Administration, Graduate School of Business and Public

Administration, to develop a "first of its kind" model for new business management direction for the public sector. The Lakewood Corporate Management Program has two phases, which will take a minimum of a year to implement:

1. An in-depth two-day seminar involving principal Lakewood managers discussing the future, trends in local government management, and how government managers compare with private entrepreneurs. The seminar, dealing with the state of the art, is designed and presented by the University of Denver faculty and practitioners from the public and business sector. The seminar is designed in such a way that Lakewood managers take an active rather than a passive part in brainstorming exercises, case studies, and discussion groups.
2. The development of five or six projects that will provide a dollar return to the city. The projects may involve (*a*) internships in the private sector (an accessible method whereby firsthand experience for skill development can be achieved on a hands-on basis); (*b*) University of Denver business management programs of over 200 training activities available to Lakewood managers; (*c*) individual projects designed by University of Denver faculty mentors (case studies, reading lists, syllabi, research studies, and independent studies); and (*d*) brokering functions conducted by University of Denver faculty members in order to match individual managers' needs with business training opportunities.

Projects coming out of phase two—those returning "hard dollars" to Lakewood—may well include:

1. Better management of personnel and physical overhead
2. Contract management of many municipal services; dealing with volume contractors for better cost efficiency, leading to smaller municipal payrolls and public capital investment
3. Time management efficiency
4. Private sector contract inspection services
5. Financial and fiscal forecasting
6. Cooperative regulations leading to better development implementation within acceptable economic time frames
7. One hundred percent automation capability
8. Innovative municipal marketing dealing with image needs determination, assessment, and programs for correction of weaknesses
9. Private-sector analytical personnel working directly with Lakewood for program improvement
10. Public/private cooperation and development of compatible management techniques.

To date, Lakewood's top managers have participated in the two-day orientation seminar, and further projects will begin as soon as possible, to maintain the momentum gained in the seminar. Five or six projects with a dollar return are being identified for phase two of the program. Individual members of Lakewood's management team will have the opportunity to work with the University of Denver and private business, through a brokerage program, to develop and implement programs leading to better efficiency and service delivery based on business techniques recognizable to the citizen.

To accomplish the Corporate Management Program, the Lakewood city council appropriated $30,000 for fiscal 1983. This sum includes necessary funding for from four to six top managers to work on program construction in cooperation with the University of Denver and various Colorado firms. For the first year of the Corporate Management Program, only those projects with a measured economic return will be considered for implementation, although other program areas will be considered in the years ahead.

The seminar

The purpose of the seminar was specifically to get Lakewood's top management to consider in depth the changes that the public sector is undergoing: management tools, techniques, and practices; external factors affecting local government; and the long-range position and role of local government. Specific objectives include:

1. Generating a "vision" of the future of management generally and public management particularly.
2. Identifying major ways in which private-sector management techniques can contribute to and influence municipal management in the future.
3. Generating interest and excitement among participants concerning subsequent phases of the program.
4. Exposing participants to resources and opportunities available through the University of Denver.

Several training/development approaches were used: small-group discussion, lecture, Delphi exercises, and multimedia presentations. The seminar was different from anything experienced before by either the faculty or the participants. Participants' interest, perspectives, and ability to conceptualize differed, and faculty made many on-the-spot changes in their presentations and approaches as the seminar unfolded. The group found that while change is easy to talk about, it is difficult to manage and operationalize.

The purpose and objectives were developed into an outline format designed to encourage participants to: (1) think about change and how to use management techniques from the corporate private sector; (2) think about the kinds of changes taking place; (3) look at the scope and character of the city of the future; (4) better understand the role and function of future managers and their place in this evolution; (5) look for problems, new tools and techniques, and applications and how these can be put together; (6) consider how to bring about change and innovation; (7) determine what to look toward in the future; and (8) consider who will be involved and how each will benefit. Specific topics included:[1]

1. Visions of the city of the future
   a. Technological introductions
   b. History/demography of the city
   c. Economics, politics, social factors
   d. Futures, trends, and forecasts
2. "Cities of the future" now
   a. Innovative city management practices
   b. Current use of private-sector techniques
   c. Current applications
3. Coping with change
   a. Adaptability and organizations
   b. Monitoring trends and forecasting impacts
   c. Dissemination of innovation
   d. Management of change and creativity
4. The municipal manager of the future
   a. What will he/she be doing?
   b. What will he/she need to know?
   c. What skills will he/she need?
5. What the private sector has to offer
   a. Management information systems
   b. Finance tools/techniques
   c. Marketing tools/techniques
   d. Production (robotics) tools/techniques
   e. Management concepts.

In summary

Underlying the Lakewood Corporate Management Program are four principles that managers of the future need to face:

1. A long-range perspective is needed by managers to integrate short-term change.
2. All organizations will undergo change, and managers must become proactive; a reactive mode is no longer feasible.
3. The private-sector corporate organization has many significant and useful tools and techniques that have public-sector application.
4. All managers will be affected by change; managing change and innovation as a result is paramount to managerial success.

1. A detailed outline of the seminar, including discussion topics, reading lists, and schedules, is available from the authors.

Public/Private Bargaining in Local Development

John J. Kirlin and Anne M. Kirlin

Local jurisdictions and developers are seeking new ways to provide capital infrastructure needed for population and job growth in California at a time when the traditional methods of providing public works are in disarray because of Proposition 13 and the general climate of fiscal stress. With increasing frequency, jurisdictions and developers "bargain" over how the capital investments needed to accommodate growth will be provided. This bargaining is project specific and is significantly less bound by legal constraints as to the forms it may take than traditional models of land-use decision-making. Bargaining is, therefore, different from taxation or development fees. Theoretically, both of these revenue generation instruments are applied uniformly and at set rates. In time, much "bargaining" may become routinized, so that it no longer warrants that label, becoming indistinguishable from taxation or fees. But for the next decade or so, and perhaps longer, bargaining will be an important feature of the land development process.

Bargaining occurs in many different arenas; almost every decision point in the land development process provides opportunity for bargaining. One important finding of this analysis is precisely that bargaining can occur in so many different arenas. Most commonly, bargaining shifts costs historically borne by the public sector to the private sector. These bargained costs are in addition to the normal development fees, dedication requirements, and taxes borne by the developer or others in the private sector. In some instances, the bargaining extends beyond capital infrastructure to include pursuit of a variety of public policy objectives and it may encompass mechanisms by which the jurisdiction participates in profits generated by the project.

While many developers, and others in both the public and private sectors, judge bargaining to be undesirable, we have concluded the opposite. Bargaining is desirable, first of all, because it is the best available alternative for financing public works. The pre-Proposition 13 system, which relied heavily on general obligation bonds, surplus revenue accumulation, and grants-in-aid from the federal government, is unlikely to return in the foreseeable future. We support the resurrection of local government capability to issue general obligation debt, but do not expect this to happen soon. So too do we support the expansion of other instruments for financing capital infrastructure, such as special assessments, but expect these instruments to never supply all needed capital investment.

Until older mechanisms for provision of capital infrastructure are resurrected or new instruments developed, bargaining must be recognized as currently contributing a very large share of public works financing at the local level. In 1980, for example, California local governments issued $76 million of general obligation debt (authorized by voters before passage of Proposition 13; because Jarvis-Gann effectively destroyed future authorizations, this instrument will soon be totally unavailable), $97 million of special assessment bonds, almost $900 million of revenue-backed bonds and $213 million of lease revenue debt instruments. A single "bargain" (Rancho Carmel, in San Diego County) will provide $85 million in capital infrastructure that would historically have been borne by the public sector. No compilation of the state-wide volume of public works provided through bargaining is available, but it must represent a substantial share of the total—almost certainly exceeding general obligation and special assessment bonds and perhaps rivaling revenue bonds.

Given the stress on public revenues, constraints upon bargaining would lead to further reductions in public works. In time, this will curtail the growth of California, driving housing prices upward, and discouraging job creation both by firms already operating in California and new firms. We judge these consequences to be undesirable in the long run and expect the pressures for growth to be so great that virtually any obstacle will be somehow overcome. Some Californians will judge a future with less growth more favorably.

Accepting bargaining as a legitimate process does not mean giving up public policy control over the extent, timing, and character of growth and development. Indeed, because bargaining occurs on a project-specific basis "above and beyond" existing taxes, dedication requirements, and development fees and can fit into whatever planning and policy making process is used by a jurisdiction, it offers new opportunities to pursue public policy objectives. This is the second reason bargaining is acceptable: it is fully consistent with strong, effective public policy.

Nor does bargaining require abridging procedural safeguards of private property rights. The statutes and court decisions supporting these rights still exist. Jurisdictions can seek to unreasonably exploit their monopoly position in the control of land use to violate rights to the use of private property. But this is not bargaining, but rather exaction, extortion, or blackmail.

One expert in local government finance and land development has used a sports analogy to express fears concerning the potential for turning bargaining into exaction. In this sport, the jurisdiction establishes the rules of the game, identifies who may play, serves as referee, controls the clock, has the right to stop the game at any time it chooses, decides who wins or loses, and may alter the outcome of the game long after it is over.

While bargaining provides no new legal safeguards against such abuses, it does afford the opportunity for landowners and developers to more openly pursue and defend their interests. The agreements struck as a result of bargaining are not always firmly rooted in the law; sometimes, this analysis reveals, they stretch the bounds of legality. But if the parties at interest—the developer and jurisdiction —do reach an agreement (without undue force on one side), it is hard for an outsider to fault the equity of that agreement. Only the affected parties know the value of what each has given and received. This is the third reason bargaining is acceptable: private property rights are not diminished.

A fourth reason to support bargaining is that the consequences of its widespread use are acceptable. In some regards, they are preferable to the pre-Proposition 13 system. For example, the ultimate incidence of increased costs imposed upon developers through bargaining should fall upon the owners of developable land. While barriers to this shift exist, such as limited supplies of developable land, it is the most likely ultimate pattern of incidence. Of course, in some locations and in the near term, developers, home purchasers, or others will bear much of the increased costs.

Under the old system, landowners could receive windfall profits if broadly funded public works projects increased the value of their parcels. As bargaining becomes more widespread, developers are likely to reduce the purchase price of land to cover these new costs, thus capitalizing the shift from public to private financing in lower prices for developable land. Beyond this general incidence effect, some potentially troublesome consequences of bargaining, such as favoring large projects proposed by large, well-funded development firms, can be addressed by specific public policies intended to counter these biases.

A fifth reason that we judge bargaining acceptable is that when both jurisdictions and developers are risk averse and prefer delaying capital outlays, they find that many forms of bargaining are preferable to the old instruments for providing public works. This is almost always the case for jurisdictions and can be so for developers.

Finally, bargaining is, according to the analysis presented here, defensible against legal attack. In particular, presumed prohibitions against "contracting away" the police powers of local jurisdictions are surmountable. Several specific approaches to the procedures used for bargaining and features to be included in any resulting contracts between jurisdiction and developer intended to minimize legal challenges are presented. A second set of legal issues, revolving around the transfer of administrative and legal tasks from the jurisdiction to the developer, is also discussed. In this case, it is suggested that the preferable strategy, both legally and politically, is for jurisdictions to develop their own expertise or seek independent consultants and counsel for assistance.

Bargaining may lead to several abuses. Because it is not legally constrained, it can be the occasion for diminishing rights to private property. This can occur if bargaining exacts so much value from a site as to raise issues of uncompensated taking of private property for public purposes. If bargaining results in unpredictable and capricious approval of proposals for changes in land uses, it can violate norms of procedural equity. Bargaining may also provide additional opportunities for bribery and influence-seeking through campaign contributions. The potential for these abuses may be reduced by various procedures. In any case, it must be noted that these abuses can occur in any system of land use. They should be guarded against, but bargaining should not be rejected because of fears of these abuses.

At a more abstract level, bargaining is another step in the movement from exclusionary zoning (which emphasized what uses were not allowed on specific parcels) toward inclusionary zoning, where public policy specifies the allowable uses. In this regard, bargaining is similar to much recent land use policy made to pursue environmental protection or social policy goals such as affordable housing. Whereas land use policies in this nation historically emphasized rights of private property, they now emphasize public policy objectives. The present land use system in California is most appropriately considered neo-feudal in character, as public jurisdictions control land uses in many of the same ways as did feudal sovereigns. Even for this reason, however, bargaining should not immediately be rejected. In the present context, the alternative to bargaining is often no change in land uses: an extreme limit upon private property rights.

Types of bargains

The arenas in which bargaining between developers and jurisdictions can occur are multiple, and so too are the types of bargains which can be reached. This section seeks to organize the bargaining taking place according to the structure of the agreements reached, that is, what the developer and the jurisdiction agree to do. In many cases, the jurisdiction's part of the bargain is granting the various approvals needed, although the jurisdiction can also undertake related public improvements or use its authority to create legal entities (e.g., assessment districts) or to issue debt at favorable terms to advance the project to completion.

To facilitate presentation of these often complex bargains, they are described from the perspective of the developer. Moreover, the term "developer" is used to designate the private sector side of these bargains, although the developer's successors in interest in the project or the project occupants may also be bound by the agreement reached. Unless otherwise stated, what the jurisdiction provides to the bargain are only needed approvals (e.g., acceptance of mitigation measures under the California Environmental Quality Act, or approval of a subdivision map).

Complex projects often include more than one type of bargain. To simplify the presentation, the terms "bargain" and "agreement" are used interchangeably to describe what may be a variety of actual devices used to effectuate the agreement reached. One of the most complex tasks confronting the developer—often requiring the services of a team of project managers, engineers, and attorneys—is to mesh all the bargaining and approvals needed into a package in a timely fashion while retaining the prospect of profits.

The following sections cover 14 types of bargains. Each is considered in turn, including a brief description of the general structure of bargain included. One or more examples are often provided for illustration.

Payments in lieu of taxes   A simple form of bargaining that arose after passage of the Jarvis-Gann Initiative requires the developer to pay to the jurisdiction an annual sum equivalent to the difference between property taxes actually received and those which would have been received had Proposition 13 not passed. This type of agreement salvaged some in-process redevelopment projects financed by allocation of tax increments to a redevelopment authority.

An example is found in the City of Santa Monica, where a downtown shopping center project under planning for more than a decade was just coming to the point of signing of final agreements when Proposition 13 passed. To save the project, the developer agreed to pay the difference between post-Proposition 13 tax receipts and the tax revenues that would have been received had the pre-13 tax rates been applied to the assessed value of the project. These payments are to be halted if Proposition 13 is declared unconstitutional or otherwise becomes inoperative or upon retirement of the tax allocation bonds financing the public improvements required for the project.

Construction of public improvements in the project area   In addition to the uniformly required dedication requirements, the developer and jurisdiction can agree that the developer construct additional public improvements in the project area. The request from the jurisdiction for such construction can arise from a general desire for their construction, but this type of bargaining appears to occur frequently in the context of environmental impact studies required by the California Environmental Quality Act (CEQA). Current CEQA procedures require the broadest ranging analysis of project environmental impacts, well beyond the physical environment, to include such issues as traffic flows, impacts upon the available capital infrastructure of the jurisdictions serving the project (e.g., storm sewer systems, water supply, schools), and upon the revenues and expenditures of the permit issuing jurisdiction. When negative impacts are discerned, mitigating measures may be required as a condition of project approval, including the construction of capital improvements.

The Aliso Viejo development in Orange County, approved in 1979, provides an example. As part of a complex package negotiated between Orange County and the developer, a project further analyzed in the next chapter, the developer agreed to construct all internal arterial highways and bike trails (in addition to the normal dedication of streets) and libraries, fire stations, and parks.

Lump sum payments from the developer to the jurisdiction, sometimes plausibly related to the project   A conceptually simple type of bargain involves a lump sum payment from the developer to the permit-issuing jurisdiction. Such a payment is commonly required as a condition of project initiation or payments can be spread over some schedule. In most such cases, the payment is related to a specific capital project to subsequently be undertaken by the jurisdiction, and this improvement is also commonly plausibly related to the project. An example of a context making such a bargain attractive to the jurisdiction can arise where a project consumes a large increment of the available unused capacity of a water supply, sewage disposal, or storm drain system. As this brings the jurisdiction closer to making a "lumpy" investment to increase system capacity, the jurisdiction is attracted to extracting a payment that can assist in covering that future capital outlay. In at least one case, however, a lump sum payment was negotiated by a jurisdiction for other purposes.

Four examples illustrate this type of bargain. When Budweiser was seeking approval of the construction of a large brewery, the City of Fairfield received $13 million towards projected increases in the city sewage and waste treatment system. In the Aliso Viejo case, the developer made payments to the county for projected future additions to water supply and waste water infrastructure. In Napa County, a developer of additional residential units at a golf and tennis resort paid the county $160,000 to improve traffic at an intersection several miles from the project but plausibly impacted by the development. Finally, in another Fairfield example, the city, acting as a redevelopment authority, assembled land for a regional shopping center, then sold that land to the developer at a price $1 million higher than its cost. Proceeds were used to purchase an additional 70 acres on the fringes of the project area, which the city will release for development controlled by its plans intended to make the uses of those parcels supportive of the city policies. The Fairfield case, an innovative and complex bargain, is examined in more detail in the next section.[1]

Public improvements constructed with repayment from charges upon later development   Another type of bargain entails the developer constructing (bearing full cost) capital improvements larger or more extensive than required for his project alone, with a portion of those costs to be recouped by charges levied on subsequent development using the infrastructure. In this type of bargain, the developer is, in essence, a lender to the jurisdiction. The developer may have different varieties of recourse of payment: no, partial, or full recourse from the jurisdiction if payment resulting from development does not occur by some specified date, or ability to compel payment from the affected property owners upon transfer of title to the property or by some specified date. Interest on the funds so expended may accrue, being added to the charge levied on beneficially impacted parcels. An assessment district may be created to provide a formal mechanism for enforcing this type of bargain.

As an example, a small rural Northern California city required a developer to install a storm drain system much larger than needed for his project to accommodate possible future development of other parcels in the vicinity. Interest accrues on the additional expenditure required ($100,000), which has been apportioned among the related parcels according to a calculation of benefit received. Owners of these other parcels are to pay their proportionate assessments, plus accrued interest, as each parcel is developed. The developer has no recourse to the city for these funds, nor does any time limit for repayment exist.

Construction of jurisdiction-desired capital improvements to gain points under a growth management plan   Some jurisdictions control growth by allocation of a predetermined number of building permits under a system in which applicants are given points under a growth management plan according to attributes of the proposed project, and building permits are allocated in descending order or point totals. Under the "Ramapo" plan, developers may acquire points by agreeing to construct capital improvements desired by the permit allocating jurisdiction.[2]

As an example of an extreme form of such a process, developers literally bid against each other in open session at a Napa City Council session, agreeing to project design features and capital improvements in efforts to increase point totals enough to obtain building permits. That growth control system has now been abandoned, but other jurisdictions continue to use point-based allocation systems.

Construction of public improvements outside the project area   Just as jurisdictions and developers may reach an agreement concerning construction of public improvements within the project area, they may do so for improvements outside of the project area. In some cases, these improvements would be related to the project (e.g., improving an arterial intersection feeding the project although at some distance), but they need not be so related.

Joint public and private use of shared facilities constructed by the developer   Another form of bargaining results in developer construction of facilities which have shared purposes, offering both public and private uses. In these cases, operation and maintenance may also be shared or be the sole responsibility of the developer or the jurisdiction.

Parking facilities for projects along the Santa Monica coast provide an example. Developers of coastal properties were required to provide more parking spaces than ordinarily required and then to provide parking to the public with the objective of improving access to the beach.

Provision of services, reducing both capital and operating budgets of a jurisdiction   Yet another way that the developer can assist a jurisdiction in meeting its needs for capital investment is to provide a service commonly provided by the jurisdiction, thereby reducing both public operating and capital budgets. This option is available in larger developments of all kinds, though apparently more common in industrial and residential projects.

Common examples in commercial and industrial projects include private provision of security forces and, less frequently, firefighting services. A few residential projects provide private security services, ranging all the way from patrols to guards at points of limited access to the project. These private security forces relate to public police forces in several different ways.[3] Planned communities, such as Leisure World, carry this much further, providing not only security services but also paramedics and recreation services. Homeowners' associations may also arrange for the private provision of services commonly provided by local government.

Maintenance and operation of public facilities and places
Only marginally different from the previous type are cases where the developer maintains or operates public facilities and places. In many cases this will not directly provide capital infrastructure nor reduce the need for public investment in capital goods, as it has the character more of ongoing, operating expense. But this type of bargain usually arises only in the context of the sort of substantial developments being discussed here and may be one of the elements that allows a successful bargain to be reached.

An example of such an agreement would be private operation and maintenance of all of the public and open spaces associated with a shopping center, even though some had been dedicated over to the local jurisdiction.

Conditions upon developers or project occupant activities which facilitate accomplishment of a jurisdiction's policies
An agreement between a developer and a jurisdiction may impose conditions upon the developer and project occupants which facilitate the accomplishment of a jurisdiction's policies. In some instances, modification of the project occurs, a case examined in the next type of bargain considered. In the present instance, the project itself is not modified, but the activities of the developer or project occupants are constrained toward achievement of a public purpose.

Returning to Santa Monica Place, the downtown shopping center, the developer leased parking for its employees from the city parking district authority. This provided revenue to assist in the retirement of bonds issued to construct parking structures serving not only the new shopping center but an older adjacent shopping mall.

Modification of project to meet public policy objectives   As suggested in discussion of the previous type, in some cases, the developer may modify the project to meet public policy objectives. Indeed, this has occurred quite frequently with proposed residential projects, which were commonly reduced in scope during the 1970's as a consequence of the environmental impact reviews required under CEQA.[4] For present purposes, however, the project modifications of interest are those that substitute for, or otherwise reduce the need for, public sector capital investment.

An example is found in bargaining over the inclusion of housing to be provided (for purchase or rental) to individuals and households of low and moderate income in residential projects. While the California Coastal Commission and some jurisdictions have established policies requiring specific ratios of such housing (inclusionary zoning policies), bargaining still occurs. In the Aliso Viejo case, for example, the developer agreed to provide 5,000 units of "affordable" housing. In Rancho Carmel, 10% of the housing is to be "affordable." Rancho Carmel, a large mixed-use project developed by Nathan Shapell in northern San Diego County, is described in the next section.

Acquisition of real property (improved or unimproved) by developer who transfers title to the jurisdiction or otherwise uses or disposes of it according to the directions of the jurisdiction   In some bargains, the developer acquires real property outside his project area and either transfers it to a jurisdiction or uses it in pursuit of a public objective.

The City of Santa Monica offers an example. There a developer purchased housing units outside the proposed project area to meet city and Coastal Commission concern for low and moderate income housing. Yountville, a small Northern California town, required a subdivider to acquire outside property to provide a preferred main access to the subdivision and to offer property outside the subdivision but owned by the subdivider to the city for the development of low and moderate income housing.

Sharing profits from the project with the jurisdiction   The jurisdiction may bargain to share in the profits generated by a development project. While the jurisdiction could commit the resulting revenue stream to purposes, including capital construction, related to the project, this was not done in two examples discussed here. Given the fiscal strains upon local jurisdictions and the uncertainties concerning long term revenues derived from any proposed project because of the willingness and capability of the governor and Legislature to move tax base around among local jurisdictions, the possibility of obtaining substantial non-tax revenues for general use is alluring to these governments.

Three examples illustrate the possibilities. The City of Napa will receive a percentage (10%) of the overage rents received when gross sales exceed a base figure on satellite shops in a shopping center project which has been approved but not yet constructed. This contract clause is expected to yield less than $10,000 annually and expires in 30 years. As is discussed more fully in the next section, the city also receives 10% of the proceeds from any refinancing of the project.

The City of Fairfield and Ernest Hahn, developer of the regional shopping center discussed previously, have entered into an agreement providing the city 10% of any net annual cash flow between $250,000 and $500,000 and 15% of net annual cash flow in excess of $500,000. The city participates in similar proportion in any transaction by which the developer receives proceeds from the project. This contract is not limited to any time period.

In a third, non-local government example, the state is leasing some state-owned resource areas to energy producing corporations on profit sharing formulas. And Cal-Trans is entering into long-term leases with developers for the use of "excess" lands. In a case in San Diego, a restaurant development will make lease payments based upon a percentage of revenues.

Private development of public property as a source of public sector revenue   Where a jurisdiction owns property or controls a resource, it may turn to the private sector for development of the property or resource as a source of revenue. These revenues can be used for any legitimate purpose, but in at least two cases are tied to capital expenditures.

Santa Clara County is developing a plan to use revenues from the disposition or development of public properties to generate revenue for planned construction of a criminal justice center project estimated to cost $70 million to $100 million. The State of California leases state-owned tidelands for oil development on the basis of profit-sharing in the revenues derived, historically earmarking the revenues received for a variety of capital construction activities (e.g., public higher education, parks and recreation, transportation, school buildings).

Case studies

This section analyzes several cases in greater depth. Even here the intention is not to give full details on any case (the legal documents effectuating the agreements described here can run to several hundred pages in length) but to give the reader enough information to provide an appreciation of the potential of this strategy for providing the capital infrastructure needed for growth. The cases discussed are among the more complex that could be chosen. While not representative of all the types of bargains enumerated in the previous section, many of those types are described. So too do a number of legal bases come into play, although redevelopment projects are over-represented as they often involve more complex bargains and thereby illustrate a richer variety of types of agreements within a single case.

Each case is presented in turn. The first three are already somewhat familiar, having been briefly described earlier. They involve redevelopment projects in the cities of Santa Monica, Napa, and Fairfield. The fourth case is the Aliso Viejo project, a very large subdivision in Orange County. Rancho Carmel, a recently approved mixed-use project in San Diego, is the fifth case. The use of public lands to raise revenues by Santa Clara County is the sixth case.

Santa Monica: a lost-tax-revenue-replacement case   Proposition 13 passed as the City of Santa Monica was in final negotiations with developers of a downtown renewal project (Santa Monica Place, a shopping center) with a total estimated cost of $18,000,000. The project was important to the city, culminating a redevelopment process that had been initiated nearly two decades previously but which had floundered several times.[5] Tax increment-backed revenue bonds were to provide financing for the city's activities in support of the development, including street reorientation, land assembly, and provision of parking. Rouse and Hahn were general partners in the development. Robinson's and the Broadway were both to build department stores in the project, with the usual provisions made for satellite shops and restaurants. The annual tax increment revenue lost as a result of passage of the Jarvis-Gann Initiative totaled $650,000, threatening the city's ability to meet its obligations, and thus the whole project.

The agreement reached among the city, general partners, and two department stores calls for payments to the city of an amount approximately equal to the tax increment lost upon passage of Proposition 13, to be paid annually until the bonds are amortized. Provisions are made to reduce or increase the payments under a number of contingencies. While the city is advantaged by this agreement in that it ensures continuation of a desired project (which will, itself, generate sales tax revenues and, hopefully, stimulate additional development in the area), the developers and department stores are also advantaged in being able to complete what they anticipate will be a profitable project. Also, they obtained a payment schedule which will probably result in annual payments less than those projected for pre-Proposition 13 taxes and which will end upon retirement of the bonds, whereas taxes would have continued in perpetuity.

A feature of this project agreed to before passage of Proposition 13 was the leasing of parking spaces for employees of Santa Monica Place in city Parking Authority structures. These structures primarily serve an adjacent, older shopping mall whose merchants were anxious about competition from Santa Monica Place. The city preferred this arrangement because it reduced the likelihood of employees searching for already congested on-street parking and helped amortize the revenue bonds which had financed construction of the parking structures. An advantage accruing to the developers was ability to devote a smaller percentage of the total square footage of the project to parking.

Napa: non-tax revenues as part of a complex financing package   The Napa case also involves a long-planned downtown renewal project threatened by the reduction in tax increment funds caused by Proposition 13. In this case, that reduction was doubly important since the proposed project was financed partially by uncommitted increment from a previous, adjacent redevelopment project and partially from the tax increment anticipated from this second phase project. The two revenue reductions totaled nearly $800,000 annually, approximately what the city originally anticipated as annual bond amortization costs of the estimated $7 million it was to spend for constructing two parking garages and reorientating streets. In addition, the city had assembled the project area land at a cost of about $800,000 and was to transfer it to the developer for $600,000, the value determined for such a large parcel through the "reuse appraisal" process often used in redevelopment projects.

As in Santa Monica, the basic concept was the standard department store anchor (here a single Rosenberg's store) plus satellite shops. In the agreement reached, the developer is committed to build a 40,000 square foot building for the department store and no fewer than 50,000 square feet of satellite shops, at an estimated total cost of $12 million. The city has a small annual participation arrangement in the project, receiving 10% of the "overage" rents on the satellite shops (with a provision to limit annual base rent increases to the Consumer Price Increase, intended to protect the city's interest through increasing the likelihood of overages). This feature of the contract between city and developer is anticipated to yield less than $10,000 annually and is limited to 30 years.

More provision under which the city is to receive 10% of the proceeds of any refinancing (or—if the refinancing lender will not make payments to the city—an alternative buyout from the developer of 10% of a "calculated" worth established as an 8.5% cap rate on the last three year's average income from the project, estimated to yield approximately $100,000 in the early years of the contract). Subsequent refinancings within the 30 year term of the agreement are subject to the same provision, which is a covenant upon the deed transferring the land.

The City of Napa is piecing together the revenue it needs to meet annual bond costs that increased interest rates have inflated to approximately $1.1 million annually. The remaining tax increment funds from the first phase plus the increment to be generated by the second phase will be committed. Instead of being abolished, the now low parking fees (five cents per hour), will be tripled in the downtown area with an anticipated yield of $250,000 annually. Much of the increased sales tax revenues and business license fees generated by the development will go to bond retirement instead of ongoing service provision, either in the project area or elsewhere in the city. The city also expects the project to enhance the value of several smaller parcels scattered on the edges of this development which it owns (totalling under four acres), and may ground lease them to developers, which would offer opportunities for greater participation.

This project has been delayed because of high interest rates.

Fairfield: the city as entrepreneur   Ernest Hahn, Inc., one of the developers in the Santa Monica case, is also the developer in the Fairfield case. The project is a regional shopping center (Solano Mall) on a 26 acre site about half a mile off Interstate 80, between San Francisco and Sacramento. As in the two previous cases, the city acquired the land as part of a redevelopment project. In addition to land assembly, it undertook public improvements to improve access to the site, to solve drainage problems in the area, and to relocate an elementary school adjacent to the projected site to a more suitable location. Included is construction of a freeway interchange without any state or federal funds.

The city generates revenues from the project in several ways, including an aggressive use of non-tax strategies. The tax revenues include the property tax increment, sales taxes, and business license fees that will be generated by the shopping center. In addition, a special assessment district encompassing the project area and adjacent areas is to be formed to assist in financing public improvements through issuance of bonds. The developer is committed to paying up to $350,000 annually in such assessments for a period not to exceed 25 years.

Non-tax revenues are substantial. The purchase price paid by the developer for the parcel netted the city in excess of $1 million more than its land acquisition costs. Receipt of these funds facilitated the city's program of land purchase in the redevelopment project area where it now owns more than 70 acres planned for future development. Additionally, the city is to receive from the developer 10% of any net annual cash flow between $250,000 and $500,000 and 15% of net annual cash flow in excess of $500,000. The city participates in the same ratio in any transaction through which the developer receives proceeds from the property (e.g., refinancing, sale, or leaseback). This participation agreement "runs with land" and binds any future holder of the developer's present interest in the property. It has no termination date, so will be reduced only if Proposition 13 is somehow repealed or ruled invalid and the city actually receives ad valorem property tax increment revenues.

Aliso Viejo: achieving multiple policy objectives in a large residential development   The Aliso Viejo project, involving construction of 20,000 new homes in one of the most desirable areas of Orange County, illustrates how a jurisdiction can achieve multiple policy objectives in a large residential development. Unlike the three previous cases, non-tax revenues will not be generated. However, extensive infrastructure ordinarily provided by the local jurisdiction will be constructed by the developer, an extension of the normal practice of a developer constructing streets and curbs then dedicating them to the local government. In addition, Orange County used the broad powers possessed by California local governments under the Subdivision Map Act (as recodified in 1974) to pursue energy conservation, open space preservation, and affordable housing policy objectives.

In 1979, at least two and one half years after the planning process for Aliso Viejo had begun, the project plan came before the County Board of Supervisors for approval. The ensuing negotiations evolved to include far more than the construction of the homes. The plan ultimately approved included the following additional features:

a 3,400 acre greenbelt; 5,000 units of affordable housing; company-provided construction of all internal arterial highways, roads, and bike trails; payment by the company for the construction of major water and wastewater infrastructure prior to actual need; and initial installations of capital facilities, including library facilities, fire stations, and parks by the company, at no cost to the county.[6]

Extensive negotiation was required to achieve the ultimate plan. The county had bargaining leverage, but had to do more than demand concessions from the developer. In return for the commitment to build affordable housing, for example, the county increased allowable project density, thus increasing the total number of houses that can be built. Spurred by the county revenue reduction caused by Proposition 13, both the county and the developer approached the negotiations with more flexibility and care than has historically been the case. Litigation against Orange County disputing the adequacy of its housing element also encouraged careful bargaining.

The Aliso Viejo Company projects that average annual county revenues will exceed average annual county costs by $2.83 million to $4.47 million upon project completion. The company's analyses also conclude that the ultimate plan has lowered county costs while increasing county revenues from those that would have been experienced had development proceeded under the county's existing General Plan.[7]

Rancho Carmel: providing capital infrastructure for a large mixed-use project   In late 1981, the San Diego City Council approved a plan for developer financing of the capital infrastructure for Rancho Carmel. The project to be completed during the next 15 years is a large mixed-use development. Situated on a parcel of nearly 1,500 acres of northern San Diego County, the project is expected to cost about $1 billion, and to include more than 7,000 dwelling units, a 1.2 million square-foot shopping center and 100 acres of light industry.

The developer, Shapell Industries, is to provide 33 separately identified capital-infrastructure projects, at a total cost of $57.5 million.[8] Included are arterial roads, freeway overpasses and interchanges, sewer mains, water system pumping stations and reservoir, parks, a library, a completely equipped fire station, and park and ride facilities. In addition, 211 acres of open space are to be dedicated to the city.

Moreover, fees will be paid for specific purposes. Approximately $370 per residential unit will be paid for community parks and recreation centers. Negotiations are under way between the developer and the Poway Unified School District to set fees that will cover construction of two new elementary schools and expansion of junior and senior high schools. These fees are estimated to be approximately $25 million.[9]

Thus, the total developer funding for capital infrastructure historically borne by the public sector will approximate $85 million in this project: $57.5 million in capital improvements, $2.6 million in park and recreation fees, and $25 million in fees for schools. In addition, open space, and the traditional internal streets, roads and water and sewer systems will be dedicated over to the city.

In this case, the developer and the jurisdiction explicitly rejected the use of assessment districts to finance the needed capital infrastructure. This was reasonable given single ownership of the land to be developed. In two nearby areas, the City of San Diego is proposing using "facilities assessment" districts plus subdivision and park fees to finance capital infrastructure because the land is held by multiple owners.[10]

As in Aliso Viejo, the jurisdiction also pursued non-fiscal policy objectives. Ten percent of the housing units in Rancho Carmel are to be "affordable." Moreover, the construction of residences is to be phased with the growth in employment opportunities offered by firms locating in the project in an effort to encourage a "self-contained" community characterized by a population which both lives and works in Rancho Carmel.

Santa Clara County: use of public lands to generate revenues
The County of Santa Clara is seeking to sell or lease county-owned land to finance a $70 million to $100 million improvement of its jails. In this case, the jurisdiction has a specific need which it plans to meet through disposition of an asset.

Following receipt of a consultant's report analyzing the need for corrections facilities for adults, the county apparently decided that it could not fund the proposed projects from tax revenues. Several months after receipt of that analysis, the county solicited bids from financial consultants to analyze how it might derive the needed revenues from sale or lease of county-owned parcels. That analysis is now under way, so it is not yet known if the county will achieve its objective.

Several other jurisdictions and at least one state agency have explored or undertaken similar joint ventures for development of publicly owned land. Included are the Bay Area Rapid Transit District, the City of Palo Alto, Cal-Trans, and the Port of Oakland. State officials urged the Los Angeles Unified School District to dispose of excess property to help meet its needs for revenues.

1. See also the selection "The Entrepreneurial Municipal Strategy" in this volume.

2. James Longtin, *California Land Use Regulations* (Westlake Village, Calif.: Local Government Publications, 1977), pp. 160–61.

3. Roland Dart, *Alternative Structures for the Provision of Police Services* (Sacramento: Dissertation presented to the Sacramento Public Affairs Center, University of Southern California, 1980).

4. Bernard Frieden, *The Environmental Protection Hustle* (Cambridge, Mass.: MIT Press, 1979).

5. Dan O'Toole, *Urban Redevelopment Strategies and Their Effects: A Comparison of the Conventional Urban Renewal Approach with That of Tax Increment Financing* (Los Angeles: Dissertation presented to the School of Public Administration and the Graduate School, University of Southern California, 1977).

6. Jack G. Raub, *The Impacts of Proposition 13 on New Development* (Costa Mesa, Calif.: Jack G. Raub Co., 1979), pp. 11–18.

7. Ibid., p. 14.

8. Public Affairs Consultants, *Rancho Carmel Community Facilities Financing Plan* (San Diego: Public Affairs Consultants, 1981).

9. Gary Shaw, "Private Money for Public Facilities, *The Tribune*, San Diego, California, October 30, 1981.

10. Ibid.

Divesting Local Functions in Pensacola

Steve Garman

Corporate America buys and sells, expands and contracts, finances and refinances, prepays interests and extends debt, all depending on a company's perception of its present market position and on its goals for the future.

Airline A might decide that it operates too few profitable long-run routes to support the ten new DC-10s ordered three years earlier. Airline B has well-established long-run routes but suffers from inadequate aircraft capacity and must wait another two years for delivery of new, larger planes. It may be in the interests of both to merge, and thus each build on the strengths of the other; or Airline A may sell its DC-10s to Airline B and limit its operation to short runs.

Every business organization has limited resources to employ in running its enterprise. Corporations which find themselves "overextended" or "spread too thin" come to the point where their resources are insufficient to maintain a profitable business. They must, therefore, identify which operations they hope will return the most and divest themselves of those operations which drain resources and do not provide adequate return on investment.

The dynamics of the private sector in a capitalistic society are well established, well understood, and well accepted. A fundamental principle guides the private entrepreneur in the ever-changing free market: build on your strengths, and to whatever extent possible, divest yourself of liabilities. A corollary principle helps make this possible: an operational liability of one company may be an asset to another.

What business are we in?

The "Law of the Situation" is a term coined by Mary Parker Follett, the first management consultant in the United States.[1] She persuaded one of her clients, a window shade company, that they were really in the light control business. The revelation opened new vistas of business opportunity previously unseen. The law of the situation asks the question "what business are we really in?"

As the external environment and internal conditions change, all businesses and other organizations must reassess their purpose and goals. Local governments, unfortunately, have assumed that they are somehow exempt from this kind of fundamental soul-searching. Cities and counties believe that they, and everyone else, already know what business they are in. In fact, nothing could be further from the truth.

Unlike a private enterprise, the *survival* of a local government may not depend on knowing what business it is in, but certainly its long-term *effectiveness* does. Local governments must discipline themselves in the process of *strategic planning*: a continual reassessment of purpose and goals in a changing society. *Only discipline enforced through strong political leadership will cause cities and counties to think strategically, rather than merely react tactically.*

Being all things to all people

City governments have historically and traditionally taken responsibility for basic urban services supported by local taxation, such as street and drainage systems, public parks and commons, fire and police protection. Today, these "general government" functions remain basic to the city government's reason for existence.

Primarily in this century, cities and urban counties have taken responsibility for a host of added activities which were previously found in the private sector, if they existed at all. They include functions as diverse as municipal airports, gas and electric utilities, zoos, transit systems, public housing projects, recreation and athletic facilities, museums, performing arts centers, seaports, marinas, hospitals, cemeteries, and many others. Unlike the general government functions, these "public enterprises" tend to be funded in whole or in part from revenues generated by the activity.

Some of these enterprises were inherited by local government because they were not financially viable elsewhere in the community. Other enterprises may have been acquired both to provide a public service and to generate revenue for the local government, while a great many erupted on the scene during the sixties and seventies when times were relatively good for local government. During that period, the federal government paid the start-up costs for constructing a host of major improvements and initiating new programs, later to be operated by the city.

Thus, American cities today often find themselves frantically attempting to manage more than their limited resources will allow. It is time for all local governments to enforce the law of the situation— to ask what business they are in, and what business they should and should not be in. Regardless of how one might feel about Reagan federalism, it is difficult to argue with the premise that when government tries to be all things to all people, it fails at everything. We tend to do one hundred things poorly rather than fifty things well.

What to keep and what to give away

Aside from the traditional urban services discussed earlier, local government activities are diverse. While it may seem appropriate to address the law of the situation by merely stating "we're in the business of offering services to the public," such an answer is not only imprecise; it ignores the issue. Local governments are so diverse and offer such a variety of services that no universal formula prescribes which activities should be retained and which should be relinquished. In deciding what to keep and what to divest, one must begin by cataloging and categorizing a particular government's activities. Pensacola, Florida, will serve as an example.

The municipal organization in Pensacola is divided into two areas of operation, each headed by a deputy city manager: (1) the general government function and (2) the public enterprise function. Further, the city council is divided into two oversight policy committees—the General Government Committee and the Public Enterprise Committee.

The general government functions are the municipal activities that generate virtually no revenue. On the other hand, enterprise functions are consciously divided into three categories:

1. Activities designed to create profit
2. Activities structured to "break even" but return no profit
3. Activities which can partially, but not completely, support themselves.

Sorting out municipal activities on the basis of revenue-raising capacity is useful in terms of strategic municipal planning and in terms of answering questions relative to the "law of the situation."

Having so categorized municipal activities, and with an understanding of the revenue-generating versus non-revenue-generating functions, a critical eye can be cast toward those activities which cost the most in terms of allocated resources and return the least. The process also includes an analysis of the legality and political feasibility of divesting an activity. Most opportunities to divest are found among the public enterprise functions. On the general government side of the ledger, fewer opportunities exist, although they do occur. Here are examples of specific functions that may be ripe for divestiture, first from the general government side, then the public enterprise side.

Investigations and jails   With increasing demands for police protection and crime control, is it possible to divest traffic accident investigation? Might that function be assumed by the state highway patrol or county police? If you must provide traffic accident investigation, must it be done with sworn personnel? Would it be possible to employ noncommissioned specialists, lower paid than trained police personnel, to fill out traffic accident forms for insurance companies and follow up with other non–law enforcement traffic accident matters?

Also, in the law enforcement area, is a municipal jail necessary? Police officers, who are law enforcement oriented, historically make bad jailers. Corrections is a field in itself and has little in common with law enforcement. Perhaps a consortium of smaller cities could create a single jail, or perhaps your county or a neighboring county would accept your prisoners.

Inspections   Many municipal inspection activities are useful areas to analyze. Are any current inspections being duplicated? Is the same sewer line being inspected by the state and the city? In Florida, for instance, a state statute is under consideration to require architects to be responsible for inspection of buildings under their design and to certify compliance of public safety and building codes—thus freeing the city of some costly and resource-draining functions.

The theatre and the sewer plant   Pensacola, in recent years, has divested itself of two municipal public enterprise functions through a strategic planning process.

In the early 1970s, at the insistence of the Environmental Protection Agency, Pensacola embarked on construction of a 23-million-gallons-per-day (MGD) capacity advance wastewater treatment plant. As inflation heated up in the late seventies, and as initial unrealistically low cost estimates were revised during construction, it became apparent that operating and debt service costs of the plant were going to mean a dramatic increase in rates. The plant offered a long-term solution to the wastewater treatment problem in that its capacity was more than double its demand when it opened in 1980, but it carried extremely high short- and mid-term costs. Further, the cost associated with operating the facility as an advanced wastewater treatment (AWT) facility could not be justified in terms of the cost/benefit difference in the quality of the effluent produced from that of a high-grade secondary treatment process.

First, the city won a battle with EPA to drop the requirement to operate at the AWT level. That created two pluses: the cost of plant operations was impressively reduced and the capacity could expand to 26 MGD as a secondary facility. Meanwhile, the county of Escambia, in which Pensacola is located, faced EPA demands to upgrade its existing treatment plants and build new plants to meet growth demand in certain areas.

Both governments decided that continuing in the sewer business was not to their advantage, and that the public was ill served under the circumstances. An independent, countywide utility authority was created, and the city and county each transferred its water and sewer systems to the authority. While Pensacola enjoyed its water system as a profit center (public enterprise—category A) the short- and mid-term liability of the sewer operation, coupled with a $10 million sale of the water system assets to the newly created authority, made the arrangement very attractive. The new plant was a liability to the city, but an asset for countywide purposes. Moreover, the $10 million received by the city was invested at relatively high rates to offset the loss of future profits from the water system.

In another instance, Pensacola has accepted a beautiful and historically significant but badly deteriorated theatre in the heart of downtown to restore into a performing arts center. During the restoration of the theatre, the drain on the time and resources of city government necessary to operate an arts theatre became more and more apparent. In short, the spirit and mind-set of city hall was ill prepared to deal with the arts very effectively.

Pensacola city government made the decision that it did not wish to be in the performing arts business. Instead, the city created an independent board to operate the theatre "lock, stock, and barrel." The board was composed of individuals knowledgeable and interested in the arts. The city agreed to subsidize the operations at the level of $100,000 per year, less than the open-ended liability of keeping it as a municipally operated facility.

A range of options

Unfortunately, it is not unusual to find a city responsible for an activity, or owning an asset, which would be better handled elsewhere. Much has been written about contracting with the private sector, but divesting goes beyond contracting out. The degree to which a local government relinquishes an activity can be seen as a continuum or a range of options. On one extreme is the traditional in-house approach, on the other, complete divestiture:

1. Activity entirely owned and operated in-house, employing a full-time civil service staff
2. Activity owned and operated in-house, but employing substantial contract personnel and other outside services
3. Activity owned and controlled by the municipality but operation entirely contracted out
4. Activity controlled by city under franchise or interlocal agreement, but owned and operated by another entity
5. Activity completely divested.

Many experiments with approaches falling somewhere on this continuum are taking place in local government today. Not every effort is a success, but these experiments are important. They illustrate an openness at least in some local governments to ask the question "what business are we in?"

The principle of divestiture in local government runs counter to the more commonly accepted practice of acquiring more and more, becoming bigger and bigger. Many city managers are guided by the principle that the way to justify a larger staff and fatter salary is to assume ever increasing responsibility. So long as city councils rewarded organizational growth, there was little personal incentive for managers to "shrink" their organizations. While they may feel or know that it is in the best interests of their city to do so, it may be against their personal interest and career path.

It is up to the manager to convince the council that his or her compensation should be based on goal achievement, which may well include successfully shrinking the municipal organization. Given the problems of cities today, a far more valid general objective would be "How much can we stop doing without impairing services?" rather than "How much more can we assume?"

Each activity of local government must be examined under the law of the situation through a strategic planning process. Applying this kind of analysis will almost invariably reveal divestiture opportunities.

1. John Naisbitt, *Megatrends: Ten New Directions Transforming Our Lives* (New York: Warner Books, 1982), p. 85.

The Alexandria Torpedo Factory

Douglas Harman

Alexandria, Virginia, is well known for its heritage of historic homes, colonial inns, and cobblestone streets. Scottish merchants founded the city in the mid-1700s as a commercial center with an active seaport link to other colonial cities. The Scottish influence led to conservative architectural styles which still exist today as well as a tradition of making effective use of available resources. This tradition continues in Alexandria and is best exemplified in the entrepreneurial efforts leading to the comprehensive redevelopment of a surplus torpedo factory.

The Alexandria Torpedo Factory and Art Center have become internationally known as a unique example of public/private cooperation and unusual planning and development utilizing obsolete industrial buildings. Although there are some unusual features to the history of the Torpedo Factory development, the local government efforts to implement this project are similar to many of the basic steps necessary for any public/private redevelopment effort. Therefore, the experience with the Torpedo Factory deserves attention as a case example of successful entrepreneurial planning.

Background

Factory buildings are not normally associated with cities having historic districts. When the Alexandria Torpedo Factory was constructed in World War I, Alexandria was simply an old industrial community pleased to have a major new factory built in its downtown area. The first large buildings constituting the Torpedo Factory were not completed until the war ended in 1919. After a short time, the Navy stopped manufacturing torpedoes at the factory. The complex did not become active again until the advent of World War II, when the Navy rapidly increased factory space and began construction of the Mark XIV torpedo for submarines and surface ships. At the end of the war, the Navy again stopped production and eventually turned the four large buildings over to the General Services Administration. Alexandria's Torpedo Factory then became a major warehouse for government material and records, the most famous of which were the Nazi war records.

The Alexandria city government involvement with the Torpedo Factory building is a record of incremental entrepreneurialism as well as a mixture of economic development and cultural and community programming. The many actions and decisions made by Alexandria government over the years reflect an evolving attitude toward these buildings and the desire to turn obsolete, underutilized buildings into a community asset. This record reflects well on the judgment of many elected and appointed officials over a period of years.

The Torpedo Factory buildings are located on the Potomac River in the heart of the Old Town area of the city. During the early 1950s, the Torpedo Factory buildings were not particularly out of place since much of the area was filled with underutilized or vacant warehouses. In the 1960s, increasing interest in the residential and commercial preservation of Old Town stimulated new uses for the eighteenth- and nineteenth-century warehouses near the river. As these old buildings were beginning to be converted into restaurants and shops, a question naturally arose about the future of the large Torpedo Factory buildings immediately adjacent to the business area then under revitalization.

In the late 1960s, city officials contacted ranking officials in the federal government and gained a sympathetic hearing. The city wanted to acquire the Torpedo Factory in order that these large gray buildings would not be a detriment to the revitalization of Old Town. The federal government declared the buildings surplus, and the city purchased them for $1.5 million in 1969.

The city gradually took possession of the properties in 1974 as the federal government moved its stored materials, furniture, and records to other locations. City officials did not make a firm decision about the future of the buildings when they were purchased. Some strongly believed that the buildings were acquired with the intention to demolish them as soon as possible. Others felt that the issue of their future use should be left to later analysis and study.

During the period of acquisition and initial possession of the property, there were changes in the elected and appointed leadership of the city. As a result, each new city council and the city managers during this period began to address the Torpedo Factory question with an eye to the future rather than the past. Clearly the buildings were not in scale with the smaller surrounding buildings. The entire complex covered 4.75 acres with a total of 380,000 square feet at a floor area ratio of 1.85. However, during the 1970s, the efforts to reutilize old industrial buildings were being given increasing attention throughout the country. San Francisco's waterfront redevelopment was one of the most prominent examples of this type of reutilization of older buildings.

In 1975 the city began studying reuse alternatives and contracted with a nationally known architect to develop proposed uses of the building and an architectural design. These plans were given to the city council in late 1975 and discussed early the next year. There was considerable controversy about the plans, which shocked many of those who felt that the buildings should be torn down in order to eliminate a conflict with the adjacent historic buildings. Some residents in Old Town were distressed that the Torpedo Factory was being considered as a multiuse commercial center. These citizens spoke out strongly against the proposal. However, other persons, including some city elected officials and staff, felt that the Torpedo Factory buildings had potential value which should be exploited.

The Art Center

In 1973 the city, in conjunction with local artists, made what was to have been a temporary use of part of the Torpedo Factory. The decision to establish a "temporary" art center came to have long-term implications for the entire complex. A local artist proposed that the Torpedo Factory be utilized as an art center during the national Bicentennial and the city's 225th birthday. Since the facility was then being vacated by the federal government and the final plans had not been made, the city council granted the artists the opportunity to convert the space into an art center and contributed $140,000 of city funds for this Bicentennial project. An operating budget of approximately $90,000 per year was also provided by the city. The local business community objected to the proposal on grounds that the art center would be undesirable competition.

The Torpedo Factory Art Center soon became a dramatic success and gained considerable attention. The concept was to have artists working in studios in the Torpedo Factory, which would be open for the public to visit and buy original art. Marian Van Landingham, a local artist who later became a delegate to the Virginia General Assembly, took a lead in putting together the concept and gathering the support in the art community for this venture. The artists made use of available surplus materials in the buildings and used funds from the city to refurbish 89,000 square feet of space into a series of studios for 176 artists in 85 studios and 4 large cooperative galleries. By the late 1970s the Torpedo Factory had become a lively Art Center with over a half million persons visiting each year. As the Art Center continued to grow and gain additional supporters, the city grappled with the increasingly complex issue of what to do with the entire complex. Before the success of the Art Center, there was substantial sentiment in favor of demolition of the factory. However, the Art

Center demonstrated that creative uses could be made of the aging factory buildings.

During this interim period, the city utilized the Torpedo Factory space in a variety of ways in addition to the Art Center. It used portions of the buildings to provide much-needed storage for city records, surplus city goods, voting machines, and material for the recreation department. Behind the Torpedo Factory was a small building which had been converted to serve the high school rowing program.

After the 1975 study recommendations were rejected by the city council, the staff faced the question of how to proceed in facilitating decisions about the future of the property. The buildings were continuing to decay, with chunks of concrete occasionally falling from the tall structures and broken glass and debris falling onto the adjacent sidewalks. These conditions could not continue indefinitely.

In 1976 the newly elected city council reflected divergent opinions about the future of the Torpedo Factory. Some members felt that the buildings should be immediately demolished. Others, influenced by the great success of the artists, felt that reutilization should be considered. The future of the facility seemed in doubt.

The design competition

In 1978 the city staff proposed to the council that the city establish a design competition to come up with the most suitable plan for the complex and recommended that the council authorize the development of a "prospectus" outlining the general goals and objectives for the Torpedo Factory. The city council approved the prospectus and authorized advertisement to encourage interested development groups to submit designs as well as specific development proposals.

In preparing the prospectus, the council addressed a number of critical issues about the Torpedo Factory. It decided that a mixed-use development should be sought in order to minimize the number of cars which might be attracted at any particular time. In addition, the prospectus required that there be a substantial reduction in the mass of the buildings, addressing the basic concern that the redevelopment not be of such a scale as to overwhelm the surrounding area. In addition, the council determined that provision should be made for the artists to continue in the complex, thus reflecting the substantial stature accorded the artists from their successful Bicentennial project.

In 1979 the city received four proposals in response to the prospectus. The one ultimately selected by the city council emphasized restoration of some of the buildings to their general appearance during World War I and new brick facades on the others. This proposal involved the following elements:

1. Demolition of the largest building in the complex and development on that site of a 460-car garage and 120 condominium residential units (both elements were through private financing)
2. A 104,000-square-foot commercial office building using the structural frame of one of the World War II buildings
3. Restoration by the city of one of the World War I buildings to house the Art Center on a permanent basis
4. Development of the pier and dock area to include retail shops, a large seafood restaurant adjacent to the river, and improved docks and piers to accommodate transient boats, visiting historic ships, and various cruise boats.

The selection process was quite intense and involved considerable public expression and controversy among the principal development groups.

Redevelopment begins

The city council selected the proposals submitted by the Alexandria Waterfront Restoration Group largely because of its architectural treatment of the buildings and desirable mixed-use elements. Metcalf and Associates and Keyes Condon Florance of Washington, D.C., designed the redevelopment plan using an interesting combination of restoration, traditional design elements, and art deco. The winning proposal did not necessarily propose the greatest financial return to the city, but it was deemed to be the most appropriate for the sensitive Old Town area (see accompanying drawings).

The Alexandria Waterfront Restoration Group purchased for $1.15 million the land and buildings constituting two of the four main Torpedo Factory buildings. The city retained ownership of the building where the artists would eventually be relocated as well as the critical space at the end of the main retail street and all of the dock and pier area adjacent to the river.

Implementing the award of the design decision involved considerable time in drafting the agreements with private developers. At each stage, city staff analyzed possible alternatives to determine ways of reducing city expenditures and maximizing the benefits of the private redevelopment effort. For example, the city handled most of the demolition work directly in order to use the more favorable financing available to the city. Otherwise, the developers' demolition costs would have been deducted from the amount provided to the city. Demolition of the largest building was expected to be very difficult because of the substantial steel reinforcement placed in the building to accommodate the very heavy loads of the factory operation. Demolition went smoothly and with fewer problems than anticipated.

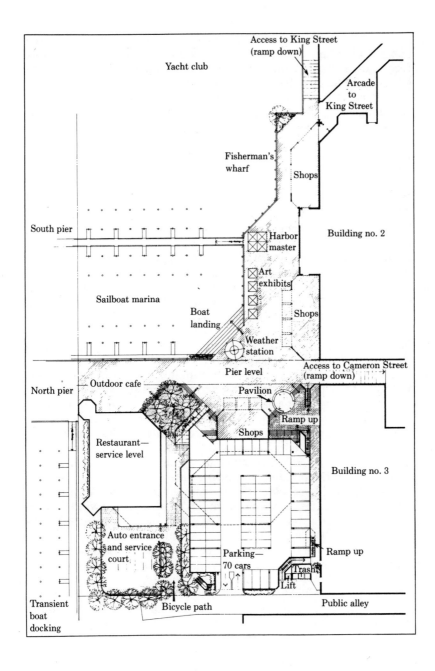

The Torpedo Factory, Alexandria, Virginia

By May 1983 substantial progress on implementing the redevelopment plan had been made. Redevelopment went forward despite record high interest rates during implementation and initial construction. The 104,000-square-foot private office building has been completed with occupancy to begin in the summer of 1983. The 460-car garage was also nearing completion at the same time with the condominium units due for completion later in the year. The city's redeveloped Art Center has opened its doors to many reviews praising the uniqueness of this facility designed to handle not only the art studios but also large receptions.

Sale/leaseback

The city also went forward with a sale/leaseback arrangement on the building to accommodate the artists. In 1982 the city council asked staff to carefully consider any opportunities under the federal tax reform acts and to look specifically at any opportunities involving the Torpedo Factory. The publicity about various local governments selling and leasing back buildings and equipment had created considerable interest. In order to address the complex financial questions, the city selected and hired a financial advisor to assist not only with the ongoing bonding programs but also with the proposed sale/leaseback arrangement with the Art Center. The concept was new to both the city staff and the developers.

As the work was progressing on Building No. 2, where the artists would be relocated, the city staff and financial advisor worked diligently to put together a sale/leaseback package for council consideration. In the past, sale of this building was viewed as unacceptable. However, in light of the unique features of the sale/leaseback provisions of federal tax law, this type of transaction became feasible because it would provide the opportunity for new revenue and allow repurchase of the building at a future date.

In the spring of 1983 the city completed its work on the sale/leaseback and came forward with an investment group willing to enter into such an agreement. This aspect of the project included authorization of bonds by the Alexandria Redevelopment and Housing Authority and the specific elements of the sale/leaseback arrangements between the city and a new private partnership created for this purpose. City staff estimated that the final agreement will net the city up to $400,000 on a "present value" basis. In addition, the complex transaction provided the city with a large capital resource during years when the city's capital budget was straining to support new facilities, including a new police headquarters and jail. The final agreement provided the city with an important cost saving.

The final sale/leaseback arrangement proved to be far more complex and less beneficial than any of the city staff originally imagined. Such arrangements are *extremely* complex, and it is very diffi-

Waterfront view

cult to assure the real financial benefits often claimed in the popular literature. The city does take a risk in such a venture, and the financial benefits must be carefully assessed as to their real economic benefit on a "present value" basis. The legal costs alone are significant.

Future phases

City staff and the private developer will be working on several aspects of the implementation of the approved development plan. Although the buildings are owned by the city, they are intended for private/commercial use. Therefore, the city staff is exploring all possible alternatives to have the construction funded by private funds on the most desirable basis possible.

The remaining aspects of the project require a continuing entrepreneurial orientation. The land on the river where the large seafood restaurant is planned is currently occupied by a small building used by the Alexandria public school rowing program. The council is not in unanimous agreement about the displacement of this program for a restaurant. Considerable attention will be given to the relocated rowing facility as well as the proposed restaurant.

The Alexandria waterfront has for thirteen years been encumbered with a lawsuit by the federal government which has made waterfront planning quite difficult. City staff did identify possible sites for relocation of the rowing program. One of the relocation sites was land occupied by a company which provides pile driving along the river. The owner of the property did not wish to sell his property. As a result, city staff came up with an exchange which provided the owner of the company two small parcels owned by the city and transit authority near Metro station areas in exchange for the waterfront land. The parcels are small but of sufficient development interest to facilitate the exchange. After protracted debates and arguments, the city council did approve the exchange of land which has made possible the development of the area behind the Torpedo Factory for a large seafood restaurant. Since the restaurant was an essential element in the overall waterfront design, it was critical that this relocation issue be resolved.

The Torpedo Factory redevelopment plan also necessitates dredging the waterfront area. The city initially took advantage of federal/state funds for planning the dock area just before the funds were cut by the federal government. Due to the extensive federal regulation of dredging and the problem of finding dredging spoil sites, dredging is extremely expensive. The city estimates that more than $2 million worth of dredging needs to be done near the Torpedo Factory to accommodate a full range of boating activities.

Conclusions and lessons learned

In 1983 the Torpedo Factory project was well on its way to completion. The new Art Center will be unique and spectacular with international recognition. The final design will allow the center to handle large convention receptions, and the facility will undoubtedly attract many major groups in the years ahead. The rehabilitated Art Center will even have an original Alexandria torpedo built there in 1944. The other elements of the project yet to be completed are the plaza behind the Torpedo Factory on the water's edge, where construction is scheduled to begin late in 1983, a small commercial building, the seafood restaurant, and related retail shops.

Once the entire project is completed, Alexandria will have a spectacular waterfront complex built from an obsolete factory which many persons wanted torn down because it was an "eyesore." Through a series of incremental and entrepreneurial efforts, the project changed from a demolition project to a complex redevelopment plan. Prior to redevelopment, the entire complex was valued at $4 million. In 1983 the city estimated that the complex would be worth approximately $31 million after completion. The Alexandria Torpedo Factory project demonstrates the value of taking advantage of available resources and the need for flexible management planning to achieve desirable community objectives.

Alexandria went forward with the Torpedo Factory project for a variety of reasons, some of which were contradictory. As the project went forward, the city became increasingly involved in key entrepreneurial elements in conjunction with the selected development group. A great deal of learning has occurred over this period. Some of the significant lessons include:

1. City-owned property should always be carefully evaluated for its potential private development value.
2. Public investment into cultural attractions (i.e., the Art Center) can stimulate private redevelopment.
3. Current tax laws need to be carefully examined for possible municipal use, such as in sale/leaseback arrangements, but optimistic projections of savings should be carefully evaluated.
4. Design and development competition programs are one means of generating developer interest and new ideas about the development approaches.
5. Development projects take considerable staff time, and cities must be willing to make available this time and/or to provide technical assistance to carry out these types of efforts.
6. It is critical that the local legislative body endorse general goals and objectives at an early point in a development project and that the staff observe these goals and objectives.

The Alexandria Torpedo Factory project is one of the most significant and complex redevelopment efforts undertaken by Alexandria. It has taken over ten years for the first phases to come to substantial completion. The entire waterfront redevelopment underscores the critical importance of entrepreneurial management.

Marketing and Entrepreneurship in Norfolk

Kenneth M. Wheeler

In Norfolk, Virginia, the business of the city government has very much to do with business these days.

The city is applying principles of marketing and entrepreneurship to three major levels of activity.

First, and most visible to the public, is a series of public/private partnerships which are transforming the downtown waterfront and other parts of the community. These efforts involve such well-known names as James Rouse and Jacques Cousteau.

A second level is city council's appropriation of large amounts of money for agencies such as the Norfolk Convention and Visitors Bureau and the city's Department of Development, as well as for activities such as Harborfest and the International Azalea Festival. The city views the expenditure of these funds as an investment in the future.

A third level involves the application of sound marketing principles to the city government itself. The city provides hundreds of public service programs ranging from the Lafayette Zoo to Lake Taylor City Hospital, from the Scope sports, cultural, and convention center to fire and police protection. Running these programs in a business-like way makes them more efficient and effective.

Along the downtown waterfront, the results of the city's partnership with the private sector are rapidly taking shape. More than $70 million in construction was underway along Waterside Drive in the spring of 1983, with $30 million more in projects on the drawing boards.

This impressive record of construction is due in large part to the leadership of Mayor Vincent J. Thomas and Dr. Mason C. Andrews, former vice mayor, as well as city manager Julian F. Hirst and assistant city manager Ronald W. Massie.

Thomas and Andrews formed a committee of business and government leaders to meet regularly and shepherd the city's development activities. A group of business leaders formed the Greater Norfolk Corporation to serve as a cutting edge for private sector involvement.

Working together, leaders among the city's elected officials, government staff, and private business groups evolved an action plan that called on everyone to participate in the way they best could. It amounted to a major marshalling of the community's resources to set a bold course for the future.

Activities were not confined to the downtown. Along the Chesapeake Bay on the northern end of the community, the city government took over an old amusement park and made its prime bayfront land available to developers. The reaction was immediate—a private company bought part of the site and built a 12-story, $9-million condominium tower, the first such high-rise on Norfolk's Chesapeake Bay shores.

On the eastern side of the city, near Norfolk International Airport, the city acquired an aging apartment complex and began converting the land to industrial uses. Again, the private sector response was almost immediate as several developers bought parcels and started construction, which included a 10-acre, $7-million office and warehouse complex built by a developer who began work on his second phase. This new Norfolk Commerce Park provided badly needed land in a city that is almost totally developed.

But the most dramatic manifestation of the city's development program came in the downtown area where the city was founded 300 years ago. Attention had been focused on the downtown waterfront by the success of Harborfest, an annual weekend festival in early summer which had its beginnings in Operation Sail in 1976.

Harborfest itself is a remarkable example of public and private cooperation for the good of the community. The brainchild of financial executive John R. Sears, Jr., and city staff member Timothy L. Jones, Harborfest has served to rekindle interest in the city's once-abandoned waterfront. Now hundreds of volunteers, working with city government support and cooperation, plan and stage the festival for more than a million visitors.

The Greater Norfolk Corporation, working in cooperation with the city government, contacted famous undersea explorer Jacques Cousteau about locating his headquarters in Norfolk. GNC's efforts resulted in the Cousteau Society's establishing its international base in Norfolk, and the society began plans for a $27 million Cousteau Ocean Center to be located on the downtown waterfront. Design work for the Cousteau Ocean Center was done by Roland Crump, who has done work for the Disney organization, among others.

And the development team put together by Mayor Thomas and Dr. Andrews continued its work to turn ideas into reality on the waterfront. The team contacted developer James Rouse about a development in Norfolk along the lines of Rouse's successful Quincy Market in Boston and Harborplace in Baltimore.

At the same time, the group worked with a local real estate firm on plans for a Virginia World Trade Center downtown. Little by little, the plans fell together, with the roles and responsibilities of the public and private agencies decided upon as decisions were needed.

In 1982 an impressive succession of groundbreakings took place all over Norfolk. Nowhere was construction more concentrated than along the city's downtown waterfront. The centerpiece was the Waterside, an 85,000-square-foot festival marketplace containing more than 100 specialty shops and eating places. The Waterside financing package was itself a tribute to public and private cooperation; even though the marketplace was built and will be managed by a private corporation, much of the funding was advanced or guaranteed by the city to ensure timely construction. The city shares as a partner in profits, as well as benefiting from increased jobs and taxes.

The city also built a major parking garage to support the facility, enlarged and landscaped a major berth for harbor cruise ships and character vessels, and devoted seven acres of prime waterfront land to Town Point Park with an amphitheater to seat 5,000, among other amenities. The city also made major improvements to Waterside Drive to handle as many as six million people expected to visit the revitalized waterfront during the first full year of operation of the Waterside.

To ensure a full schedule of activities for visitors, the city worked with the board of directors of Harborfest, which changed its name to Festevents and contracted with the city to assume the task of creating a festive atmosphere in the downtown through a variety of special promotions, performances, and almost anything else to draw people.

In addition to Festevents, the city provides funds to several other agencies and offices that contribute to the economic well-being of the community. Harborfest has gotten its seed money from the city, although in recent years the Harborfest volunteers have raised considerable funds through corporate sponsorships and through a percentage of concession revenues during Harborfest.

The city also funds the Norfolk Convention and Visitors Bureau, which is operated by the private nonprofit Community Promotion Corporation, and the Department of Development, which operates as a department of city government.

The city also provides funding through the Norfolk Chamber of Commerce for the International Azalea Festival, held in April of each year as a tribute to spring and to the North Atlantic Treaty Organization, whose Atlantic headquarters are in Norfolk.

The motivation for all this funding, which runs well over $1 million a year in tax funds, is a belief that these activities constitute an investment in Norfolk's future, much as a private company would invest funds in its own research and development activities. In business, it takes money to make money. The city government in Norfolk recognizes that it takes money for the city to realize its objectives of strengthening the local tax base and providing job opportunities for present and future citizens.

And the city government has also applied the principles of marketing to its own city-run programs. The city realizes that it is, in fact, a municipal service corporation chartered by the state of Virginia to provide local services for the residents of Norfolk. Those services should be provided in the most efficient and effective way possible, and the application of marketing techniques to city operations is one good way to increase efficiency.

The city's Department of Communications and Marketing works with all of the government's departments, bureaus, and divisions on marketing problems. The department recently put together and implemented a graphics identification program to be used by all city government operations. The program was developed with the dual objectives of esthetics and practicality, and many operational staff executives who would be using the program were involved in its development. The result has been a graphics program that achieves the city government's communications and marketing objectives while being easy to use.

Throughout the city government, sound business principles are applied to operations to make them more businesslike and therefore of better service to the people of the community.

City
Gift
Catalogs

In the last few years many local governments have used "gift catalogs" to supplement tax revenues by attracting donations and contributions from members of the community. These catalogs, sometimes paid for by advertising, describe equipment, materials, and
services needed by the local government, with price tags attached.
They provide an opportunity for individuals, service clubs, neighborhood or school groups, and businesses to make tax-deductible contributions to the municipality.

Gift catalogs have multiple advantages. Not only do they stimulate private-sector giving to the government, but they also involve
citizens in community services and impress on them the actual costs
involved in services that are often taken for granted.

On the following pages are reproductions of sample "offerings"
from gift catalogs published by St. Petersburg, Florida; Scottsbluff,
Nebraska; Anaheim, California; and Reno, Nevada.

THE PARKS

Plants and trees	$50 - up
Bird seed supply especially for creatures of Boyd Hill Nature Trail	$15
Adventure playground equipment	$5,000 - up
Benches	$200 each
BBQ grills	$250
Picnic tables	$400
Outdoor portable public address system for city-wide events	$3,000
Padded folding chairs for public gatherings	$50 each
Banquet tables	$100 each
Utility maintenance vehicles	$6,000
Tractors (farm type)	$15,000
Small riding mowers	$1,000
Seven-gang mowers	$35,000
Renovation of boat dock at Bay Vista Park	$70,000
Outdoor public activity shelters	$3,500
Electric tram for handicapped and non-pedestrian users of Boyd Hill Nature Trail	$13,000
Meeting, concession and restroom facilities for Puryear Park	$60,000
Purchase of Little Bayou Park, ten ecologically sensitive acres at Fourth Street and 54th Avenue South - total acquisition cost, $750,000. Funds available, $330,000	$420,000

Source: St. Petersburg, Florida

Help-The-Zoo

In 1975 a group of concerned citizens started the "Help-The-Zoo" Fund. The money in this fund is donated and as in the case of the construction of the new Mammal House is combined with City funds to install improvements to the Zoo. We as a community have a lot to be proud of in the Zoo and in order to keep this facility going, continued citizen support will be needed. Donations for the Zoo can be made to the "Help-The-Zoo" Fund and may be designated to one of the following projects:

1. Construction of new
   restrooms $35,000
2. New & replacement fencing $10,000
3. Additional playground
   equipment $200-$5,000
4. Benches $100
5. Picnic tables $150-$400
6. Purchase of diet supple-
   ments for the animals $50-$500
7. Construction of new animal
   shelters $1,000-$10,000

Other areas where volunteer services are needed at the Zoo include:

Loan of baby animals for Children's Zoo during spring and summer months.

Volunteer labor to supervise Children's Zoo on week-ends in the summer—includes feeding and watering the animals, litter clean-up and general supervision.

Volunteer Zoo guides—trained by Zoo personnel to give tours to school groups and other groups as requested (spring and summer).

Source: Scottsbluff, Nebraska

Department of Parks and Recreation
A Park Is for Sharing—and Caring

"A park is the purest of human pleasures. A source of wonder, delight, exultation and inspiration, the park has always been an allegory of man's relationship to nature." Francis Bacon

Adopt-A-Park

Neighborhood involvement in park maintenance has always been important to the Park Maintenance Division. It has become more important in recent years as fewer dollars are available for parks. A formal Adopt-A-Park Program was developed in 1981. This program provides small monthly payments to groups and individuals who work in park areas to reduce litter and control other maintenance problems. The list of parks currently included in the Adopt-A-Park Program is provided below. Another list of parks which are in need of special attention is also provided. You can provide either the funds for the monthly fee to be paid for adoption of the park or you may want to adopt the park as your community service project. This program does not provide for purchase of equipment, trees, supplies, shelters, etc. but you can also get involved by donating these items.

Parks	Duties	Payment
1. Frank Park (May & Sept.)	litter clean-up, clean shelters	$40/mo
2. Broadway Mini Park	litter clean-up	$30/mo
3. Pioneer Park and Tower Park	litter clean-up, clean shelters, clean restrooms on week-ends	$50/mo
4. Band Park and Broadway Parkings	litter clean-up	$40/mo
5. Overland Park	litter clean-up	$30/mo
6. Veterans Park	litter clean-up	$30/mo
7. Lacy Park	litter clean-up, clean shelters, clean restrooms on week-ends, water new trees	$50/mo

Source: Scottsbluff, Nebraska

nature needs

A nature walk in Oak Canyon Nature Center or a visit to our Nature Mobile to take time out to relate to and appreciate nature. Our 58 acre Nature and Interpretive Center located in Oak Canyon gives thousands of visitors a close-up view of local animal and plant life. Help us in teaching ecology and improving our environment by purchasing one or more of the following:

Garden Tools $5-25

Insect Spreading Boards $8

Binoculars 7 × 35 .... $25

Hummingbird Feeders $30

Spotting Scopes
w/Tripods $100

Fields Interpretive
Center $100

Dissecting Scopes $150

Mounted Gray Fox $175

Mounted Racoon $200

Mounted Bobcat $250

Mounted Dove $35

Mounted
Great-Horned Owl $100

Source: Anaheim, California

office supplies

Flyers for playgrounds, and program information for all activities rely on office supplies and equipment. Any donation earmarked for this area will be put to good use. A few specific items needed are:

Therapeutic Recreation Letterhead $50

IBM Typewriter $900

Xerox Copier $2,000

Printing of Brochures .... Any amount
Ads available for $500 and up

Postage Money .... Any amount
To help mail program information to the community

staff needs

Rent A Leader! Recreation Leaders are needed throughout the City for a variety of programs and supervision of parks and facilities. You can buy an hour of happiness for a child for as little as $2.90 an hour! The more you donate, the more you will help in keeping youngsters busy in constructive activities.

Recreation Aides .... $2.90 hr.

Recreation Leaders .... $3.18 hr.

Recreation Directors .... $4.12 hr.

Source: Anaheim, California

DREAMS

COMMUNITY/RECREATION CENTER

Imagine a complex including gymnasiums, meeting rooms, dance studio, arts and crafts center, exercise rooms, auditorium with a stage seating for several hundred, etc., etc. This is our dream for the future—a community/recreation center. The perfect project for the entire community.

Cost: .... 5 million

Source: Reno, Nevada

Municipal Home Insurance

Charles W. Thompson

Homeowners insurance has not been a customary part of municipal administration. But when you think about it, neither have microprocessors, computer-aided dispatch, probeye, tax increment financing, and municipal equity in shopping centers. All of which points out not only the changes that have occurred in municipal administration but, more significantly, the changing attitude and concepts of the public toward government.

Historical connections

Actually, the concepts underlying municipal home insurance (MHI) are not new at all. The reality is that we have come back to a place of origin. In the colonial period, the early fire insurance companies organized local townspeople into paid fire brigades and paid them out of premiums. In other words, fire protection was financed from homeowners insurance premiums.

As cities grew, it became apparent that fire in one structure was a threat to adjacent buildings and even the entire neighborhood. A simple volunteer fire brigade was not adequate to meet the needs. This was especially true when different fire insurance companies held the insurance on adjoining structures—neither would fight the fire in the other's building!

General municipal fire protection became a public necessity. The big change was in the way the service was financed. Cities assumed the costs of fire protection, along with other related services, while fire insurance companies merely underwrote the risks, along with other home-related risks.

Over the years, the insurance industry has pressed public agencies to hire more firefighters, purchase more fire apparatus, build larger water reservoirs and transmission mains, enact stricter building regulations, and develop more and better accessibility to new developments.

In short, the growth and development of both fire-protection
and fire-homeowners insurance has paralleled the growth and matu-
ration of American cities.

What is municipal homeowners insurance?

Simply stated, MHI is a type of voluntary homeowners insurance
requiring compliance by the homeowner with all significant public
safety codes and regulations; this makes the homeowner eligible to
purchase insurance coverage. The program also provides for payment
to the city of any excess premiums above losses and expenses.

The fundamental philosophy underlying MHI is simply that financial self-interest can produce an effective partnership between
city public safety agencies and homeowners. The product of that
partnership should be tangibly lower insured loss experience among
the program participants. Lower losses, in turn, permit reduced insurance rates for homeowners and premium dividends for the cities
involved.

The basic approach involves a joint effort between public and
private enterprise brought together in a voluntary relationship to
help solve an old problem. This approach allows each participant to
do what it does best and to remain in its traditional role. Through a
cooperative relationship, the insurance is provided, marketed, and
adjusted by private-sector insurance companies and agents for those

---

As soon as people began to band together for the common good, there
was an inherent conflict between the necessity to have laws that apply
to everyone and a desire for individual freedom that would allow a
range of choices and personal successes. Practically from the dawn of
civilization, there has been a conflict between what is the public interest and what is private enterprise.

If you subscribe to the theory that necessity is the mother of invention, then it is interesting to note that two of the biggest human
institutions have the same mother. Necessity for protecting life and
property from unnecessary loss has resulted in the formation of two
structures: the government's attempts at public safety, expressed in
the form of police and fire departments, and private enterprise's development of the insurance industry, which is reflected in life insurance,
medical insurance, and fire and theft insurance.

Recently there has been an effort to get the two children spawned
by the concept of saving life and property to work more closely together. Not unlike people who experience sibling rivalry, government
and private enterprise are experiencing a real conflict over just exactly
who "mother liked best."

Source: Ronny J. Coleman, Director of Fire Protection, San Cle-
mente (California) Fire Department, "Private or Public—A Question
of Priorities," unpublished paper.

homeowners who have voluntarily undergone a comprehensive home safety analysis performed under a city home safety and security program. This home safety analysis covers all principal areas of home safety—fire, theft, building, and liability exposures.

It is also important to point out some of the distinctions between early concepts of MHI and today's model. Several years ago, we spoke of "municipal fire insurance." This was an idea which would have placed the city in an insurer's role. The city would continue to provide fire protection and would insure the homeowner against fire loss. Premiums would go into a municipal trust fund, generate interest income, and pay for losses and some or all fire protection costs. The idea is similar to self-insurance programs in which cities self-insure against general liability, workers compensation, and medical claims.

The idea of municipal fire insurance was never seriously considered by any city in the United States, although somewhat similar programs have been espoused in a few other nations. This concept, however, was the beginning of later developments which have incrementally led to municipal homeowners insurance programs. MHI is an outgrowth of American fire insurance history and U.S. concepts of private enterprise.

The development of MHI

As pointed out, MHI has developed over a period of time and has had many contributors. In the early days of my city management career in Ohio, I tried to generate interest in a plan which was a modified version of municipal fire insurance. The modification was an attempt to enlist the support of local insurance agents to sell the policies and receive a commission for their efforts. The idea was not well received, and after a brief time it was dropped although not forgotten.

Later, in California, working with Joe Baker, then city manager of Burbank, another endeavor was launched to revive the idea. The city attorneys were asked to make a study of the idea, and through the local state assemblymen, an attorney general's opinion was secured. These legal reviews pointed out the many problems a city would encounter if it should attempt to become directly involved in underwriting private risks.

At this point, it was learned through the Institute of Local Self Government in Berkeley, California, that a similar thrust was being made by a group of municipal officials in northern California. Under the lead of fire chief Byron Channey (then at Mountain View, now at Palm Springs), similar concepts were being explored.

As events developed further in the early 1970s, the U.S. Fire Administration sponsored a comprehensive investigation into the feasibility of the concept. Technical support for this research was provided by the Mission Research Corporation of Santa Barbara, headed by William C. Hanna. The feasibility study examined several alternative forms of MHI, ranging from mandatory versions to completely voluntary forms and "franchise" approaches.

Using this research and later studies made under the auspices of the Federal Emergency Management Agency (FEMA, of which the U.S. Fire Administration is now a part), a group of municipal officials from southern California developed a model which could be inaugurated in several cities and have more or less universal applicability.

This group, headed by the author and Rod Sackett, director of management services for the city of Orange, consulted many municipal officials from the Los Angeles and Orange County area—city managers, fire chiefs, city attorneys, police chiefs, risk managers, and building officials. Academic and private-sector interests also were involved.

After several insurance companies were approached, the AVCO Financial Insurance Group joined with the ad hoc committee to develop the program model. Richard Zizian, then director of marketing for AVCO, represented the company on the committee. The model was developed with the following objectives as guides:

1. To develop, through mutual interest, a partnership between private enterprise and local government to carry out a program to serve the interests of both
2. To improve public and home safety and security
3. To gain greater cost effectiveness of the homeowners insurance expenses through (a) lower insurance premiums; (b) providing financial support for public safety operations from existing insurance premiums; and (c) allowing insurance rates to be developed commensurate with local loss experience and local public safety effectiveness and performance.

The problems associated with mandatory forms of MHI and the risks associated with city participation as an underwriter were resolved. This resolution took the form of a very flexible program which is legally, politically, and economically much more acceptable to cities.

This program flexibility was achieved by setting up a variety of alternative choices regarding the degree of involvement on the part of the city. In addition, since Mill Valley, California, adopted the program in 1982, the program has been expanded and modified (Vern Hazen, city manager of Mill Valley at the time of adoption, was a member of the ad hoc development committee; he is now city manager of Escondido, California). Therefore, it now appears that a wide variety of choices are open to cities, allowing a tailor-made plan to suit virtually any local circumstance.

General provisions of the MHI program

There are several plans in which a city, or group of cities, can enter into MHI, depending on the extent to which it wishes to become involved. These plans range from a *master policy plan* to a *unilateral offer plan*. These plans are now being marketed as the Cooperative Home Insurance Program or CHIP. The general provisions of the plans are, however, all the same, the difference being in the role played by the city.

The key element in MHI—the element which may determine its real profitability to cities—is the *home safety analysis*. This analysis is, in effect, a broad or comprehensive inspection of the home, examining the major aspects of safety and security. As such, it is primarily concerned with factors which constitute the major contributing share of home losses. Whether the losses are from fire, burglary, or liability may vary somewhat from city to city and from time to time, but the home safety analysis can be tailored to the city's specific situation. The model program includes a checklist of the principal items in tune with general building and safety codes and items that experience has shown to be most important.

This checklist was developed with the involvement of fire chiefs, police chiefs, building officials, risk managers, and insurance specialists. The use of this checklist and the conduct of the home safety analysis, however, *must be performed as a part of the city's safety education program*. Its primary purpose should never be enforcement. Obviously, a city official cannot and should not ignore any life-threatening violation, but it would be better to call such violations to the homeowner's attention and allow ample time for correction before beginning even a preliminary enforcement effort.

The home safety analysis is an educational and prevention-oriented program and is strictly voluntary on the part of the homeowner. Once the analysis has been completed, the homeowner is left with a copy, together with any other safety education material the city wishes to distribute. The city inspectors/analysts are not to discuss home insurance, and the city does not market it; that is left to the insurance agent or insurance service bureau.

The city's business is, and traditionally has been, public safety. Cities know the safety business, and virtually all cities have safety and inspection programs conducted through their police, fire, and building departments. The home safety analysis under MHI takes the major ingredients of each, together with a few aspects relating to liability, and puts them together in checklist form. Inspection teams could be set up utilizing fire companies, police cadets, and/or building inspectors.

It would appear to be most appropriate for a two-person team to conduct the analyses, and all participants should receive special orientation and instruction regarding the checklist, public relations tips, and admonishment about discussions of insurance. In this fashion, costs of inspection should not be much beyond present costs, and the added benefits in public safety and public relations should make it doubly worthwhile.

At any rate, the more effectively the home safety program can be performed, the more benefits it will produce in terms of (1) insurance cost reductions to the homeowner; (2) lower fire service costs to the taxpayer; (3) lower burglary and fire loss to the homeowner; (4) lower police investigation costs to the city; and (5) lower liability costs to both homeowner and city.

Once the home safety analysis is completed, the homeowner can, if he or she chooses, contact the insurance carrier. The homeowner must authorize the city to provide a copy of the home safety analysis to the insurance company or give the company his copy. If the inspection does not indicate any major problems or hazards, the home and homeowner will be recognized as a good risk and become eligible for coverage under MHI.

Since insurance premiums come due throughout the year, the home safety analysis program can be programmed on a regular basis. Public safety retirees could be used in this program, but it should not require the addition of new personnel.

The single most important and unique feature of MHI is the development of premium dividends returnable to the city. Dividends are defined as those premiums remaining after insurance company retention, agent's commissions, and loss-related costs are paid. Homeowners would rather see some part of the premiums they must pay remain in the city to help defray the costs of city public safety programs. The amount actually returned depends on an unknown— that is, how much loss there will be. History indicates that in some years the losses will be very low, while in other years they may be very high. If losses exceed premiums, the city will receive nothing and will have paid out whatever the inspections cost.

A study of loss ratios of twenty-three major insurance companies on their homeowners policies over a three-year period (1978–79 through 1980–81) reveals a low of 42 percent and a high of 79 percent. The annual averages were 51 percent, 58 percent, and 64 percent, respectively. It should be noted that these are nationwide figures and were achieved without the benefit of a home safety analysis. *A basic premise of the MHI program is that the home safety analysis will present a preferred risk and will result in lower losses.*

To support this premise, pilot and demonstration programs have been conducted in numerous cities. These tests have been held on a variety of police activities (burglary prevention and neighborhood watch) and fire safety activities. The results of these programs have generally been positive, although the programs have not, for the most part, been systematic and ongoing.

Among the things that are known about safety is that people who observe safety measures have fewer and less severe accidents. A clean, well-maintained, and orderly residence and surrounding yard is less likely to have fires and liability exposures than one with "accident invitations" all around. Smoke detectors, burglar alarms, and deadbolts also have been shown to be worthwhile. These are among the things looked for and taught during the home safety analysis.

In addition, the fact that a city can realize substantial revenue from this program provides an incentive to city staff and management to make their community safer.

Homeowners policies can vary, but the basic policy now available is comparable to other policies. Coverages are available in a comprehensive package as in other homeowners policies, and are available for single-family, condominium, and mobile homes provided the owner occupies the unit as a principal place of residence (when Mill Valley started, only single-family units were eligible). The program continues to provide all the usual homeowners insurance package policy coverages, including fire, theft, and comprehensive personal liability.

Rates and rate structures vary from community to community and from state to state. Rates also may vary even within a city. Generally, the premiums for MHI will fall in the lower quarter of those offered by carriers writing insurance locally. Initial rates will be established on the basis of an assessment of the community's housing stock, public safety system, and historical loss experience. As loss data accumulate, rates will be adjusted actuarially according to local loss control performance. Thus, the city and the insured citizens have a direct and significant influence on their own insurance rates. Although these plans have been developed and are ready to implement, there is still room for a city to negotiate. Some fine tuning may be needed to tailor the program to a city's unique circumstances.

Insurance premiums will be retained initially by the insurance carrier and a statewide pool will be established to generate an adequate reserve for losses and expenses. The required premium level is $1,000,000 annually, in aggregate, for all pool participants. When this level is reached, premium dividends will be distributed and continue as long as the required premium level is maintained. A common loss ratio, developed by all pool participants, will be used in determining the dividend. The dividends will then be distributed according to each city's contribution, pro rata, to the earned premium in the state pool. Participation in the state pool will not be required of all cities; larger cities may initially be able to support their own individual programs or a group of cities may organize themselves—through a joint powers agreement or intercity contract, for example—to establish a more regionalized program.

Establishment of the statewide pool increases every city's prospect for success. Shock losses will be better absorbed on a statewide basis, especially when the program is in its infancy. Smaller cities which would not be able to support MHI because of inadequate premium volume can, therefore, participate and generate dividends in a timely manner through the pool, along with larger cities.

The prepayment of premiums by MHI insureds is what makes it possible for the insurance carrier to make money on the program; the carrier retains the investment income from the cash flow.

In general, the distribution of premium revenues will be as follows:

1. The insurance carrier initially retains approximately 20 percent to cover administrative expenses, reinsurance, and taxes. This retention may be adjusted as actual costs are determined. It is realistic to think that this amount could be reduced over a period of time to perhaps 15 percent.
2. The managing general agency retains approximately 2½ percent to cover legal work in each state, seminars for cities to explain the program, assistance in the formation of JPAs, and the selection of an exclusive local agency to represent MHI in the community. After the initial startup, this may be reduced to 1½ to 2 percent after the third or fourth year.
3. The local insurance agency retains up to 12 percent to cover marketing expenses, quotations, policy issuance, billing, and policy servicing. This amount, like the others, could be reduced conceivably to as low as 8 to 10 percent after a few years.
4. The balance of 65 to 75 percent is available for paying claims and for dividends to the cities.

Claims will be handled by professional adjusting firms under contract to the insurance carrier in each community.

Reinsurance arrangements are currently such that a maximum of $50,000 will be charged against the pool for any single loss, regardless of the carrier's payment to the insured. For example, for a covered loss of $135,000, only $50,000 would be charged to the pool; the balance of $85,000 would be paid by the carrier's reinsurer. The loss pool is also protected against catastrophic loss in the same way, with a maximum chargeable limit. At this time, the catastrophe level is still under negotiation with the reinsurer. However, the stop loss is anticipated to be between $400,000 and $500,000.

With losses controlled at 50 percent or lower, and administrative costs held to about 35 percent, at least 15 percent of the premium dollars will be "unused" and will be available for payment to cities as premium dividends. Naturally, higher or lower loss ratios proportionally influence profitability of the program.

Profitability may generally be estimated in the following way: If

$300 is an average annual premium for homeowners insurance, then $45 per policy will be available to the city each year for a loss ratio of 50 percent. The number of policies involved may be estimated as the number of owner-occupied single-family, condominium, and mobile home dwellings multiplied by the expected market penetration of about 30 percent. So for a city with 25,000 eligible occupancies (a city of approximately 100,000 population), annual revenues of about $335,000 can be expected. The number of home visits required can be expected to be about 1.5 times the number of policies sold. However, not all policies fall due at the same time, and inspections can be spread throughout the year.

The program is structured so that the city incurs no liability whatsoever for losses. If losses exceed premiums, the city receives nothing—the city's only obligation is to continue to offer a home safety analysis.

As implied above, the city can enter the program in several ways. First, the city can hold a master policy on behalf of all eligible homeowners. It is a nonexclusive contract which spells out the legal and financial relationship between the city and the insurance carrier. This requires city council approval and a city announcement to homeowners of its availability. The homeowner simply gets a policy endorsement to the master policy.

Another approach is for a city simply to endorse the program and announce that the safety analysis is available, leaving everything else to the insurance agency. Under this approach, the city council takes no official action regarding a master policy, only that the city approve the program. The arrangements governing the return of dividends to the city are contained in an endorsement to the homeowners policy.

Under any arrangement, it would appear advisable for the city to insist on an equitable and professional claims handling program. The fairness and objectivity of this element of the program is vital to any insurance plan. The managing general agent will have this responsibility.

Implementation

It should be obvious that MHI represents a departure for local public administration. It is a new way of doing things and, like all new things, will be viewed with curiosity and suspicion. Also, as with all new ventures, a great deal of misinformation will be generated. Unfortunately, a great deal of this misinformation, or lack of knowledge concerning the plan, will come from insurance people.

Positions taken by various detractors range from statements that it will take money away from local agents to expressions that it will be too costly to administer. The fact that these positions are inconsistent has not kept them from being expressed.

The essential points are that a great deal of information and edification are needed in advance. Again, as with all new plans and ideas, there must be very thorough preparation in order to inaugurate a successful program.

In view of this particular obstacle, it appears that a grouping of cities under a joint-powers type agreement whereby the joint powers board would be assigned this task could very well be a preferred implementation strategy. Such an arrangement has many successful precedents to follow, as evidenced by the many associations handling workers compensation insurance programs and municipal liability programs.

From a public standpoint, the market surveys that have been conducted to date show an overwhelmingly positive reaction. MHI simply expands the choices a homeowner has available and improves competition in the marketplace, and it allows monies that the homeowner/taxpayer *already* pays to be more effectively used for public safety activities—the very programs which are designed to lessen those risks covered by his or her insurance.

MHI is one of the few really innovative insurance ideas to be developed in recent times. It undoubtedly will be adjusted and modified as it matures through experience. Despite the fact that it will continue to evolve, it is a fully developed and viable program. It is an idea whose time has finally arrived. It promises to be one of the major events of this century in its potential impact on local municipal administration. It was designed by public officials, for public purposes, in the public interest. It deserves the very serious consideration of public administrators and officials.

PART 4

Conclusion

Strategies for Change in Local Government

James L. Mercer, Susan W. Woolston,
and William V. Donaldson

Most local government managers continue to do things as they always have in the belief that it may be all right for some other local government to try a new idea or device, but they could never get away with it in their city or county. Opposition from the union, the city council, the county commission, or the community may be the reasons given.

This article will discuss the problem of fear of innovation. All the good ideas in the world are worthless unless they are put to some use. Good intentions and conference attendance by themselves will not make the next decade one of local government renaissance. Only the application of the knowledge we now have about improving the performance of government will let local government meet the needs of its citizens within the fiscal limits the economy and the taxpayer revolt have created.

Increasing opportunities for innovation

Let us examine ways managers can increase opportunities for innovation and improve chances for success. If the line of resistance to change were in a constant place, evaluating the possibilities of success for a particular innovation or change would be much easier. But events constantly alter the position of that tolerance line, and it is in a different place for different issues and at different times. For example, there may be a great deal of room for innovation in the fire service but little in the police service. A tight budget may increase willingness to accept innovation in highway construction but reduce it in

Reprinted, by permission of the publisher, from *Managing Urban Government Services* by James L. Mercer, Susan W. Woolston, and William V. Donaldson, pp. 213-224 © 1981 by AMACOM, a division of American Management Associations, New York. All rights reserved.

refuse collection services. The line of resistance is not in the same position in one local government as it is in another. This means that one city's or county's experience with change is not always a useful guide in introducing that same change in another jurisdiction.

The first step for the would-be innovator is to locate the line of resistance for a particular issue and take full advantage of the opportunity for change it gives. The best method for locating the line of resistance on a particular issue is to use the trial balloon, or run-it-up-the-flagpole-and-see-who-salutes method. Fortunately, there are a number of warning signals before one reaches the line of resistance. But a manager who is convinced of the reasonableness of an idea for change may overlook the warning and cross the line of resistance without being aware of it. If relationships with the council or commission and the community have been good, that manager probably will survive the resulting storm, but the chances for success the next time he or she introduces a change will be diminished.

In addition to the well-meaning manager who blunders over the line of resistance to change, either through ignorance or in an excess of enthusiasm, some managers deliberately adopt a policy of brinkmanship. Such a manager often accomplishes a great deal and is certainly fun to watch at work. He or she is constantly at war with members of the council or commission, the news media, or some other segment of the community. The immediate results of kamikaze managers are often impressive, but the improvements they bring to government often don't last longer than their job tenure. The objective of good management should be to create an atmosphere that encourages innovation, thought, efficiency, and individual development. Knowing where the line of resistance to change is on any issue and developing the skills to increase the tolerance for change can create a management structure that increases individual innovation and resultant improvements in operating effectiveness.

This article will deal with three issues: locating the resistance to the change line; factors external to the manager that change the position of this line; and ways in which the manager can change it by personal action.

The first requirement for locating the line of resistance to change is a thorough knowledge of the community. It is important to know the position of each council or commission member on any issue and what the newspaper's editorial policy is likely to be when the issue is raised. Informal discussions of the issue with members of the council/commission can be helpful if they are kept as general as possible. They provide an ideal opportunity to educate the council or commission member and to suggest to him or her a number of alternate courses of action. A serious mistake managers make is to expect council or commission members to instantly take a stand on an issue before they have had an opportunity to thoroughly understand it or to understand their constituents' interest in it.

The reporters who cover the city hall or the county courthouse on a day-to-day basis can help a manager discover the line of resistance to change on a given issue. They often have their own opinions which may or may not reflect the editorial opinions of their newspapers. It is worth knowing what these opinions are and how strongly they are held. Opinion polling and attitude sampling can give a manager a general feeling of the public's interest in any given issue and how strongly various opinions are held. The leadership of neighborhood organizations and other community leaders are sounding boards that can help a manager measure support or opposition on a particular issue. Not only will a manager locate the line of resistance by understanding the community but he will also learn what segments of the community have a particular interest in the issue at hand.

As the manager attempts to locate the line of resistance to change on a specific issue, one of the most frequent responses will be, "We tried that before and it didn't work." An examination of the issue will often reveal that what was tried and allegedly failed was the will of the bureaucracy and not the idea, or it was an entirely different problem and solution.

What happened in the past has great value in helping to predict the future location of the line of resistance to change. The passage of time, however, often changes the problem, the people who were concerned with it, and attitudes in general, so that what happened in the past is not a precise guide to the future.

Because the line of resistance may change during the implementation of any new program, it is sometimes difficult to predict the effect or consequences of the proposed change. One way to handle this is to take all reasonable precautions and then start implementing the change. If things get too complicated, a manager can always back off.

Another less risky method by which a manager may evaluate resistance to change for a given issue is to create a model that will let him or her predict the consequences of the change without having to make a major commitment to it. Many city or county services, such as refuse collection, police patrol, and the distribution of fire stations, lend themselves very well to the modeling technique. Even if the model isn't precise, the effort to quantify will give a manager some new insights into the proposed change and the effect it may have on the community.

Similar to the model, but a little more risky, is the pilot project. On a number of issues a manager may create a small-scale test of what he or she wants to do, one that will minimize the consequences of failure. This will also give the manager an opportunity to assess the opposition to the particular change. The difficulty with pilot projects is that they may not predict what will happen on a larger scale. They should, however, at least reveal problems of management and community acceptance that will help the manager decide whether to go on with the project.

Experience will help a manager monitor the council or commission, news media, and public as an issue develops, so that he or she can accurately assess the chances of success on any issue. It is often better to back off if defeat is inevitable, because that leaves the option of trying again when chances are better. An old and wise manager once said, "Change is to government as a racehorse is to a track. A horse will be around again if you don't shoot it the first time."

The art of perceiving changes in the position of the resistance line caused by external events lies in utilizing those influences to increase the likelihood of successful innovation. Often the changes that influence the position of the line of resistance are at first perceived as disasters. No matter how bad an event may initially seem, it almost always creates an opportunity to initiate change. A good example of chaos creating opportunities for change was the havoc wreaked on the Mississippi Gulf Coast in 1969 by Hurricane Camille. Out of that disaster came much better emergency preparations planning that helped save lives and reduce property damage when a hurricane hit much of the same area in 1979. The fiscal crisis that will be with most governments throughout the 1980s will create many opportunities to innovate in areas of productivity and efficiency.

Revenue reduction, cost increases, and taxpayer dissatisfaction all reduce the resistance to change on the part of citizens, council/commission, and employees. Natural and man-made disasters give the manager an opportunity to review how the city/county delivers a given service and to introduce changes in that delivery system.

The discovery of dishonesty on the part of public employees offers opportunities for introducing changes. If the manager is willing to look at fundamental changes in the system rather than cosmetic changes that most likely will increase costs, the discovery of corruption or inefficiency in a governmental operation is a golden opportunity for making changes that have been deferred too long.

Systems that seem to function satisfactorily, even if inefficiently, often break down and reveal their true nature under pressure. A flood, a large snowstorm, an employees' strike, and similar disasters provide the opportunity to reexamine what local government is doing and to make some substantial changes in its operation. There will also be some opportunities for change that will arise from positive actions. New federal programs will create new, if limited, fiscal resources for local governments, and local periods of prosperity will bring new or increased tax revenues. If the new revenues produced by windfalls of this sort are perceived as a signal to return to the "good old days" of expanding governmental services, however, they will only increase the problems local government will face in the future.

The prospects of increased revenues rejuvenate moribund bureaucracies and create a different set of problems for the manager than those caused by failures of public systems. The failure of a public system to function well in the face of a challenge often brings about the least useful reaction from its managers at the very time that the organization should be most free to innovate and that creativity from employees is most needed. The organization is likely to turn in upon itself, becoming more centralized, more cautious, and more vocal in defending the way it has been doing things. The result of this "wagon circling" is a large expenditure of energy, both inside the organization and in its relationships with the rest of the world. Affixing and avoiding blame become a preoccupation inside the organization and with its outside detractors and supporters. The effect of this is more likely to produce another set of regulations, checks, and controls rather than any positive changes in the organization. If anything, the organization becomes more cautious and its employees less likely to advocate any change that might attract attention to them.

The skilled manager can see beyond the point of affixing blame and realizes that the opportunity for positive change in the organization has been increased by the anxiety about inquiry into reasons for past failures. Positive approaches to fundamental management improvement will be welcomed by the organization's detractors and its defenders.

The more closely a manager examines the location of the line of resistance to change, the more he or she realizes its position is constantly changing and that this position is affected by a wide variety of events. Watching these changes for opportunities to introduce new ideas and for warnings of when to slow down will improve the efficiency of government, with a modest risk to the manager. The manager need only have a general idea of what he or she wants to accomplish and a closet full of projects to select from when the opportunity presents itself. Over a period of time, major changes can be made in the way the government operates, and the manager will find that the tolerance to change will increase as the organization performs more efficiently and as the manager anticipates problems and implements solutions.

The resulting rate of progress will probably satisfy most managers and will certainly improve the efficiency of most governmental organizations, but it may not be fast enough to suit some managers. A manager may decide he or she would like to be able to influence the line of resistance to change without having to wait for external events to accomplish this. For this manager, the ability to manipulate the level of resistance to change is of value. The deliberate and planned increase in an organization's tolerance to change can be risky, but the feeling of accomplishment and control it provides far outweighs the risks involved.

It is this ability to influence the line of resistance to change that lies at the very heart of the art of management and, like all art, it is something that has to be practiced to be learned. Some may object that this involves manipulating people and events, a proper role for the elected leader but not for the appointed manager, or that there is something inherently wrong with trying to change attitudes and circumstances to achieve a predetermined goal. Manipulation is only a more realistic description of leadership, and a proper inquiry into its morality should examine its methods and its goal, but not its use.

Following are some suggestions that the manager can use to influence the position of the line of resistance to change as it applies to a specific local government. With experience and reflection most managers will be able to add to this list.

Often the manager is the only person who is likely to accept leadership in the publicly unexciting project of increasing the efficiency of government. No end of leadership will be discovered if you talk about cutting taxes and increasing services, but that leadership will evaporate if you are interested in increasing accountability and productivity. A smart manager will not confuse leadership with public credit for accomplishment. He or she will work with the elected officials to encourage them to take public leadership in improving governmental performance and will give them credit for accomplishment. The manager's reward for increasing efficiency in government is in knowing that he or she did it and in seeing the staff stretch to exercise their creativity.

Because of the groups they represent or because of their peculiar association with an issue, some people are able to increase the level of resistance to change on some issues more than others. The shop steward in the local government garage is much more likely to get the mechanics in that garage to accept work standards than is a bright, young budget analyst from the management office. The manager who wants to increase the tolerance of change in the organization will spend time understanding who has a special interest in any planned change and what that interest is. A manager will try to develop leadership on the issue of concern from among the people who are affected by it and will even try to convince the affected group that the desired change was really their idea.

The quality of support for the change a manager wants to make is important, but so is the size of that support. Special interest groups have demonstrated the effectiveness of creating the illusion of broad support from relatively small groups. If, at the first council/commission discussion of a change the manager proposes, all the council/commission sees is a chamber full of opponents, it may be difficult to convince the elected members that they are the only people in the local government who are opposed to the proposed change. A group of supporters who appear at the start of any discussion will not only convince the council/commission that there are two sides to the issue but will produce much better balanced media coverage.

The most difficult problem to solve in an attempt to increase the level of tolerance to change is that the people who are opposed to a given idea have a much stronger motivation to oppose it than its supporters have to support it. The effect of self-serving opposition is to distort the apparent position of the line of resistance to change. Public attitude and opinion polls are helpful tools the manager can use to accurately locate the line of resistance to change and to demonstrate its location to members of the council/commission. They are also helpful in demonstrating to the media the narrow base of support that most active opposition groups have.

There are few issues that do not have current or potential partisans on both sides. The thoughtful manager will identify both and be sure the group that supports his/her ideas for change are heard from. As an example of this principle, imagine the manager who has decided the city/county could make substantial savings by privatizing a section of the refuse collection in the jurisdiction. If the first public discussion of the idea at the council/commission meeting is attended by 500 refuse collectors, organized by their union representative, discussing how these poor people are going to be thrown out of jobs, the issue suddenly becomes, both to the council/commission and the public at large, the prosperous, well-upholstered city/county manager versus the poor, hardworking garbageman. A little thought on the manager's part would have brought the realization that there probably are as many poor people who would benefit by privatization and that the private collectors could probably fill the council/commission chamber with "Ma and Pa" operators who are struggling to make a living with one truck. The result would have been a balanced picture of the effect of the change that would not pit the manager against the group and would, in effect, develop allies and sympathy.

Unfortunately, there are not always organized groups who will support the manager's position, and it may be necessary for the manager to organize his or her own support. Citizen volunteers who explore and recommend solutions to problems are often an effective means to develop a constituency for change. Neighborhood organizations and citizen action groups who have the opportunity to think through a problem can sometimes put the manager in the position of appearing to be pushed into recommending a change that was already intended. There is often an unspoken competition between the council/commission and the manager that groups opposed to the manager's recommendation can exploit. If the council's/commission's perception is that the manager is being pushed by an outside group, this possibility is much less likely to develop.

The level and direction of media coverage has a major influence on the location of the line of resistance to change on most issues. By choosing what issues to cover and by the extent of the coverage, the media can decrease or increase the manager's chances of success in getting a particular innovation adopted. Unfortunately, many managers confine their media contacts to news conferences and complaints to the editor about stories they didn't like. The more open the manager is in dealing with the media, and the more he or she is willing to spend time discussing ideas and plans with them, the better the coverage will be.

The use of a paid public relations person to act as a buffer between the manager and the media is a mistake. The media perceive it as an attempt to avoid them and the taxpayers see it as a use of their money to trumpet the virtues of a government they probably don't like anyway. It is wise for a manager to remember that radio and television are concerned with audio and visual images and that controversy creates better images than agreement. It is imperative that there is always an image friendly to the manager's position available to counteract the image that opposition presents.

Most reporters are anxious to present both sides of an issue. It is up to the manager to see that his or her side has as much visual appeal as that of the opponents. A group of city/county employees protesting layoffs is a less damaging public issue if it is balanced by a group of citizens demanding a tax cut.

Radio and television generally deal with ideas that can be explained in less than 30 seconds. A good manager will practice presenting ideas in a short time frame and will understand that most reporters from television and radio don't really understand what is going on in local government and don't have time to learn. Because of the nature of the print media, newspaper reporters have a great deal more time to explain issues and usually are willing to do some research to develop enough background to explain the issue well. The more time the manager can spend with newspaper reporters, the less likely a story in the paper will be superficial. Although editors and publishers do not write the day-to-day news, they generally make the decisions about what news will be featured and what the editorial position of the newspaper will be. It is therefore a good idea for the manager to report to them periodically about what's going on in local government.

The business community, in theory at least, is an ally of the manager in wanting to improve productivity and efficiency in government. The business community can contribute valuable expertise and, by its approval of a plan the manager wants to implement, can substantially raise the line of resistance to change. It can also help the local government gain a reputation for innovation and productivity that will increase receptiveness to new ideas in the future.

Practical Management Series

**The Entrepreneur
in Local Government**

Text type
Century Schoolbook

Composition
Unicorn Graphics
Washington, D.C.

Printing and binding
R. R. Donnelley & Sons Company
Harrisonburg, Virginia

Paper
International Springhill, 55#

Cover design
Rebecca Geanaros